WHAT LIFE
COULD MEAN
YOU

Alfred Adler (1870–1937) was born in a suburb of Vienna, the
son of a Jewish grain merchant. He became a medical doctor and
was one of the first to take a serious interest in the theories of
Sigmund Freud, recognizing that they opened up a new phase in
the development of psychiatry and psychology. He joined Freud's
discussion group and in 1910 became President of the Vienna
Psychoanalytic Society. Shortly afterwards the divergence
between his views and those of Freud and Jung led to his
resignation.

It is clear both that Adler's work is deeply indebted to his one-
time colleague, and that from the beginning he had an
independent approach to formulating the problems of human
psychology and finding solutions to them. In 1912 he formed the
Society for Individual Psychology, which stressed the importance
of taking a broad and responsive view of the human personality,
rather than adherence to the strict scientific principles of the
Freudians. He died in 1937, while on a lecture tour in Scotland,
and his name is bracketed with those of Freud and Jung as one of
the three great fathers of modern psychotherapy.

Colin Brett is an Adlerian counsellor and former Training Officer
of the Adlerian Society of Great Britain. He currently works as a
freelance management consultant and Adlerian Counsellor
Trainer in Great Britain, Ireland and South Africa. He is the
translator of Adler's *Understanding Human Nature* and editor of
Understanding Life, both published by Oneworld.

ALSO PUBLISHED BY ONEWORLD

Social Interest, Adler, ISBN 1–85168–156–6
The Freud–Adler Controversy, Handlbauer, 1–85168–127–2
Understanding Life, Adler, ISBN 1–85168–128–0
Understanding Human Nature, Adler, ISBN 1–85168–157–4

WHAT LIFE
COULD MEAN
TO YOU

alfred adler

Edited by Colin Brett

ONEWORLD

OXFORD

WHAT LIFE COULD MEAN TO YOU

Oneworld Publications
(Sales and Editorial)
185 Banbury Road
Oxford, OX2 7AR
England

Oneworld Publications
(US Marketing Office)
160 North Washington St, 4th floor
Boston, MA 02114
USA

First published in Great Britain in 1931
First published by Oneworld Publications 1992
Reprinted 1994
© this edition Oneworld Publications 1998

A CIP record for this book is available from the British Library

ISBN 1–85168–158–2

Cover design: Peter Maguire
Cover illustration: All M. C. Escher
works © Cordon Art – Baarn – Holland
All rights reserved
Printed and bound by WSOY, Finland

CONTENTS

FOREWORD

What Life Could Mean To You has a great deal of meaning for me. It was the first of Adler's books that I read more than fifteen years ago. I was a BBC producer at the time, making programmes for non-academic school leavers on non-curriculum subjects: leaving school and starting work, or not starting work as the case might be; programmes about self-awareness, relationships with family and friends and the other sex. I seemed to have been working in the field of personal relationships all my life. And yet I knew of Adler only vaguely.

So who was Alfred Adler? He was born in Vienna in 1870 and is often linked with his contemporaries and sometime colleagues, Sigmund Freud and Carl Gustav Jung. He had decided by the age of five that he would be a doctor in order to 'fight death'. He was the second child in a family of six. He suffered from rickets as a child as well as spasms of the glottis. When Adler was three, his younger brother died of diphtheria in the cot beside him. A year later, he himself was seriously ill with pneumonia. Small wonder that he had a strong desire to make people more healthy.

He studied medicine at the University of Vienna and was first an eye specialist and then a general practitioner. He was ahead of his time even then. He preferred not to treat the symptom in isolation but to try to understand the whole personality of his patients and take into account their social setting and how they reacted to it.

His earliest publications were *Health Book for the Tailoring Trade* and *Study of Organ Inferiority and its Psychical Compensation*. He very soon entered the field of neurology and psychiatry, where his ability to understand the whole personality in a commonsense way was invaluable.

In 1902 Freud asked Adler to join his weekly discussion circle. Because he was interested in Freud's work (Freud was fourteen years older and already widely known), he joined the psychoanalytic circle even though, from the beginning, he openly disagreed with some of Freud's theories. Adler was never a pupil of Freud's; indeed, he was highly esteemed by him, and was a contributing, articulate member of the circle as well as the co-editor of *The Psychoanalytical Journal*. He was eventually named Freud's successor as president of the Vienna Psychoanalytic Society. However, their theoretical differences increased and, along with six others, he resigned from the circle in 1911 when Freud insisted that everyone agree with his sexual theories. Adler objected to 'accepting the doctrine of sexual impulses in the neurotic or normal individual as the basic factor in psychic life. They are never causes but elaborated material and a means of personal striving'.

Adler and his colleagues eventually called their new school the Society for Individual Psychology. The word *individual* was used to emphasize the uniqueness and indivisibility of the personality. In the year following his resignation he published *The Neurotic Constitution*.

During the First World War, Adler served as an army physician in the neuro-psychiatric section of a military hospital. Here he became more and more aware of the contribution he felt he must make to spreading the commonsense ideas that he considered so vital for human beings to put into practice if they were to generate courage, develop their social interest (community spirit) and help humankind to live in harmony.

After his service in the war, his enthusiasm for developing the idea of social interest and involvement in the community grew. He eventually developed more than thirty child-guidance clinics in Vienna. He demonstrated his techniques to large groups of professionals and lay people – an idea that had not been used before. Like so many other Jewish people of his generation, he had to flee Europe and, in 1935, he settled in the United States where he was already well known. A Chair of Medical Psychology was especially created for him at the Long Island College of Medicine.

Adler continued to lecture and see clients in America and many European countries. At the age of sixty-seven he had a punishing schedule of fifty-six lectures, to be delivered in four different countries in one month. He had already completed his work in Paris, Brussels and Holland and had given one lecture to the students at Aberdeen University when, on May 28, 1937, he died of a sudden heart attack while taking a morning walk.

Adler's contribution to modern thinking is very great indeed. Although he wrote more than 300 books and articles, his greatest efforts were concentrated on lecturing and giving public demonstrations. During his lifetime, when confronted by the fact that the principles he had formulated so painstakingly were being appropriated by others without crediting him as the source, he simply said that it did not matter. What mattered was that his principles were recognized as being useful and were helping to create a climate of equality in which everyone could reach their full potential and contribute to society as a whole, realizing that they were different from, but equal to, other people.

Today, more than sixty years after Adler's death, the struggle for equality has never been stronger or more widespread. In our schools, pupils refuse to respond to autocratic treatment; teachers protest when their worth as professionals is not recognized. Parents set up pressure groups to obtain adequate education for their children; at the same time they have become aware that their children will no longer do as they are told, but will respond to being given choices and responsibilities. Gay men and lesbians demand the right to be recognized; black people push forward in their struggle to be seen as equals. A man is no longer the 'lord and master' of his home but is expected to be in partnership with the woman in his life. Workers strike when arbitrary decisions are made by management without consultation. We cannot be treated as equals unless we first firmly believe in our own equality. We believe we are equal when we feel confident about relating to other human beings.

Counsellors and therapists trained in Adlerian methods are working in the United States, Canada, Great Britain, Germany, Israel and many other countries throughout the world in schools, with parenting groups, with physically and mentally handicapped children and their families, with delinquents, criminals and with a wide variety of people who want to improve their work-life, their family situation or their ability to form intimate relationships.

In Adler's words, 'No experience is in itself a cause of success or failure. We do not suffer from the shock of our experiences – the so-called *trauma* – but instead make out of them whatever suits our purposes. We are not determined by our experiences but are *self-determined* by the meaning we give to them . . . As soon as we find and understand the meaning a person ascribes to life, we have the key to the whole personality.' Adler was the first to admit that there was nothing new in this idea. Epictetus (c. AD 50–120), who was born a slave and became a philosopher, is reported to have said much the same: 'Men are not worried by *things*. When we meet with difficulties, become anxious or troubled, let us not blame others but rather ourselves, that is, our ideas about things.' And John Milton wrote in the first book of *Paradise Lost*: 'The mind is its own place, and in itself / Can make a Heaven of Hell, a Hell of Heaven.'

Adler, with his creative mind and scientific background, was able to see all problems as social problems. Individual Psychology allows no room for blame but makes us responsible for our own choices and the way we decide to deal with their consequences. We are self-determining and creative; we are goal-directed even though we may be unaware of what those goals are, and Adler sees each of us as a unity. Once we recognize our goal we can see the purpose of our behaviour.

For Adler the answer to life's problems lies in 'social interest' – a feeling of connectedness with the whole of humanity that we must put into action if we are to contribute fully to society. 'It is the individual who is not interested in his fellow human beings who has the greatest difficulties in life and causes the greatest injury to others. It is from among such individuals that all human failures spring.'

After attending a residential weekend organized by the Adlerian society, I eventually became an accredited Adlerian counsellor. All the work I do is firmly based on Individual Psychology because, in almost all cases, it works. People can gain insight into the mistaken notions they created in childhood about themselves and others and, in a very short time, they can take positive steps to regain the enabling power that they gave away when they were too young to know the implications it would have for the rest of their lives.

I hope that you will find some of the optimistic thoughts expressed by Adler as useful as I have and that you will understand, as he did, that we can choose to change.

Rita Udall
Vice Chair,
Council of the British Adlerian Society

NOTE TO THE 1998 EDITION

The intention behind this new, revised and updated edition is to offer a complete guide to Adler's work on personal development that will appeal not just to Adlerian counsellors but also to students of psychology and interested laypersons. Consequently, sections of the text have been re-ordered to improve the flow of argument, sub-headings have been added for greater clarity, and certain expressions have been updated in accordance with contemporary usage. Readers should also note that instead of using 'she' or 'he', the plural pronoun has been used where applicable.

*This book is dedicated to
the human family in the hope
that its members may learn
from these pages to
understand themselves better.*

1

THE MEANING OF LIFE

Human beings live in the realm of *meanings*. We do not experience things in the abstract; we always experience them in human terms. Even at its source our experience is qualified by our human perspective. 'Wood' means 'wood in its relation to humankind', and 'stone' means 'stone as a factor in human life'. Anyone who tried to consider circumstances, to the exclusion of meanings, would be very unfortunate: he would isolate himself from others and his actions would be useless to himself or to anyone else; in a word, they would be meaningless. But no human being can escape meanings. We experience reality only through the meaning we ascribe to it: not as a thing in itself, but as something interpreted. It is natural to conclude, therefore, that this meaning is always more or less unfinished, or incomplete, and even that it can never be altogether right. The realm of meanings is thus the realm of mistakes.

If we asked someone, 'What is the meaning of life?', they would probably be unable to answer. For the most part, people do not trouble themselves with the question or try to formulate any answers. It is true that the question is as old as humanity itself and that in our own time young people – and older people too – will sometimes demand, 'But what is life *for*? What does life mean?' However, it is fair to say that they only ask these questions when they have suffered some sort of setback. As long as life is smooth and they are not confronting difficult tests, the question is never put into words. It is, rather, in their actions that people inevitably pose these questions, and answer them. If we closed our ears to words and concentrated on observing actions, we would find that each person has formulated their own individual 'meaning of life', and that all their opinions, attitudes, movements, expressions, mannerisms, ambitions, habits and character traits are in accordance with this meaning. Each person behaves as if they could rely upon a certain interpretation of life. In all their actions there is an implicit summing up of the world and of themselves; a verdict, 'I am like this and the universe is like that'; a meaning given to oneself and a meaning ascribed to life.

There are as many meanings ascribed to life as there are human beings and perhaps, as we have suggested, each meaning is mistaken to some extent. No one knows the absolute meaning of life, and thus any interpretation that is at all serviceable cannot be called absolutely wrong. All meanings are variations between these two limits. Among these variations, however, we can distinguish some that work well and some that are less effective; some where the mistake is small and some where it is large. We can discover what it is that the better interpretations have in common and what it is that the less satisfactory interpretations lack. We can derive from these a common measure of the truth, a common meaning, which enables us to decipher reality in so far as it concerns humankind. Again, we must bear in mind that 'true' means true for humankind, true for the purposes and aims of human beings. There is no other truth than this. Even if another truth existed, it would not concern us. We could never know it; it would be meaningless.

THE THREE TASKS OF LIFE

All human beings live under three main constraints, and it is these constraints that they must take into account. They make up reality, since all the problems or questions that face human beings arise from them. We are always forced to answer these questions and deal with these problems because they constantly confront us, and in our answers we will find our personal conception of the meaning of life.

The first of these constraints is that we are living on the crust of this small planet, earth, and nowhere else. We must live with the resources and the restrictions of the earth as best we can. We must develop both our bodies and minds so that we can continue our personal lives on earth and help to ensure the continuance of humankind. This is one inescapable problem that challenges everyone. Whatever we do, our actions are our own answer to the situation of human life: they reveal what we think necessary and fitting, possible and desirable. Every answer must take into account the fact that we are a member of the human race and that humanity inhabits this earth.

Now if we consider the weakness of the human body and the potential danger this places us in, it becomes very important for us to reappraise our answers, to make them far-sighted and coherent, for the good of our own lives and the welfare of humankind. It is as if we were faced with a problem in mathematics; we must work to find a solution. We cannot proceed haphazardly or by guesswork, but must work consistently, using all the means at our disposal. We are unlikely to find an absolutely perfect answer that establishes the truth once and for all; nevertheless, we must use all our skill to find an approximate answer. Moreover, we must constantly struggle to find a better one, and all the answers must take into account the fact that we are earthbound, with all the advantages and disadvantages that our position entails.

Here we come to the second constraint: none of us is the only member of the human race. There are others around us, and we exist in association with them. The weakness and the limitations of individual human beings make it impossible for them to achieve their own aims in isolation. If they lived on their own and tried to meet their problems by themselves they would perish. They would not be able to continue their own life, nor would they be able to continue the life of humankind. Thus they are always tied to others, owing to their own weaknesses, shortcomings and limitations. The greatest contribution to an individual's own welfare and to that of humankind is fellowship. Every answer to the problems of life, therefore, must take into account this constraint; it must be formulated in the light of the fact that we are living in association with other people and that we would perish if we were alone. If we are to survive, even our emotions must accord with this greatest of problems, purposes and goals: the continuance of our personal life and of the life of humankind on this planet that we inhabit together with our fellow human beings.

There is a third constraint governing us: human beings are made up of two sexes. The preservation of individual and of communal life must take account of this fact too. The problem of love and marriage belongs to this third constraint, and no man or woman can go through life without addressing it. Whatever human beings do when confronted by this problem constitutes their answer to it. There are many different ways in which human beings attempt to solve the problem. Their actions always reveal what they believe to be their only solution to it.

These three constraints, therefore, pose three problems: first, how to find an occupation that will enable us to survive under the limitations set by the nature of our home planet; second, how to find a position among our fellow human beings, so that we can co-operate and share the benefits of co-operation; and third, how to accommodate ourselves to the fact that there are two sexes and that the continuance of humankind depends upon the relations between them.

Individual Psychology has found that all human problems can be grouped under these three main headings: occupational, social and sexual. It is in their response to these three problems that individuals unfailingly reveal their own personal interpretation of the meaning of life. Suppose, for example, we consider a person whose love-life is unsatisfactory or non-existent, who fails to exert himself in his profession, who has few friends and who finds contact with his fellow human beings painful. From the self-imposed limits and restrictions in his life we may conclude that he sees *being alive* as a difficult and dangerous thing, entailing few opportunities and many failures. His narrow field of action can be construed as expressing the opinion: 'Life means protecting myself against harm, barricading myself in and escaping unscathed.'

Suppose, on the other hand, we consider a person who has a love relationship that is an intimate and full co-operation, whose work results in useful achievements, who has lots of friends and whose contacts with people are wide-ranging and fruitful. We may conclude that such a person sees life as a creative task, offering many opportunities and no irreversible setbacks. His courage in confronting all the problems of life is to be construed as saying: 'Life means being interested in people, being part of the whole, and contributing my share to the welfare of humankind.'

SOCIAL FEELING

It is here that we find the common elements of all mistaken 'meanings of life' and of all true 'meanings of life'. All those who seem to have failed – neurotics, psychotics, criminals, alcoholics, problem children, suicides, sexual deviants and prostitutes – have 'failed' because they are lacking in fellow-feeling and social interest. They approach the problems of occupation, friendship and sex without the confidence that they can be solved through co-operation. The meaning they ascribe to life is a private meaning: no one else benefits from their personal achievements. Their goal of success is in fact a goal of mere fictitious personal superiority, and their triumphs have meaning only to themselves.

Murderers, for example, have confessed to a feeling of power when they held a weapon in their hands, but clearly they were confirming their importance only to themselves. To the rest of us, it is unthinkable that the mere possession of a weapon could confer any superior worth. A private meaning is in fact no meaning at all. True meaning is only possible in communication: a word that meant something to one person only would really be meaningless. It is the same with our aims and actions: their only true meaning is their meaning for others. Every human being strives for significance, but people always make mistakes if they do not recognize that their own significance lies in their contribution to the lives of others.

There is a story about the leader of a small religious sect. One day she called her followers together and informed them that the end of the world would take place on the following Wednesday. Her followers were very impressed and promptly sold their property, abandoned all worldly considerations, and waited in anticipation for the promised catastrophe. Wednesday passed without any unusual occurrences. On Thursday they came to ask for an explanation. 'Look at this mess you got us into', they said. 'We abandoned all our security. We told everybody we met that the end of the world was coming on Wednesday, and when they laughed at us we were not discouraged, but repeated that we had it on infallible authority. Wednesday has come and gone and the world is still here around us.' 'But my Wednesday', said the prophetess, 'is not your Wednesday.' In this way, falling back on a private meaning, she protected herself against criticism. For a private meaning can never be put to the test.

The mark of all true 'meanings of life' is that they are common meanings – they are meanings in which others can share, and meanings that others can accept. A valid solution to the problems of life will always set an example for others also, for in it we shall see common problems met in a successful way. Even genius is to be defined as no more than supreme usefulness: it is only when a person's life is recognized by others as having significance that we call them a genius. The meaning expressed in such a life will always be, 'Life means making a contribution to the whole'. We are not referring here to professed motives, since we ignore such claims and look instead at concrete achievements. The people who meet the problems of human life successfully act as if they recognize, fully and spontaneously, that the fundamental meaning of life is interest in and co-operation with other people. Everything they do seems to be guided by the interests of their fellow beings, and where they encounter difficulties they try to overcome them in ways that do not impinge on the welfare of others.

To many people, perhaps, this is a new point of view, and they may doubt whether we are right to say that the meaning of life really is contribution, interest in others and co-operation. They may ask, 'But what about individuals? If they are always considering other people and devoting themselves to their interests, surely their own individuality suffers? Is it not necessary, in the case of some individuals at least, that in order to develop properly they must first consider themselves? Are there not some individuals who should learn, first of all, to guard their own interests or to strengthen their own personalities?'

This view, I believe, is a great mistake, and the problem it raises is a false problem. If human beings, in the meaning they ascribe to life, wish to make a contribution, and if their emotions are all directed towards their goal, they will naturally be bound to develop in ways that best enable them to make their contribution. They will fit themselves for their goal: they will develop a sense of social feeling and go on to become skilled in this through practice. Once the goal has been determined, the training will follow. Then and only then will they begin to equip themselves to solve the problems of life and to develop their abilities. Let us take the example of love and marriage. If we are interested in our partner, if we are doing our best to ease and enrich our partner's life, we will naturally make the best of ourselves that we can. If we think that we must develop our personality in a vacuum, without any intention of contributing to another's life, we will simply become domineering and unpleasant.

There is another hint from which we can infer that the true meaning of life depends on contribution and co-operation. If we look around us today at the inheritance we have received from our ancestors, what do we see? All that survives of them is the contributions they have made to human life. We see cultivated ground; we see roads and buildings. The fruits of their experience of life are communicated to us in traditions, philosophies, the sciences and the arts, and in techniques for dealing with our human situation. All these things came down to us from people who contributed to human welfare.

What has happened to everyone else? What has happened to those who never co-operated, who ascribed other meanings to life, who asked only, 'What can I get out of life?' They have left no trace behind them. Not only are they dead; their lives were futile. It is as if our earth itself had spoken to them and said, 'We don't need you. You are not fit for life. There is no future for your aims and strivings, for the values you held dear, for your minds and souls. Be off with you! You are not wanted. Die out and disappear!' The last judgement for people who ascribe to life any other meaning than co-operation is always, 'You are useless. Nobody wants you. Go!' In our present culture, of course, we can find many imperfections. Where we find that it is unsatisfactory, we must change it; but the change must always be one that further contributes to the welfare of humankind.

There have always been people who understood this fact, who knew that the meaning of life was to be interested in the whole of humankind, and who tried to develop social interest and love. In all religions, we find this concern for the salvation of humankind. In all the great movements of the world, people have been striving to increase social interest, and religion is one of the greatest strivings in this direction. Religions however, have often been misinterpreted, and it is difficult to see how they can do more than they are doing already, unless by a closer application to this common task. Individual Psychology arrives at the same conclusion in a scientific way and proposes a scientific method to achieve it. This, I believe, is a step forward. Perhaps science, by increasing people's interest in their fellow human beings and in the welfare of humankind, will be able to achieve more in this area than other movements, whether political or religious, have ever managed to do. While we approach the problem from a different angle, the intention is the same – to increase interest in others.

Since the meaning we ascribe to life becomes, as it were, the guardian angel or pursuing demon of our life, it is clearly very important to understand how these meanings come to be formed, how they differ from one another, and how they can be corrected if they involve big mistakes. This is the role of psychology, as distinct from physiology or biology: to provide us with an understanding of *meanings* and the way in which they influence human actions and human fortunes.

FORMATIVE CHILDHOOD EXPERIENCES

From our earliest days the first gropings for this 'meaning of life' can be discerned. Even babies strive to ascertain their own powers and their share in the life around them. By the end of the fifth year of life, children have adopted a unified and crystallized pattern of behaviour, with their own distinct style of approaching problems and tasks which we would call their 'life style'. They

At this age lack knowledge, skills + experience so how can this be so?

have already fixed their deepest and most lasting conception of what to expect from the world and from themselves. From now on, the world is seen through an established scheme of apperception. Experiences are interpreted before they are accepted, and the interpretation is always in accordance with the original meaning that the child has ascribed to life.

Even if this meaning is very seriously mistaken, even if our misguided approach to our problems and tasks results in continual misfortune and unhappiness, we do not readily relinquish it. Mistakes in our perception of the meaning of life can only be corrected by reconsidering the situation in which the faulty interpretation was made, recognizing the error and revising the scheme of apperception. In rare circumstances, perhaps, the consequences of a misguided approach may force individuals to revise the meaning they have ascribed to life. They may then succeed in adjusting their approach by themselves. They will never take this step, however, without some social pressure, or without realizing that to continue with the old approach is self-destructive. Generally, the most effective way individuals may revise their life style is with the assistance of someone trained in psychology, in the understanding of these meanings, who can help them to discover the original error and suggest a more appropriate meaning.

Let us take a simple illustration of the different ways in which childhood situations may be interpreted. Unhappy experiences in childhood may be given quite opposite meanings, and so result in contrasting interpretations of the meaning of life for different individuals. For example, one person with unhappy experiences behind him may only dwell on them in so far as they indicate a remedy for the future. He will think, 'We must make an effort to remove such unfortunate situations and ensure that our children grow up under better conditions.' Another person with similar experiences may feel, 'Life is unfair. Other people always have the best of it. If the world treated me like that, why should I treat the world any better?' This is why some parents say of their children, 'I had to suffer just as much when I was a child, and I came through it. Why shouldn't they?' A third person may feel, 'I should be excused for everything I do because of my unhappy childhood.' In each case, their interpretations of the meaning of life will be evident in their actions, and they will never change their actions unless they change their interpretations.

This is where Individual Psychology diverges from the theory of determinism: no experience is in itself a cause of success or failure. We do not suffer from the shock of our experiences – the so-called *trauma* – but instead make out of them whatever suits our purposes. We are not determined by our experiences but are *self-determined* by the meaning we give to them; and when we take particular experiences as the basis for our future life we are almost certain to be misguided to some degree. Meanings are not determined by situations. We determine ourselves by the meanings we ascribe to situations.

Physical disadvantages

There are, however, certain childhood situations from which a seriously mistaken meaning is frequently drawn, and the majority of failures come from children who have experienced these situations. Children who suffer from physical handicaps, diseases, or illnesses during their infancy fall into this category. Such children experience many hardships and find it difficult to feel that contributing to society is what life is all about. Unless someone close to them can draw their attention away from their own problems and interest them in others, they are likely to become preoccupied entirely with themselves. It is also possible, in today's society, that their feelings of inferiority are reinforced by the pity, ridicule or ostracism of their peers. These are all circumstances in which such children may become introverted, lose hope of playing a useful part in society, and consider themselves personally humiliated by the world.

I was the first person, I think, to describe the difficulties that confront a child whose organs are imperfect or whose glandular secretions are abnormal. This branch of science has made extraordinary progress, but hardly along the lines in which I would have liked to see it develop. From the beginning, I was looking for ways of overcoming these difficulties, rather than a basis for blaming such failure on genetic or physical conditions. No physical defect *compels* an individual to develop a distorted life style. We never find two children whose glands have the same effects on them. Indeed, we often see children who overcome their difficulties and who, in overcoming them, develop unusual faculties for usefulness.

Because of this, Individual Psychology is not a very good advertisement for schemes of eugenic selection. Many of the most eminent people, people who made great contributions to our culture, began life with physical imperfections; many suffered from ill-health and some died young. It is often from those people who struggled hard against difficulties, both physical and material, that advances and inventions have come. The struggle strengthened them and they went further ahead than they would otherwise have done. We cannot judge from physical signs alone whether the mind will develop in a bad or good way. Hitherto however, the majority of children who started life with physical and endocrine disadvantages have not been trained in the right direction. Their difficulties have not been understood and they have for the most part become very self-centred. This is why we find so many failures among children whose early years were burdened with physical disabilities.

Pampering

Birth order affects?

The second situation that often leads to mistaken interpretation of the meaning of life is that of the pampered child. Spoilt children are brought up to expect their wishes to be law. They are given prominence without working to deserve it and they will generally come to demand this prominence as a birthright. In consequence, whenever they are not the centre of attention and when other people do not make the consideration of their feelings a primary objective, they will be very much at a loss. They will feel their world has failed them. They have been trained to take, not to give. They have never learned any other way of facing problems. Others have been so subservient to them that they have lost their independence and do not know that they can do things for himself. Their main object of interest was themselves, and they never learned the use and necessity of co-operation. When they are confronted by difficulties, they only have one method of coping with them – to make demands on other people. They believe that if they can regain their position of prominence, they can force others to recognize that they are special and should be granted everything they want. Then and only then will their situation improve.

As adults, these spoilt children are perhaps the most dangerous group in our community. Some of them may make great protestations of goodwill; they may even become very 'lovable' in order to secure an opportunity to dominate others; but they go on strike when asked to co-operate like ordinary human beings, in ordinary human tasks. There are others who are revolt more openly: when they no longer find the easy warmth and acquiescence to which they were accustomed, they feel betrayed. All of society, they feel, is hostile to them and they try to revenge themselves upon others. And if society shows hostility to their way of living (as it probably will) they take this hostility as a new proof that they are *personally* ill-treated. This is the reason why punishments are never any use. They simply confirm the opinion that 'everyone is against me'. But whether spoilt children go on strike or revolt openly, whether they try to dominate through weakness or to take their revenge through violence, they are in fact acting on the basis of the same mistaken view of the world. We even find people who try both methods at different times. Their goal remains unaltered. They feel that the meaning of life is to be first, to be recognized as the most important, to 'get everything I want', and as long as they continue to ascribe this meaning to life, every method they adopt will be mistaken.

Neglect

The third situation in which a mistake can easily be made is that involving neglected children. Such children have never known what love and co-operation can be. They construct an interpretation of life that simply does not include these positive forces. It is easy to understand how, when they face the problems of life, they will overrate their difficulty and underrate their own capacity to meet them with the help and goodwill of others. They have found society cold and unfriendly and will expect it always to be cold and unfriendly. In particular, they will not realize that they can *win* affection and esteem by doing things that are useful to others. They will thus be suspicious of others and unable to trust themselves.

There is really no experience that can take the place of unselfish, disinterested affection. The most important task of a parent is to give a child their first experience of a trustworthy 'other person'. Later, parents must broaden and deepen this feeling of trust until it includes the whole of the child's environment. If they fail in the first task – to gain the child's interest, affection and co-operation – it will be very difficult for the child to develop social interest and a sense of fellowship with others. Everybody has the capacity to be interested in others, but this capacity must be trained and exercised or its development will be retarded.

If we could study extreme cases of neglected, hated or unwanted children, we would probably find that they were blind to the existence of co-operation, isolated, unable to communicate with others and completely ignorant of everything that would help them get along with other human beings. But, as we have already seen, individuals in these circumstances would perish. The fact that children survive infancy is proof that they have been given a certain amount of care and attention. There are, therefore, no cases of totally neglected children; rather, we are dealing with those who have received less than usual consideration, or who were neglected in some respects, though not in others. In short, it is sufficient to say that neglected children ares ones who never really found a trustworthy 'other person'. It is a very sad comment on our civilization that so many failures in life are children who were orphaned or abandoned, and that we must include such children, on the whole, in the category of neglected children.

These three situations – physical disadvantages, pampering, and neglect – offer great temptations to draw mistaken conclusions about the meaning of life. Children who have experienced these situations will almost always need help in revising their approach to problems. They must be helped to a better understanding of what life is about. If we have an eye for such things – which really means, if we have a true interest in them and have trained ourselves in this direction – we shall be able to see their interpretation of life in everything they do.

FIRST MEMORIES AND DREAMS

An investigation of dreams and associations may prove useful: the personality is the same in dreaming life as in waking life, but in dreams the pressure of social demands is less acute and the personality will be revealed because there will be fewer safeguards and concealments. The greatest help of all however, in unlocking the meaning individuals ascribe to themselves and to their life, is their store of memories. Every memory, however trivial they may consider it, is important because by definition it represents to them something *memorable*, and it is memorable because of its bearing on life as they picture it. It says to them, 'This is what you must expect', or 'This is what you must avoid', or even, 'Such is life!' Again we must stress that the experience itself is not as important as the fact that this particular experience persists in memory and is used to crystallize the meaning ascribed to life. Every memory is a chosen reminder.

The memories of early childhood are especially useful in showing how long individuals have had a particular approach to life, and in revealing the circumstances in which they first formulated their attitude to life. The earliest memory of all has a very notable place for two reasons. First, it encapsulates the fundamental estimate individuals make of themselves and their situation. It is their first summing-up of appearances, and their first more or less complete symbol of themselves and the demands made on them. Second, it is their subjective starting point, the beginning of the autobiography they have made for themselves. Consequently, we can often find in it the contrast between a perceived position of weakness or inadequacy and the goal of strength and security that they regard as their ideal. It is of no importance for the purposes of psychology whether the memory individuals consider the earliest is really the first event that they can remember – or even whether it is a memory of a real event. Memories are important only for what they represent, for their interpretation of life and their bearing on the present and future.

Let us look at a few examples of first memories and see the 'meaning of life' that they exhibit. 'The coffee pot fell off the table and scalded me.' Such is life! We ought not to be surprised to find that the woman whose history began in this way was pursued by a feeling of helplessness, and overstated the dangers and difficulties of life. Neither should we be surprised if, in her heart, she reproached other people for not taking sufficient care of her. Somebody had been very careless to leave such a small child exposed to danger in this way. A similar picture of the world is portrayed in another first memory: 'I remember falling out of a pram when I was three years old.' With this first memory went a recurrent dream: 'The world is coming to an end and I wake up in the middle of the night to find the sky bright red with fire. The stars all fall and we collide with another planet. But just before the crash I wake up.' When this patient, a student, was asked if he was afraid of anything, he answered, 'I'm afraid that I won't make a success of life', and it is clear that his first memory and his recurrent dream act as discouragements and confirm his fear of failure and catastrophe.

A boy of twelve, who was brought to the clinic because of enuresis (bed-wetting) and continual conflicts with his mother, gave as his first memory: 'Mother thought I was lost, and ran into the street shouting for me, and was very frightened. All the time I was hiding in the cupboard in the house.' In this memory we can discern the interpretation: 'Life means getting attention by causing trouble. The way to gain security is through deceitfulness. I am overlooked, but I can fool others.' His enuresis was an appropriate means of keeping him at the centre of worry and attention, and his mother confirmed his interpretation of life by her anxiety and fussing over him.

As in the previous examples, this boy had early on gained the impression that life in the outside world was full of dangers, and he had concluded that he was only safe if others were apprehensive on his behalf. This was the only way he could reassure himself that they were there to protect him if he needed it.

This is the earliest memory of a woman of thirty-five: 'While I was on the stairs in the dark, a boy cousin, a little older than

myself, opened the door and came down after me. I was very
frightened of him.' It seemed probable from this memory that she
was unaccustomed to playing with other children, and that she
was especially ill at ease with the other sex. A guess that she was
an only child proved correct, and she was still, at the age of thirty-
five, unmarried.

A more highly developed social feeling is shown in the
following: 'I remember my mother letting me wheel my baby sister
in the pram.' In this instance however, we might look for signs of
being at ease only with weaker people, and perhaps of dependence
upon the mother. It is always best when a new child is born to
gain the co-operation of the older children in taking care of it, to
interest them in the new addition to the family and allow them to
share responsibility for its welfare. If parents can gain their co-
operation, older children will not be tempted to regard the
attention given to the baby as a diminution of their own
importance and resent it.

The desire to be with other people is not always an indication
of a real interest in others. One girl, when asked for her first
memory, replied: 'I was playing with my elder sister and two girl
friends.' Here we can certainly see a child training to be sociable.
However, we obtain a new insight when she mentions as her
greatest fear, 'I am afraid of being left alone.' We shall look,
therefore, for signs of a lack of independence.

As soon as we find and understand the meaning a person
ascribes to life, we have the key to the whole personality. It is
sometimes stated that it is impossible to change human character,
but this view can only be held by those who have never found the
key to the situation. As we have already seen, no argument or
treatment can be successful if it fails to discover the original error,
and the only possibility for improvement lies in training the person
to adopt a more co-operative and courageous approach to life.

THE IMPORTANCE OF LEARNING TO CO-OPERATE

Co-operation is the only safeguard we have against the
development of neurotic tendencies. It is therefore very
important that children should be trained and encouraged in

You can still be neurotic & co-operative!

co-operation, and should be allowed to find their own way amongst children of their own age, in common tasks and shared games. Any barrier to co-operation will have serious consequences. Spoilt children, for example, who have learned to be interested only in themselves, will take this lack of interest in others to school with them. Their lessons will interest them only in so far as they think they can gain their teachers' favour. They will listen only to what they consider advantageous to themselves. As they approach adulthood, the result of their lack of social feeling will become more and more evident. When they first misconstrued the meaning of life, they ceased training themselves for responsibility and independence. By now they are painfully ill-equipped for any of life's tests and difficulties.

We cannot blame adults for children's early mistakes. We can only help them to remedy them when they begin to suffer the consequences. We do not expect children who have never been taught geography to score high marks in an examination paper on the subject. Similarly, we cannot expect a child who has never been trained in co-operation to respond appropriately when tasks that demand co-operation are set before them. But all of life's problems demand an ability to co-operate if they are to be resolved; every task must be mastered within the framework of human society and in a way that furthers human welfare. Only individuals who understand that life *means* contribution will be able to meet their difficulties with courage and with a good chance of success.

If teachers, parents and psychologists understand the mistakes that can be made in ascribing a meaning to life, and provided they do not make the same mistakes themselves, we can be confident that children who lack social feeling will eventually develop a better sense of their own capacities and of the opportunities in life. When they meet problems, they will not stop trying; they will not look for an easy way out, try to escape or throw the burden onto the shoulders of others; they will not demand extra consideration or special sympathy; they will not feel humiliated and seek revenge, or ask, 'What is the use of life? What do I get from it?' They will say, 'We must make our own lives. It is our own task and we are capable of performing it. We are masters of our own actions. If something new must be done or something old replaced, no one can do it but ourselves.' If life is approached in this way, as a co-operation of independent human beings, there are no limits to the progress of our human civilization.

2

MIND AND BODY

THE INTERACTIONS OF MIND AND BODY

People have always debated whether the mind governs the body or the body governs the mind. Philosophers have joined in the controversy and taken one standpoint or the other. They have called themselves idealists or materialists, they have presented arguments by the thousand, and the question still seems as thorny and unresolved as ever. Perhaps Individual Psychology can contribute towards a solution, for in Individual Psychology what we are really concerned with are the daily interactions of mind and body. Individuals – mind and body – come to us for treatment, and if our treatment is misconceived we will be unable to help them. Our theory must therefore grow from experience and must stand the test of application. We have to deal with the results of these interactions, and have the greatest incentive to find the right point of view.

The findings of Individual Psychology remove much of the tension from this problem. It no longer remains a simple 'either/or' issue. We see that both mind and body are expressions of life: they are parts of life as a whole. We begin to understand their reciprocal relations within that whole. Human life depends on movement, and it would not be sufficient for a human being to develop only physically, because movement implies a governing intelligence. A plant is rooted: it stays in one place and cannot move. It would be very surprising, therefore, to discover that a plant had a mind, or at least a mind in any sense that we could comprehend. Even if a plant could foresee consequences, that faculty would be useless to it. What advantage would there be for the plant to think: 'Here is someone coming. In a minute he will

tread on me, and I will be crushed underfoot'? The plant would
still be unable to move out of the way.

All moving beings, however, can foresee events and decide on
the direction in which to move. This implies that they have
minds or souls.

Sense, sure, you have,
Else you could not have motion.
                    Hamlet, Act III, Scene 4

This ability to anticipate and direct movement is the central
principle of the mind. As soon as we have recognized it we can
understand how the mind governs the body: it sets the goals of
movement. Merely to initiate a random movement from moment
to moment would never be enough: there must be a goal for such
strivings. Since it is the function of the mind to decide the
objective of movement, the mind is in the driving seat. Yet the
body also exerts an influence on the mind since it is the body that
must be moved. The mind can only move the body in accordance
with its physical capabilities and within its limitations. If, for
example, the mind proposes to move the body to the moon, it will
fail unless it discovers a technique that overcomes the body's
limitations.

Human beings move more than any other creatures. Not only
do they move in more ways – as we can see in the complicated
movements of their hands – but they are also more capable of
influencing the environment through their movements. We might
expect, therefore, that foresight would be very highly developed in
the human mind, and that people would show the clear evidence
of purposive striving to improve their lot.

In every human being moreover, we can discover, behind all
partial movements towards partial goals, one single, inclusive
movement. All our strivings are directed towards a feeling of
security, a feeling that all the difficulties of life have been
overcome and that we have finally emerged safe and victorious, in
relation to the whole situation around us. With this goal in view,
all movements and expressions must be co-ordinated and unified.

The mind is thus compelled to develop as if to achieve a final ideal goal.

It is the same with the body. The body also strives to be a unity; it too develops towards an ideal goal pre-existent in the embryo. If, for example, the skin is broken, the body sets to work to make itself whole again. The body, however, is not simply left alone for its potentialities to unfold; the mind can help it in its development. The value of exercise and training, and of hygiene in general, has been amply proved. All these are aids for the body, supplied by the mind in its striving towards the final goal.

From the very first days of life up to the last, this partnership of growth and development continues. Body and mind co-operate as indivisible parts of one whole. The mind is like a motor, dragging with it all the potentialities it can discover in the body, helping to bring it to safety and impregnability. In every movement of the body, in every expression and symptom, we can see the stamp of the mind's purpose. A person moves: there is meaning in that movement. Individuals move their eyes, their tongue, the muscles of their face: their face has an expression, a meaning. They are the mind that puts meaning there. Now we can begin to see what psychology, or the science of the mind, really deals with. The purpose of psychology is to explore the meaning of all the expressions of an individual, to find out about his or her goal, and to compare it with the goals of others.

In striving for the final goal of security, the mind is always faced with the necessity of making that goal concrete; of calculating where security lies and how it might be reached. Here, of course, it is possible to take a wrong turning, but without a definite goal and chosen direction there could be no movement at all. If I move my hand, I must already have a purpose for the movement in mind. The direction the mind chooses may, in the event, lead to disaster, but it is chosen because the mind mistakenly conceives it as the most advantageous. All psychological mistakes are thus mistakes in choosing the direction of movement. The goal of security is common to all human beings, but some of them are wrong in their conclusions about where to find it, setting off in the wrong direction, therefore, and going astray.

If we see an expression or symptom and are unable to recognize the meaning behind it, the best way to understand it is, first of all, to reduce it in outline to a bare movement. Let us take, for example, the act of stealing. To steal is to remove property from another person and to take it for oneself. Let us now examine the goal of the movement: the goal of stealing is to enrich oneself, and to feel more secure by possessing more. The starting point of the movement is therefore a feeling of being poor and deprived. The next step is to find out in what circumstances individuals are placed and in what conditions they feel deprived. Finally, we can see whether they are going the right way about changing these circumstances and overcoming their feeling of being deprived. Are they going in the right direction, or have they mistaken the method of securing what they desire? We need not criticize their final goal, but we may be able to point out that they are going the wrong way about achieving it.

As we noted in Chapter 1, in the first four or five years of life individuals establish the unity of their mind and form the relations between mind and body. During this period they take the qualities they have inherited and the impressions they receive from their environment and adapt them to their pursuit of superiority. By the end of the fifth year their personality has formed. The meaning they ascribe to life, the goal they pursue, their style of approach and their emotional disposition have all been determined. They can be changed later, but only if they can free themselves from the misguided attitudes they acquired in childhood. Just as all their previous thoughts and deeds were in accordance with their interpretation of life, so now, if they are able to correct their mistaken apperception, their new thoughts and deeds will be in accordance with their new interpretation.

It is through their senses that individuals come into contact with their environment and receive impressions from it. We can see, therefore, from the way they train their bodies, the kind of impression they are prepared to receive from their environment and the use they are trying to make of their experience. If we notice the way they look and listen and what it is that attracts their attention, we can learn a great deal about them. This is the reason postures are so important. They show us how individuals have trained their senses and how they are using them to select impressions. Every posture has a meaning.

Now we can add to our definition of psychology. Psychology is the understanding of individuals' attitudes towards the sensory impressions received by their bodies. We can also begin to see how the great differences between human minds have arisen. A body that is ill-adapted to the environment and has difficulty in fulfilling the demands of that environment will usually be experienced by the mind as a burden. For this reason, children who have been born with physical disadvantages tend to be slower in their mental development too. It is harder for their minds to influence, move and control their bodies towards a position of superiority. A greater effort of mind is needed, and their mental concentration must be greater than anyone else's if they are to secure the same ends. So their minds become overburdened and they become self-centred and egotistical. When children are always concerned with their physical imperfections and their difficulties with movement, they have no attention to spare for the things outside themselves. They find neither the time nor the freedom to take an interest in others. In consequence, they grow up with a lesser degree of social feeling and a less developed ability to co-operate.

Physical disadvantages offer many handicaps but these handicaps by no means represent an inescapable fate. If the mind is active in its own right and works hard to overcome obstacles, individuals may very well become just as successful as those who born without handicaps. Indeed, children with physical disadvantages very often accomplish, in spite of their handicaps, more than children who start off with every advantage. A boy, for example, may suffer unusual stress through defective vision. He concentrates harder than his keen-sighted peers on trying to see; he gives more attention to the visible world, and is more interested in distinguishing colours and forms. In the end, he comes to have a much greater appreciation of the visible world than children who never strain their eyes to see it. Thus an imperfect organ can turn out to be the source of great advantages – but only if the mind has found a way of overcoming such imperfections.

Among painters and poets a great proportion are known to have suffered from imperfect vision. These imperfections were overcome by well-trained minds, and finally they could use their eyes to better purpose than others with perfect vision. The same kind of compensation can be seen, perhaps more easily, among left-handed children whose left-handedness has not been recognized. At home, or at the beginning of their school days, they were trained to use their imperfect right hands. Thus they were really not well equipped for writing, drawing or craftwork. We might expect that if the mind can overcome such difficulties, this imperfect right hand would often develop a high degree of skill. This is precisely what happens. In many instances left-handed children develop better handwriting than others, more talent for drawing and painting, or more skill in craft. By finding the right technique, by motivation, training and practice, they have turned disadvantage into advantage.

Only children who desire to contribute to the whole, and whose interest is not centred on themselves, can successfully teach themselves to compensate for defects. If children desire only to rid themselves of difficulties, they will continue to lag behind. They can keep their courage up only if they have a goal in mind for their efforts, and if the achievement of this goal is more important to them than the obstacles that stand in the way.

It is a question of where their interest and attention are directed. If they are striving towards an object outside themselves, they will quite naturally train and equip themselves to achieve it. Difficulties will be seen merely as hurdles to be cleared on the way to success. If, on the other hand, their interest lies in stressing their own limitations or in fighting these limitations with no purpose except to be free of them, they will not be able to make real progress. A clumsy right hand cannot be trained into a skilful right hand by thinking about it, by wishing that it were less clumsy, or even by avoiding situations in which clumsiness is inevitable. The clumsy hand can become skilful only through exercise in practical activities, and the incentive to do well in the future must be more deeply felt than the feeling of discouragement about one's present clumsiness. If children are to marshal their powers and overcome their difficulties, there must be a goal for their movements outside themselves; a goal based on interest in reality, interest in others and interest in co-operation.

A good example of a hereditary characteristic and the use to which it may be turned was found during my investigations into families who suffered from hereditary kidney defects. Many children in these families suffered from enuresis. The physical disability is genuine. It can show up in the kidney or the bladder or in the existence of *spina bifida*, and often a corresponding defect of the lumbar segment can be suspected from a naevus or mole on the skin in that area. The physical defect, however, by no means accounts fully for the enuresis. The children are not completely at the mercy of their organs; they use them in their own way. Some children, for example, will wet the bed at night but never wet themselves during the day. Sometimes the habit will disappear suddenly, following a change in the environment or in the attitude of the parents. Enuresis can be overcome if the children cease to use their disability for their own mistaken purposes.

Most children who suffer from enuresis, however, are given incentives not to overcome it, but to continue it. A skilful parent can give the appropriate training, but if the parent is not skilful this tendency persists unnecessarily. Often, in families who suffer from kidney or bladder troubles, there is too much stress on everything to do with urinating. Parents will then mistakenly try very hard to stop the enuresis. If children notice how much value is placed on this issue, they will probably resist. It will give them an excellent opportunity to assert their opposition to this kind of training. Children who resist the treatment that their parents give will always find a way to attack them at their point of greatest weakness.

A very well-known sociologist in Germany has discovered that a surprising proportion of criminals had parents whose occupations related to the discouragement of crime, such as judges, police or prison wardens. Often the children of teachers are obstinate academically. My own experience has borne this out, and I have also found a surprising number of neurotic children among the children of psychologists, and of delinquent children among the offspring of ministers of religion. In a similar way, children whose parents place too much stress on urinating have a splendid opportunity of showing, through their enuresis, that they have wills of their own.

Enuresis can also provide us with a good example of how dreams are used to stir up emotions appropriate to the actions we intend. Children who wet their bed frequently dream that they have got out of bed and gone to the toilet. In this way they have excused themselves; now it is perfectly legitimate for them to wet their bed. Bed-wetting serves several purposes: to attract attention, to subordinate others, to keep their attention by night as well as by day. Sometimes it is used to antagonize them too; the habit is a declaration of war. Whichever way we look at it, it is obvious that enuresis is really a creative expression: children are speaking with their bladder instead of their mouth. The physical weakness merely provides them with a way to express their opinion.

Children who express themselves in this way are always suffering from stress of some kind. Generally they belong to the class of spoilt children who have lost their place at the centre of attention. Another child has been born, perhaps, and they find it more difficult to get the undivided attention of their parents. Enuresis thus represents an attempt to make closer contact with their parents, even by unpleasant means. It says, in effect, 'I am not as grown-up as you think: I still need to be looked after.'

In different circumstances, or with a different physical defect, they would have chosen other means of achieving this end. They might have used sound, for example, to make contact, in which case they would have been restless and cried during the night. Some children walk in their sleep, have nightmares, fall out of bed, or become thirsty and call for water. The psychological background that gives rise to all these expressions is the same. The choice of symptom depends in part on the child's physical make-up and in part on the environment.

Such cases show very clearly the influence that the mind exerts over the body. In all likelihood the mind not only affects the choice of a particular physical symptom but also governs and influences the whole constitution. We have no direct proof of this hypothesis, and it is difficult to see how such a proof could ever be established. The evidence, however, seems clear enough. If a boy is timid, his timidity is reflected in his whole development. He will not concern himself with physical achievements; or, rather, he will not imagine that they are within his reach. Consequently, it will not occur to him to train his muscles in an efficient way, and he will ignore all the impressions from outside that would normally be a stimulus to muscular development. Other children, who allow themselves to take an interest in the training of their muscles, will make better progress in physical fitness than the timid boy whose interest is blocked.

We can reasonably conclude from such observations that the whole form and development of the body is affected by the mind and reflects its errors or deficiencies. We can often observe physical conditions that are plainly the end result of mental and emotional problems, where individuals have not found a satisfactory means of compensating for a physical difficulty. The endocrine glands themselves, for example, can certainly be influenced in the first four or five years of life. While glandular defects do not have a compulsive influence on conduct, they are continuously affected by the whole environment, by the direction from which children seek to receive impressions, and by the creative activity of their minds.

THE ROLE OF FEELINGS

'Culture' is the name we give to the change the human race has made in its environment. Our culture is the result of all the movements that people's minds have initiated for their bodies. Our work is inspired by our minds, which direct and assist the development of our bodies. In the end we will find that every human expression is filled with the purposiveness of the mind. It is by no means desirable, however, that the mind should overestimate its own importance. If we are to overcome difficulties, physical fitness is necessary. The mind is engaged, therefore, in governing the environment in such a way that the body can be protected from sickness, disease and death, damage, accidents and functional failures. This is why we have evolved the ability to feel pleasure and pain, to imagine and to identify ourselves with good and bad situations.

Feelings prepare the body to meet a situation with a specific response. Fantasy and identification are methods of prediction, but there is more to them than that. They stir up appropriate feelings to which the body will respond. In this way, the individuals' feelings are shaped by the meaning they ascribe to life and the goal they have set for their strivings. To a great extent, though feelings rule their bodies, they do not depend on them: they will always depend primarily on their goal and their consequent life style.

Clearly, individuals' life styles are not the only factors that govern their behaviour. Their attitudes do not cause their actions without further help. To result in action, they must be reinforced by feelings. What is new in the outlook of Individual Psychology is our observation that feelings never contradict the life style. Where there is a goal, feelings always adapt themselves to its attainment. This takes us, therefore, beyond the realm of physiology or biology; the origin of feelings cannot be explained by chemical theory or predicted by chemical examination. In Individual Psychology we must presuppose the physiological processes, but we are more interested in the psychological goal. For example, we are not concerned with the influences of anxiety on the sympathetic and para-sympathetic nerves so much as with its purpose and goal.

With this approach, anxiety cannot be taken as arising from the suppression of sexuality, or as the legacy of disastrous birth experiences. Such explanations are wide of the mark. We know that children who are accustomed to being accompanied, helped and supported by their parents may find that exhibiting anxiety – from whatever source – is a very effective means of controlling them. Nor are we satisfied with a physical description of anger;

our experience has shown us that anger is a device used to dominate a person or a situation. While we can take it for granted that all our physical and mental characteristics are inherited, our attention must be directed to the use made of this inheritance in striving to achieve a definite goal. This, it seems, is the only real psychological approach.

In all individuals we see that feelings have grown and developed in a direction and to a level that were essential to the attainment of their personal goal. Their anxiety or courage, cheerfulness or sadness, have always agreed with their life style: their relative strength and dominance have accorded exactly with our expectations. People who accomplish their goal of superiority through sadness cannot be cheerful and satisfied with their accomplishments. They can only be happy when they are miserable! We also notice that feelings appear and disappear at will. Patients suffering from agoraphobia lose feelings of anxiety when they are at home or when they are dominating others. All neurotic patients exclude every aspect of life in which they do not feel strong enough to achieve dominance.

Emotions are as fixed as one's life style. Cowards, for example, are always cowards, despite their arrogance with weaker people or courage when they are shielded by others. They may triple-lock their doors, protect themselves with guard dogs and burglar alarms and still insist that they are as brave as lions. Nobody will be able to prove their feelings of anxiety, but the cowardice of their character is amply displayed by the trouble they take to protect themselves.

Sexuality and love give a similar testimony. Sexual feelings always arise when individuals have a sexual goal in mind. By concentrating on their sexual goal, they manage to exclude any conflicting tastes and incompatible interests, and are thus able to evoke the appropriate feelings and functions. When these feelings and functions are lacking, as expressed in impotence, premature ejaculation, deviance and frigidity, it is clear that they have been unwilling to exclude inappropriate tastes and interests. Such abnormalities are always induced by a mistaken goal of superiority and a mistaken life style. We always find in such cases a tendency to expect consideration from the partner rather than to give it, a lack of social feeling, and a lack of courage and optimism.

A patient of mine, a second child, suffered very profoundly from inescapable feelings of guilt. Both his father and elder brother set great store by honesty. When the boy was seven years old, he told his teacher at school that he had done a piece of homework by himself although, as a matter of fact, his brother had done it for him. The boy concealed his guilty feelings for three years. At last he went to see the teacher and confessed his awful lie. The teacher merely laughed at him. Next he went to his father in tears and confessed a second time. This time he was more successful. The father was proud of his boy's love of truth; he praised and consoled him. But in spite of the fact that his father had absolved him, the boy continued to be depressed. We can hardly avoid the conclusion that this boy was concerned with proving his great integrity and scrupulousness by blaming himself so bitterly for such a trifling misdemeanour. The high moral tone of his home gave him the incentive to excel in integrity. He felt inferior to his elder brother in schoolwork and social success, so he tried to achieve superiority through a sideline of his own.

Later in life he suffered from other forms of self-reproach. He masturbated and never completely eradicated his cheating at school. His feelings of guilt always intensified before he took an examination. As he went on, he developed more and more difficulties of this sort. Because of his sensitive conscience he was much more heavily burdened than his brother, and thus he always had an excuse whenever he failed to match his brother's attainments. When he left university, he planned to obtain technical work, but his compulsive guilt feelings troubled him so much that he spent the whole day praying to God to forgive him. This of course left him no time for work.

By now his mental condition had deteriorated to the extent that he was sent to a mental hospital, where he was considered incurable. After a time, however, he improved and left the hospital, but asked permission to be readmitted if he should suffer a relapse. He left his job to study the history of art. The time of his examinations approached. He went to church on a public holiday, prostrated himself before the congregation and cried out, 'I am the greatest sinner of all'. In this way, once again, he succeeded in drawing attention to his sensitive conscience.

After another period in hospital he returned home. One day he came down to lunch naked. He was a well-built man and in this respect could compete well with his brother and with other people.

His feelings of guilt were devices to make him appear more honest than others, and this was his way of struggling to achieve superiority. His struggles, however, were directed towards the useless side of life. His avoidance of examinations and employment is evidence of cowardice and a heightened feeling of inadequacy, and his whole neurosis was a deliberate exclusion of every activity in which he was afraid of failing. The same striving for superiority by underhand means is evidenced in his self-abasement in the church and his sensational entrance into the dining room. His life style demanded this behaviour, and the feelings he induced were entirely appropriate to his aims.

Another piece of evidence will perhaps show more clearly the influence of the mind on the body, since it relates to a more familiar phenomenon that results in a temporary physical condition rather than a permanent one. It is the fact that, to a certain degree, every emotion finds some bodily expression. Individuals will show their emotion in some visible form; perhaps in their posture and attitude, perhaps in their face, perhaps in the trembling of their limbs. Similar changes could be found in the organs themselves. If they flush or turn pale, for example, it means the circulation of the blood is affected. Anger, anxiety, sorrow and every other emotion find expression in our 'body language', and each individual's body speaks a language of its own.

When one person is in a frightening situation, they tremble; another's hair will stand on end; a third will have heart palpitations. Still others will sweat or choke, speak in a hoarse voice, or cower and shrink back physically. Sometimes the balance of the body is affected, or there may be loss of appetite or vomiting. With some people it is the bladder that is affected by such emotions; with others it is the sex organs. Many children feel sexually stimulated when taking an examination, and it is well known that criminals will frequently go to a brothel or to their lovers after they have committed a crime. In the realm of science, we find some psychologists who claim that sex and anxiety go together, and others who claim the two things are not even remotely connected. Their point of view is a subjective one, based on personal experience. That is why some see a connection, while others do not.

All these responses belong to different types of individuals. Research would probably reveal that such responses are to some extent hereditary. Certain physical expressions of this kind will often give us hints about the weaknesses and peculiarities of a family as a whole. Other members of the family may show very similar physical responses to a given situation. What is most interesting here, however, is to see how, through the emotions, the mind is able to act as a trigger to physical conditions.

Emotions and their physical expression tell us how the mind is acting and reacting in a situation it interprets as favourable or unfavourable. In an outburst of temper, for example, individuals wish to overcome their difficulties as quickly as possible. The best way, it seems to them, is to hit, accuse or attack another person. The anger, in its turn, influences the organs. It mobilizes them for action or tenses them up. Some people have stomach trouble when they are angry, or go red in the face. Their circulation is altered to such a degree that a headache ensues. One would generally expect to find suppressed rage or humiliation behind attacks of migraine or habitual headaches; and, with some people, anger results in trigeminal neuralgia or epileptic fits.

The means by which the emotions influence the body have never been completely explored, and we may never fully understand them. Mental tension affects both the voluntary and the involuntary nervous system. Where there is tension, there is action in the voluntary nervous system. Individuals drum on the table, bite their lips or shred paper. If they are tense, they seem compelled to move in some way. Chewing a pencil or their nails gives them an outlet for their tension. These movements show us that they feel threatened by some situation. It is the same whether they blush when they are among strangers, start to tremble, or exhibit a tic; these are all caused by anxiety and tension. By means of the involuntary nervous system, the tension is communicated to the whole body. Thus with every emotion the whole body is subjected to tension. The manifestations of this tension, however, are not always as clear as these examples, and we only refer here to those physical symptoms whose connection with nervous tension is clear and obvious.

If we delve more deeply we shall find that every part of the body is involved in an emotional expression, and that physical expressions are the consequences of interaction between the mind and the body. It is always important to look for these reciprocal actions of the mind on the body and of the body on the mind, since they are two parts of the whole with which we are concerned.

It would be reasonable to conclude from such evidence that one's life style and corresponding emotional disposition exert a continuous influence on the development of the body. If it is true that children's characters and life styles are formed very early in their life, we ought to be able to discover, if we are experienced enough, the resulting physical expressions in later life. Brave people will show the effects of their mental attitude in their physique. Their body will be differently built, their muscle tone will be firmer, the carriage of their body will be more upright. It is probable that posture has a considerable influence on the development of the body and may account in part for the better muscle tone. The expression of the face is different in the brave person and, in the end, the whole cast of the features is influenced. Even the shape of the skull may be affected.

It would be difficult to deny nowadays that the mind can influence the workings of the brain. Pathology has shown cases where an individual has lost the ability to read or write through an injury to the left hemisphere of the brain, but has been able to regain this ability by training other parts of the brain to take over this function. This often happens when an individual has a stroke and there is no possibility of repairing the damaged part of the brain. Other parts of the brain compensate, and so restore the functions of the organs. This fact is especially important in helping to demonstrate the possible educational application of Individual Psychology. If the mind can exercise such an influence over the brain, if the brain is no more than the tool of the mind – its most important tool, but only a tool nevertheless – then we can find ways to develop and improve this tool. No one need remain inescapably bound by the limitations of their brains all their life: methods may be found to train the brain, to make it better fitted for life.

A mind that has fixed its goal in a mistaken direction – and, for example, is not developing the ability to co-operate – will fail to exercise a helpful influence on the growth of the brain. For this reason we find that many children who lack the ability to co-operate show, in later life, that they have not fully developed their intelligence or their ability to understand. Since adults' whole bearing reveals the influence of the life style they built up in their first four or five years, since the results of their view of the world and the meaning they have ascribed to life are plain for all to see, we can discover the blocks in co-operation from which they are suffering, and help to correct their failures. In Individual Psychology we have already established the first steps towards this science.

MENTAL CHARACTERISTICS AND PHYSICAL TYPES
Many authors have pointed out a constant relationship between the expressions of the mind and those of the body. None of them, it seems, has attempted to discover the bridge or causal relationship between the two. Kretschmer, for example, has described how, by studying a person's physical characteristics, we can discover corresponding mental and emotional ones. He is thus able to distinguish types into categories into which he fits a great proportion of humankind. There are, for instance, the pyknoids, round-faced individuals with short noses and a tendency to

corpulence – the people of whom Shakespeare's Julius Caesar speaks:

> Let me have men about me that are fat;
> Sleek-headed men and such as sleep o' nights.
> *Julius Caesar*, Act I, Scene 2

Kretschmer correlates specific mental characteristics with such a physique, but his work does not make clear the reasons for this correlation. In our own society, individuals of this physique do not appear physically disadvantaged; their bodies are well suited to our culture. Physically they feel they are as good as anyone else. They have confidence in their own strength. They are not tense and, if they wished to fight, they would feel capable of fighting. They have no need, however, to look on others as their enemies or to struggle with life as if it were hostile. One school of psychology would call them extroverts, but would offer no explanation. We should expect them to be extroverts, however, because their bodies are not a source of anxiety.

A contrasting type that Kretschmer distinguishes is the schizoid, who either looks childlike or is unusually tall, long-nosed, and with an egg-shaped head. Schizoids, Kretschmer believes, are reserved and introspective. If they suffer from mental disturbances, they become schizophrenic. They are of the type of which Caesar says:

> Yond Cassius has a lean and hungry look;
> He thinks too much; such men are dangerous.
> *Julius Caesar*, Act I, Scene 2

Perhaps these individuals suffered from physical defects and grew up more self-centred, more pessimistic and more 'introverted'. Perhaps they made more demands for help, and when they found that they were not given sufficient attention, became bitter and suspicious. We can find, however, as Kretschmer admits, many mixed types, and even pyknoid types who have developed with the mental characteristics he has attributed to schizoids. We could understand this if their circumstances had trained them in this direction, making them timid and discouraged. We could probably, by systematic discouragement, make any child into a person who behaved like a schizoid.

With long experience, we can recognize from all these partial expressions the extent of a person's ability to co-operate. Without knowing it, people have always been looking for such signs. The necessity for co-operation makes constant demands on us, and hints have already been discovered, not scientifically but intuitively, which show us how to orient ourselves better in this chaotic life. In the same way we can see that, before all the great upheavals of history, the mind of the people had already recognized the necessity for change and was striving to achieve it. So long as the striving is purely instinctive, mistakes can easily be made. People have always disliked individuals with very noticeable physical peculiarities, shying away from disfigurement and deformity. Without knowing it, they were judging these people to be less fitted for co-operation. This was a great mistake, but their judgement was probably based on experience. The way had not yet been found to increase the degree of co-operation in individuals who suffered from these peculiarities. Their handicaps were therefore overemphasized, and they became the victims of popular superstition.

Let us now summarize our position. In the first four or five years of life, children unify their mental strivings and establish the root relationships between their mind and body. A fixed life style is formed, with corresponding emotional and physical habits and traits. It incorporates a specific degree of co-operation, large or small, and it is from this degree of co-operation that we learn to evaluate and understand individuals. For example, in all failures the common denominator is a poor ability to co-operate. We can now give yet another definition of psychology: it is the under-standing of deficiencies in co-operation. Since the mind is a unity and the same attitude to life runs through all its expressions, all of an individual's emotions and thoughts must be consistent with their life style. If we see emotions that apparently cause difficulties and run counter to the individual's own welfare, it is completely useless to begin by trying to change these emotions. They are a true expression of the individual's life style, and they can be uprooted only if they change it.

Here Individual Psychology gives us a special hint for our educational and therapeutic outlook. We must never treat one symptom or one single aspect of someone's personality. We must discover the wrong assumption people have made in choosing their life style, the way their mind has interpreted their experiences, the meaning they have ascribed to life, and the actions with which they have responded to the impressions received from their body and environment. This is the real task of psychology. Proper psychology does not involve sticking pins into children and seeing how high they jump, or tickling them and seeing how much they laugh. These enterprises, so common among modern psychologists, may in fact tell us something of an individual's psychology, but only in so far as they give evidence of a fixed and personal life style.

Life styles are the proper subject matter of psychology and the material for investigation, and psychologists who treat any other subject matter are occupied, in the main, with physiology or biology. This holds true of those who investigate stimuli and reactions, those who attempt to trace the effect of a *trauma* or shocking experience, and those who examine inherited abilities and observe how they develop. In Individual Psychology, however, we consider the psyche itself, the unified mind. We examine the meanings individuals ascribe to the world and to themselves, their goals, the direction of their strivings, and the way they approach the problems of life. So far, our best guide towards understanding individuals is the degree of their ability to co-operate.

3

FEELINGS OF INFERIORITY
AND SUPERIORITY

THE INFERIORITY COMPLEX

The 'inferiority complex', one of the most important discoveries of Individual Psychologists, has become world famous. Psychologists from many different schools or branches of the science have adopted the term and use it in their own practice. I am not at all sure, however, that they always fully understand it or use it in the right way. It is never helpful, for example, to tell patients that they are suffering from an inferiority complex. To do so would only emphasize their feelings of inferiority without showing them how to overcome them. We must recognize the sense of inadequacy that is revealed in their life style and encourage them at the very point where their courage fails them.

All neurotic people have an inferiority complex. They are defined by the kind of situation in which they feel unable to live a useful life, and by the limits they have set on their efforts and activities. Giving their problem a name is no help at all. We cannot make them courageous by saying, 'You are suffering from an inferiority complex', any more than we can help someone with a headache by saying, 'I can tell you what is wrong with you. You have a headache!'

Many neurotic people, if they were asked whether they felt inferior, would answer 'No'. Some would even answer, 'On the contrary. I feel superior to the people around me.' We do not need to ask: we need only observe their behaviour, which reveals the tricks they use to reassure themselves of their importance. If we see someone who is arrogant, for example, we can guess that he feels, 'Other people are likely to overlook me. I must show them that I am somebody important.' If we see someone who gesticulates strongly when he speaks, we can guess that he feels, 'My words would not carry any weight if I did not emphasize them'.

Behind all types of superior behaviour, we can suspect a feeling of inferiority which calls for very special efforts of concealment. It is as if a person feared that he was too short and walked on tiptoe to make himself seem larger. Sometimes we can see precisely this behaviour when two children are comparing their height. The one who is afraid that he is shorter will stretch up and hold himself very stiff: he will try to seem bigger than he is. If we asked such a child, 'Do you think you are too short?' we would hardly expect him to admit to it.

We cannot assume, therefore, that an individual with strong feelings of inferiority will appear to be a submissive, quiet, restrained, inoffensive sort of person. Feelings of inferiority can express themselves in a thousand ways. Perhaps I can illustrate this by telling the story of three children on their first trip to the zoo. As they stood before the lion's cage, one of them hid behind his mother's skirts and said 'I want to go home'. The second child stood where he was, very pale and trembling, and said, 'I'm not a bit frightened'. The third glared at the lion fiercely and asked his mother, 'Shall I spit at it?' All three children really felt afraid, but each expressed his feelings in his own way, in keeping with his life style.

To a certain degree we all experience feelings of inferiority, since we all find ourselves in situations we wish we could improve. If we have kept our courage, we shall set about ridding ourselves of these inferiority feelings by the only direct, realistic and satisfac- tory means – that of improving the situation. No human beings can bear a feeling of inferiority for long; they will be thrown into a state of stress that demands some kind of action. But suppose an individual is discouraged; suppose they cannot imagine that if they make realistic efforts they will improve their situation. They will still be unable to bear their feelings of inferiority. They will still struggle to get rid of them. But the methods they try will not get them any further forward. Their goal is still 'to be superior to difficulties', but instead of overcoming obstacles they will try to persuade, even force themsleves, into *feeling* superior. Meanwhile their feelings of inferiority will intensify, because the situation that produces them remains unaltered. Since the root cause is still there, every step they take will lead them further into self-deception, and all their problems will press in upon them with greater and greater urgency.

If we looked at their actions without understanding, we would think them aimless. They would not impress us as designed to improve the situation. As soon as we see, however, that they are occupied, like everyone else, in striving for a feeling of adequacy, but have given up hope of ever changing their situation, all that they do begins to make sense. If they feel weak, they create situations where they can feel strong. They do not train themsevles to be stronger, to be more adequate. Instead, they train themsleves to *appear* stronger in their own eyes. Their efforts to fool themselves will only be partially successful. If they feel unequal to their problems at work, they may attempt to reassure themselves of their own importance by being a tyrant at home. However much they deceive themselves in this way, their real feelings of inferiority will remain. They will be the same old feelings of inferiority provoked by the same old situations. They will constitute the permanent undercurrent of the individual's psychological make-up. In such cases we may truly speak of an inferiority complex.

It is time now to give a precise definition of the inferiority complex. The inferiority complex manifests itself in the presence of a problem for which individuals are not properly adapted or equipped, and highlight their conviction that they are unable to solve it. From this definition we can see that anger can be as much an expression of an inferiority complex as tears or excuses. As feelings of inferiority always produce stress, there will always be a compensatory movement towards a feeling of superiority, but it will not be directed towards solving the problem. The movement towards superiority will thus be towards the useless side of life. The real problem will be shelved or put to one side. Individuals will try to restrict their field of action and will be more concerned with avoiding defeat than with pressing forward to success. They will give the impression of hesitating, of standing still, or even of retreating in the face of difficulties.

Such an attitude can be seen very clearly in cases of agoraphobia. This symptom is an expression of the conviction, 'I must not go too far. I must keep myself to familiar circumstances. Life is full of dangers and I must avoid them.' Where this attitude is held consistently, the individual will keep to one room, or will retire to bed and stay there.

The most thoroughgoing expression of a retreat in the face of difficulties is suicide. Here, face to face with all the problems of life, individuals give up, and express their conviction that there is nothing they can do to improve things. The striving for superiority that is present in cases of suicide can be understood when we realize that suicide is always a reproach or a revenge. Suicide victims always lay the responsibility for their death at someone else's door. It is as if they said, 'I was the most vulnerable, most sensitive person in the world, and you treated me with the utmost brutality.'

To some degree or other, all neurotic people restrict their field of action and their contacts with the world. They try to keep at a distance the three real, pressing problems of life and confine themselves to situations in which they feel able to dominate. In this way they build themselves a narrow cell, close the door and spend their life protected from the elements. Whether they dominate by bullying or by whining will depend on their upbringing: they will choose the device which they have found most effective for their purposes. Sometimes, if they are dissatisfied with one method, they will try the other. In either case the goal is the same – to gain a feeling of superiority without working to improve the situation.

For example, discouraged children who find that they can best get their own way by tears will be a cry-baby. The cry-baby leads directly to the adult melancholic. Tears and complaints – which I call 'water-power' – can be an extremely effective weapon for disrupting co-operation and enslaving other people. With cry-babies, as with people who suffer from shyness, embarrassment and feelings of guilt, we can see the inferiority complex on the surface. These people readily admit their weakness and their inability to look after themselves. What they would like to hide is their obsessive goal of supremacy, their desire to be first at all costs.

Children given to boasting, on the other hand, appear at first sight to have a superiority complex. If, however, we examine their behaviour rather than their words, we soon discover their unadmitted feelings of inferiority.

The so-called Oedipus complex is in reality nothing more than a special instance of the 'narrow cell' of the neurotic person. If individuals are afraid to meet the problem of love in the world at large, they will not succeed in ridding themselves of their neurosis. If they confine themselves to the family circle, it will not surprise us to find that their sexuality is expressed within these limits. Because of feelings of insecurity, they have never looked beyond the few people with whom they are most familiar. They are afraid they may not be able to dominate other people as they are accustomed to dominate those in his own circle. The victims of the Oedipus complex are children who were spoilt by their parents, who were brought up to believe their every wish was law, and who never realized that they could win affection and love by their independent efforts outside the bounds of the home. In adult life such people stay bound to their parents. In love they do not look for an equal partner, but for a servant; and the servant of whose support they are most sure is their parent. We could probably induce an Oedipus complex in any child. All we should need is for his mother to spoil him, and refuse to interest him in other people, and for his father to be comparatively indifferent or cold.

All the symptoms of neurosis give a picture of restricted movement. In stammering speech we can see a hesitant attitude. A residue of social interest drives stammerers to make contact with other people, but their low self-esteem and fear of failing the test are in conflict with their social interest, so they hesitate in their speech. Children who are 'backward' at school, men and women who are still without an occupation at the age of thirty or more, people who have evaded the problem of marriage, compulsive neurotics who continually repeat the same actions, insomniacs who are always too weary to face the tasks of the day – all of them reveal an inferiority complex that forbids them to make progress in solving the problems of life. People whose sexuality is characterized by masturbation, premature ejaculation, impotence and deviance all show a faulty approach to life, caused by a feeling of inadequacy in their approach to the other sex. The concomitant goal of supremacy will suggest itself if we ask, 'Why such feelings of inadequacy?' The answer can only be, 'Because individuals have set themselves an impossibly ambitious goal.'

We have said that feelings of inferiority are not in themselves abnormal. They are the cause of all improvements in the human condition. Scientific progress, for example, is possible only when people are conscious of their ignorance and their need to prepare themselves for the future; it is the result of the strivings of human beings to improve their lot, to learn more about the universe and to be better able to deal with it. Indeed, it seems to me that all our human culture is based upon feelings of inferiority. If we can imagine disinterested observers visiting our planet, they would surely conclude, 'These human beings, with all their associations and institutions, with all their striving for security, with their roofs to keep off the rain, their clothes to keep them warm, their paved streets to make travel easier – obviously they feel they are the weakest creatures on earth.' And in some ways human beings *are* the weakest creatures on earth. We do not have the strength of the lion or the gorilla, and many animals are better equipped than we are to face the difficulties of life alone. Some animals compensate for their weakness by association – they join together in herds – but human beings need more varied and more fundamental co-operation than we can find anywhere else in the world of nature.

Human children are especially weak; they need care and protection for many years. Since all human beings have at one time been the youngest and weakest of creatures, and since humankind, without co-operation, would be completely at the mercy of its environment, we can understand how children who have not trained themselves in co-operation will be driven towards pessimism and a persistent inferiority complex. We can also understand that life will continue to pose problems even for the most co-operative individuals. No individuals will ever find themselves in the position of having reached their final goal of superiority, of being complete masters of their environment. Life is too short, our bodies are too weak, the three problems of life will

NOT true!

always demand richer and fuller solutions. We can always find an interim solution, but we can never feel completely satisfied with our achievements. The striving will continue in any case; but in the case of the co-operative individual it will be hopeful, useful striving, directed towards a real improvement in our common situation.

Nobody will worry, I think, about the fact that we can never reach our ultimate goal. Let us imagine a single individual, or humankind as a whole, having reached a position where there were no further difficulties. Surely life in these circumstances would be very dull: everything could be foreseen, everything calculated in advance. Tomorrow would bring no unexpected opportunities and there would be nothing to look forward to in the future. Our interest in life comes mainly from our uncertainty. If we were all sure about everything, if we knew all there was to know, there would be no more discussions or discoveries. Science would come to an end; the universe around us would be nothing but a twice-told tale. Art and religion, which provide us with an ideal to aim for, would no longer have any meaning. It is our good fortune that life's challenges are inexhaustible. Human striving is never-ending and we can always find or invent new problems, and create new opportunities for co-operation and contribution.

But neurotic people's development is blocked at the very beginning. Their solutions to life's problems remain at a superficial level and their personal difficulties are correspondingly great. The more normal individuals devise increasingly meaningful solutions to their problems; they can move on to new difficulties and arrive at new solutions. In this way they become capable of contributing to society. They do not lag behind and become a liability to their fellow human beings; they do not need or demand special consideration. Instead, they proceed with courage and independence to solve their problems in accordance with their social feeling as well as their own needs.

THE GOAL OF SUPERIORITY
The goal of superiority is personal and unique to each individual. It depends upon the meaning they ascribe to life. This meaning is not merely a matter of words. It is revealed in the life style and

runs through it like a strange melody of the individual's own creation. They do not express their goal in such a way that we can formulate it conclusively. Rather, they express it obliquely, so that we have to guess at it from the clues they give. Understanding someone's life style is like understanding the work of a poet. Poets use only words, but their meaning is more than the mere words they use. The greatest part of their meaning must be deduced by study and intuition; we must read between the lines. So too with that most profound and intricate creation, a personal philosophy of life. Psychologists must learn to read between the lines; they must learn the art of perceiving hidden meanings.

How could it possibly be otherwise? We decide what life means to us in the first four or five years of our existence. We do not do so by a mathematical calculation, but by groping in the dark, by experiencing feelings we cannot wholly understand, by catching hints and fumbling for explanations. Similarly, we decide on our goal of superiority by groping and guesswork; it is a lifelong urge, a dynamic tendency, not a charted and geographically determined point. Nobody is conscious of their own goal of superiority to the extent that they can describe it in full. Perhaps they know their professional aims, but these are no more than a small proportion of their strivings. Even if the goal has been clearly defined, there can be a thousand ways of striving towards it. One person, for example, will want to be a doctor, but to be a doctor may mean many different things. Not only may they wish to be a specialist in one particular field of medicine, they will show in their professional life their own peculiar degree of interest in themselves and interest in others. We shall see how far they train themselves to be of help to their fellow human beings and what limits they set for their helpfulness. They have made this profession their aim as a compensation for a specific feeling of inferiority; and we must be able to guess, from their behaviour in their profession and elsewhere, the specific feeling for which they are compensating.

We very frequently find, for example, that doctors were confronted with the realities of death quite early in their childhood. Death was the aspect of human insecurity that made the greatest impression on them. Perhaps a sibling or a parent died, and their later training developed towards finding a way, for themselves and others, of feeling more secure against death. Others may make it their declared goal to be a teacher, but we are well aware how many different kinds of teachers there are. If teachers have a low degree of social feeling, their goal of superiority in being a teacher may be to be a big fish in a small pond. They may feel secure only with those who are weaker and less experienced than themselves. Teachers with a high degree of social feeling will treat their pupils as their equals; they will genuinely wish to contribute to the welfare of humankind. We need only mention here how different the capacities and interests of teachers may be, and how clearly their behaviour points to their personal goals. When a goal is clearly defined, the individual's potentialities must be curtailed and limited to fit this goal; but the overall goal, which we will call the prototype, will always push and pull at these limits and find a way, under any conditions, to express the meaning that the person ascribes to life and their final ideal striving for superiority.

With every individual, therefore, we must look below the surface. Individuals may change the way in which they define and declares their goal, just as they may change one expression of their declared goal, namely their occupation. Consequently, we must look for underlying coherence, for the unity of the personality. This unity is fixed in all its expressions. If we take an irregular triangle and rotate it into different positions, each position will seem to give us quite a different triangle; but if we look hard we shall discover that it is the same triangle all the time. So, too, with the prototype. Its content is never fully expressed by any single aspect of behaviour, but we can recognize it in all its expressions. We can never say to a person, 'Your striving for superiority would be fully satisfied if you did this or that . . .' The striving for superiority remains flexible; and, indeed, the nearer to health and normality individuals are, the more they can find new openings for their strivings when they are blocked in one particular direction. It is only neurotic people who look at the goal they have set for themselves and say, 'I must have this or nothing.'

We should be careful not to make too hasty an assessment of any particular striving for superiority, but we can find in all goals one common factor – a striving to be god-like. Sometimes we find children who express themselves quite openly in this way, and remark, 'I should like to be God'. Many philosophers have had the same idea. There are also some teachers who want to train and educate children to be like God. In old religious disciplines the same objective is visible: disciples should educate themselves in such a way that they become god-like. This concept of god-likeness appears in a more modest form in the idea of 'superman'; and it is revealing – I shall not say more – that Nietzsche, when he became insane, signed himself in a letter to Strindberg, 'The Crucified'.

Insane people often express their goal of god-like superiority quite openly: they will assert, 'I am Napoleon', or 'I am the Emperor of China'. They wish to be the centre of worldwide attention, to be constantly in the public eye, to be in radio contact with the whole world and overhear every conversation. They wish to predict the future, and to possess supernatural powers.

In a more moderate and reasonable way, perhaps, the same goal of god-likeness is expressed in the desire to know everything, to possess universal wisdom, or in the wish to perpetuate our life. Whether it is our earthly life we desire to perpetuate, or whether we imagine ourselves as coming to earth again and again in many incarnations, or whether we foresee immortality in another world, these expectations are all based upon the desire to be like God. In religious teachings it is God who is the immortal being, who survives through all time and eternity. I am not discussing here whether these ideas are right or wrong: they are interpretations of life, they are *meanings*, and to some degree we are all caught up in this meaning – God and god-likeness. Even the atheist wishes to conquer God, to be higher than God; and we can recognize this as a peculiarly strong goal of superiority.

Once a person's goal of superiority has been defined, there are no mistakes made in their life style; all actions are consistent with that goal. The habits and behaviour of the individual are precisely right for attaining their declared goal, and they are beyond all criticism. The life style of every problem child, every neurotic, every alcoholic, criminal or sexual deviant reflects the behaviour appropriate to achieving what they take to be the position of superiority. It is impossible to criticize their behaviour in itself; it is exactly the behaviour they ought to display if they are pursuing such a goal.

A boy at one school, the laziest boy in the class, was asked by his teacher, 'Why do you do so badly in your schoolwork?' He answered, 'If I am the laziest boy here, you will always give me lots of your time. You never pay any attention to good boys, who never disturb the class and do all their work properly.' So long as his aim was to attract attention and to control his teacher, he had found the best way to do it. It would be no use trying to get rid of his laziness: he needed his laziness for his goal. From this point of view he was perfectly in the right, and if he changed his behaviour he would be a fool.

Another boy was very obedient at home but he seemed to be stupid; he was backward at school and not at all quick-witted at home. He had a brother two years older than he was, and his brother was quite different in his life style. He was intelligent and lively but he was always getting into trouble because of his impudence. The younger brother was one day overheard saying to the older brother, 'I'd rather be as stupid as I am than as impudent as you are'. His apparent stupidity may be seen as an expression of intelligence once we realize that it was his way of achieving his goal: to keep out of trouble. Because of his stupidity, less was demanded of him, and if he made mistakes he was not blamed for them. Given his goal, he would have been a fool not to be stupid!

Up to the present day, problems have usually been treated by tackling the symptoms. Individual Psychology is entirely opposed to this approach, both in medicine and in education. When children are backward in arithmetic, or have bad school reports, it is useless to concentrate our attention on these particular aspects and try to improve them. Perhaps they want to upset the teacher, or even to escape school altogether by getting themselves expelled. If we prevent them from using one method, they will find a new way to reach their goal.

It is just the same with adult neurotics. Suppose for example, they suffer from migraine. These headaches can be very useful to them and they may occur at the precise moment when they have greatest need of them. Through these headaches they may avoid confronting the problems of life. The headaches may come on whenever they are obliged to meet new people or make a decision. At the same time, they may assist in tyrannizing over their office staff or their partner and family. Why should we expect them to give up such a proven device? The pain they give themselves, from their point of view, is no more than a wise investment; it brings in all the returns they could wish for. No doubt we could frighten them out of their headaches by giving them an explanation that would shock them, just as shell-shocked soldiers were sometimes frightened out of their symptoms by electric shocks or fake operations. Perhaps medical treatment would provide relief and make it more difficult for them to continue with the particular symptom they have chosen. But, so long as their goal remains the same, if they give up one symptom they must find another. 'Cured' of their headaches, they will develop insomnia, or some other fresh symptom. So long as their goal remains the same, they must continue to pursue it.

Some neurotic people can drop symptoms with astonishing rapidity and take on new ones without a moment's hesitation. They become virtuosos of neurosis, continually extending their repertoire. Reading a book on psychotherapy will suggest to them still more nervous troubles that they have not yet had the opportunity of trying out. What we must always look for is the purpose for which the symptom is adopted and the consistency of this purpose with the general goal of superiority.

Suppose in my classroom I sent for a ladder, climbed up it, and perched on top of the blackboard. Anyone seeing me would probably think, 'Dr Adler is crazy'. They would not know what the ladder was for, why I climbed it, or why I was sitting in such an uncomfortable position. But if they knew, 'He wants to sit on the blackboard because he feels inferior unless he is physically higher than other people; he only feels secure if he can look down on his class', they would not think I was quite so crazy. I would have chosen an excellent way to attain my declared goal. The ladder would then seem a very sensible device, and my efforts to climb up it would appear well planned and executed.

Only on one point would I be crazy – my interpretation of superiority. If I could be convinced that my declared goal was badly chosen, then I could change my activity. But if the goal remained, and my ladder was taken away, I would try again with a chair; and if the chair was taken away, I would see what I could do by jumping and climbing, and pulling myself up by my own strength. It is the same with all neurotic people: nothing is wrong with their choice of means – they are beyond criticism. It is only the declared goal we can improve. With a change of goal, their mental habits and attitudes will also change. They will no longer need the old habits and attitudes, and new ones, fitted to their new goal, will soon replace them.

Let us look at the example of a woman of thirty who came to me suffering from anxiety and an inability to make friends: this woman could not successfully earn her own living, and in consequence was still a burden on her family. She would take small jobs from time to time as a secretary, but unfortunately her employers would always make amorous advances to her and scare her so much that she had to leave the office. Once, however, she found a place where her employer was less interested in her and made no advances at all. She felt so humiliated that she left this job too. She had been receiving psychiatric treatment for many years – eight years, I believe – but her treatment had not succeeded in improving her sociability or putting her in a position where she could earn her living.

When I saw her, I traced back her life style to the first years of her childhood. No one can understand the grown-up without first learning to understand the child. She had been the youngest in her family, very pretty, and spoilt and indulged beyond belief. Her parents were very well off at the time, and she had only to express a wish for it to be granted. 'Why', I said when I heard this, 'you were brought up like a princess.' 'That's odd', she replied.

'Everybody used to call me Princess . . .' I asked her what her earliest recollection was. 'When I was four years old', she said, 'I remember going out of the house and finding some children who were playing a game. Every so often they jumped up and called out, "The witch is coming". I was very frightened and when I got back home, I asked an old woman who was staying with us whether there were really such things as witches. She answered, "Yes, there are witches and burglars and robbers, and they will all come after you."'

From this we can see that she was afraid to be left alone. She expressed her fear in her whole life style. She did not feel strong enough to leave home, and those at home had to support her and look after her in every way. Another early recollection was as follows: 'I had a piano teacher, a man, and one day he tried to kiss me. I stopped playing and went and told my mother. After that, I didn't want to play the piano any more.' Here, too, we can see that she trained herself to put a great distance between herself and men, and her sexual development was in accordance with the goal of protecting herself against love. She felt that to be in love was a weakness.

Here I must say that many people feel weak if they are in love, and to a certain degree they are right. If we are in love we must be tender, and our interest in another human being leaves us vulnerable. Only individuals whose goal of superiority is never to be weak or exposed will avoid the mutual dependence of love. Such people shy away from love and are ill-prepared for it. Often you will find that if they feel in danger of falling in love, they turn the situation to ridicule. They laugh and make jokes and tease the person by whom they feel threatened. In this way they try to rid themselves of their feeling of weakness.

This girl, too, felt weak in relation to love and marriage, and in consequence she was much more strongly affected than she needed to be when men made advances to her at work. She could see no way out other than to run away. While she was still confronted with these problems, her mother and father both died and with them the 'princess's' court almost ended too. However, she managed to find relatives to come and look after

her, but her position was not nearly so satisfactory. After a while
her relatives would become very bored with her and would stop
paying her the attention she felt she needed. She scolded them
and told them how dangerous it was for her to be left alone, and
in this way she staved off the tragedy of being left to her own
devices.

I am convinced that if her family had given up bothering about
her altogether, she would have gone mad. The only way to
accomplish her goal of superiority was to force her family to support
her and allow her to exclude all the problems of life. She kept in
her own mind the image, 'I do not belong to this planet, but to
another planet where I am a princess. This poor earth does not
understand me or acknowledge my importance.' One step further
would have led her to insanity, but so long as she had some small
resources of her own and could still persuade relatives or family
friends to take care of her, there was no need for the final step.

Here is another case where both the inferiority complex and
the superiority complex can be clearly recognized. A girl of
sixteen was sent to me, who had been stealing since she was six or
seven and staying out at night with boys since she was twelve.
When she was two years old her parents had divorced after a long
and bitter personal struggle. She was taken by her mother to live
with her in her grandmother's home, and her grandmother, as so
often happens, proceeded to indulge and pamper the child. She
had been born when the struggle between her parents was at its
height and her mother had not welcomed her arrival. She had
never liked her daughter and considerable tension existed
between them.

When the girl came to see me I talked with her in a friendly
way. She told me, 'I don't really enjoy stealing things or running
about with boys, but I've got to show my mother that she can't
control me.'

'You do it for revenge?' I asked her. 'I suppose so', she
answered. She wanted to prove that she was stronger than her
mother, but she had this goal only because she felt weaker. She
felt her mother disliked her and she suffered from an inferiority
complex. The only way she could think of to assert her superiority

was to cause trouble. When children commit thefts or other delin-
quencies, it is usually for revenge.

A girl of fifteen disappeared for eight days. When she was
found she was taken to the juvenile court, and there she told a
tale of having been kidnapped by a man who had bound her and
kept her locked in a room for eight days. No one believed her.
The doctor spoke privately with her and urged her to tell the
truth. She was so angry with him for not accepting her story that
she slapped him in the face. When I saw her, I asked her what she
wanted to be, and showed her I was interested only in her welfare
and in what I could do to help her. When I asked her for a dream,
she laughed and told me the following: 'I was in a bar. When I
went out, I met my mother. Soon my father came, and I asked my
mother to hide me, so that he would not see me.'

She was afraid of her father and was fighting him. He used to
punish her, and because she was afraid of punishment she was
forced to lie. If we ever hear of a case of lying, we must look for a
severe parent. There would be no sense in lying unless the truth
were felt to be dangerous. On the other hand, we can see that this
girl co-operated to some extent with her mother. She then
admitted to me that someone had enticed her into a bar and she
had spent the eight days there. She was frightened of confessing
because of her father, but at the same time her actions had been
prompted by the desire to get the better of him. She felt
subjugated by him, and she could feel superior to him only by
hurting him.

How can we help people who have taken the wrong turning in
their search for superiority? It is not difficult if we recognize that
the striving for superiority is common to everyone. We can then
put ourselves in their place and sympathize with their struggles.
The only mistake they make is that their strivings serve no useful
purpose. It is the striving for superiority that motivates every
human being and is the source of every contribution we make to
our culture. The whole of human life proceeds along this great
line of action – from below to above, from minus to plus, from
defeat to victory. The only individuals who can really meet and
master the problems of life, however, are those who show in their

striving a tendency to enrich everyone else, those who forge ahead in such a way that others benefit too.

If we approach people in the right way, we shall not find them hard to convince. All human judgements of value and success are founded, in the end, upon co-operation; this is the great universal truism of the human race. All that we ask of conduct, of ideals, of goals, of actions and traits of character, is that they should serve the cause of human co-operation. Nobody is completely devoid of social feeling. The neurotic person and the criminal also know this open secret; we can see their knowledge in the pains they take to justify their life styles or to put the blame on someone else. They have lost the courage, however, to conduct their lives in a useful way. An inferiority complex tells them, 'Success in co-operation is not for you'. They have turned away from the real problems of life and are engaged in shadow-boxing to reassure themselves of their strength.

In our human division of labour there is room for a great variety of goals. Perhaps, as we have seen, every goal may involve some small degree of mistakenness, and we could always find something to criticize. But human co-operation has need of many different kinds of excellence. To one child, superiority will seem to lie in mathematical knowledge, to another in art, to a third in physical strength. Children with a weak digestive system may come to believe that the problems confronting them are mainly problems of nutrition. Their interest may turn towards food, since in this way they believe they can better their situation, and in consequence they may become an expert cook or a professor of nutrition. In all these special goals we can see, together with a real compensation for difficulties, some exclusion of possibilities, some training towards self-limitation. We can understand, for example, that philosophers must exile themselves from society from time to time, to think and write books. But the inevitable mistake involved with each goal is never great if a high degree of social interest accompanies the goal of superiority.

4

EARLY MEMORIES

KEYS TO THE PERSONALITY

Since the struggle to reach a position of superiority is the key to the whole personality of individuals, we meet it at every point of their psychic development. Having recognized this fact, we can use it to understand their life style. There are two important points to remember. First, we can start wherever we like: every expression will lead us in the same direction – towards the one motive, the one theme, around which her personality is built. Second, a vast store of material is provided for us. Every word, thought, feeling or gesture contributes to our understanding. Any mistake we might make in evaluating too hastily one facet or expression of personality can be checked and corrected by reference to a thousand others. We cannot finally decide the meaning of one facet until we can see the part it plays in the whole; but every facet is saying the same thing, and prompts us towards the solution.

We are like archaeologists who find fragments of earthenware and tools, the ruined walls of buildings, broken monuments and leaves of papyrus, and from these fragments proceed to infer the life of a whole city that has perished. But we are dealing not with something that has perished, but with all the interrelated facets of a human being, a living personality that can set before us a kaleidoscope of new manifestations of its own interpretation of life.

It is not an easy task to understand a human being. Individual Psychology is perhaps the most difficult of all psychologies to learn and to practise. We must always listen for the whole story. We must be sceptical until the key becomes self-evident. We must gather hints from a multitude of small signs – from the way a person enters a room, the way they greet us and shake hands, the way they smile, the way they walk. We may go astray on one point, but others are always available to correct or confirm our impressions. Treatment itself is an exercise in co-operation and a test of co-operation. We can succeed only if we are genuinely interested in others. We must be able to see through their eyes and hear through their ears. They must contribute their part to our shared understanding. We must work out their attitudes and difficulties together. Even if we felt we had understood them, we would have no proof that we were right unless they also understood themselves. A tactless truth can never be the whole truth; it shows that our understanding was insufficient.

It is perhaps from a failure to understand this point that other schools of psychology have derived the concept of 'negative and positive transferences', factors that are never met in Individual Psychology treatment. To indulge patients who are accustomed to being indulged may be an easy way to gain their affections, but their desire for domination will be apparent underneath. If we slight them and overlook them, we may easily incur their enmity. They may discontinue the treatment, or they may continue it in the hope of justifying themselves and making us sorry. We cannot help them either by indulging them or by slighting them; we must show them the interest of one human being towards another. No interest could be more genuine or more objective. We must co-operate with them in finding their mistakes, both for their own benefit and for the welfare of others. With this aim in view we shall never run the risk of generating 'transferences', of posing as authorities, or of putting them in a position of dependence and irresponsibility.

Among all psychic expressions, some of the most revealing are individuals' memories. Their memories are the reminders they carry about with them of their own limitations and of the meaning of events. There are no 'chance memories'. Out of the incalculable number of impressions that individuals receive, they choose to remember only those which they consider, however dimly, to have a bearing on their problems. These memories represent their life story, a story they repeat to themselves for warmth or comfort, to keep them concentrated on their goal, or to prepare them, by means of past experiences, to meet the future with a tried and tested approach. The use of memories to stabilize a mood can be clearly seen in everyday behaviour. If individuals suffer a setback and are discouraged by it, they recall previous setbacks. If they are melancholy, all their memories are melancholy. When they are cheerful and courageous, they select quite different memories. The incidents they recall are pleasant, they confirm their optimism. In the same way, if they are confronted with a problem, they will summon up memories that help to shape the attitude with which they will meet it.

Memories thus serve much the same purpose as dreams. Many people, when they have decisions to make, will dream of an examination they have successfully passed. They see their decision as a test, and try to re-create the mood in which they have previously been successful. What holds true of the variations of mood within an individual life style, holds true also of the structure and balance of moods in general. Melancholy people could not remain melancholy if they dwelt on their good moments and their successes. They say to themsleves, 'I have been unlucky all my life', and select only those events they can interpret as instances of their unhappy fate.

EARLY MEMORIES AND LIFE STYLES

Memories can never run counter to one's life style. If an individual's goal of superiority demands they should feel, 'Other people always humiliate me', they will choose to remember incidents they can interpret as humiliations. As their life style changes, their memories will change too. They will remember different incidents, or they will put a different interpretation on the incidents they remember.

Early memories are especially significant. To begin with, they show the life style in its origins and in its simplest expressions. We can judge from these early memories whether children were pampered or neglected; how far they were trained for co-operation with others; whom they preferred to co-operate with; what problems confronted them, and how they struggled against them. In the early recollections of children who suffered from visual difficulties and who trained themselves to look more closely, we shall find impressions of a visual nature. Their recollections will begin, 'I looked around me . . .', or they will describe colours and shapes. Children who had physical difficulties, who wanted to walk or run or jump, will show these interests in their recollections. Events remembered from childhood must be very close to the main interest of individuals; and if we know their main interest, we know their goal and personal life style. It is this fact which makes early memories of such value in vocational guidance. In them we can find, moreover, the children's relationships with their mother, father and other members of the family. It is comparatively unimportant whether the memories are accurate or not; what is most valuable about them is the fact that they represent the individual's judgement: 'Even when I was a child, I was such and such a person', or 'Even as a child, I saw the world like this'.

Most illuminating of all is the way children begin their story, the earliest incident they can recall. The first memory shows the individual's fundamental view of life, their first satisfactory expression of their attitude. It allows us to see at one glance what they have taken as the starting point for their development. I would never investigate a personality without asking for the first memory.

Sometimes people do not answer, or profess that they do not know which event came first, but this itself is revealing. We can gather that they do not wish to discuss their fundamental philosophy of life, and that they are not prepared to co-operate. In general, however, people are perfectly willing to discuss their first memories. They take them as mere facts, and do not realize the meaning hidden in them. Scarcely anyone understands a first memory, and most people are therefore able to confess their purpose in life, their relationships with others and their view of the environment in a perfectly neutral and natural manner through their first memories. Another point of interest in first memories is that their compression and simplicity allows us to use them for group investigations. We can ask a school class to write their earliest recollections and, if we know how to interpret them, we have an extremely useful picture of each child.

Shape peoples' personalities

ANALYSING EARLY MEMORIES

Let me, for the sake of illustration, give a few first memories and attempt to interpret them. I know nothing about the individuals other than the memories they recount – not even whether they are children or adults. The meaning we find in their first memories would have to be checked against other expressions of their personality, but we can practise our skills by taking them as they stand and sharpening our ability to guess the rest. We will then know what might be true, and will be able to compare one memory with another. In particular, we will be able to see whether individuals are moving towards co-operation or away from it, whether they are bold or timid, whether they wish to be supported and watched or to be self-reliant and independent, and whether they are prepared to give or are anxious only to receive.

1. '*Since my sister . . .*' It is important to notice which people occur in first memories. When a sister occurs, we can be pretty sure that the individual has felt very much under her influence. The sister has overshadowed the other child's development. Generally we find a rivalry between the two, as if they were competing in a race, which clearly offers additional difficulties in development. Children cannot extend their interest to others as effectively when they are preoccupied with rivalry as they can when they co-operate on friendly terms. We must not jump to conclusions, however. Perhaps the two children were good friends.

'*Since my sister and I were the youngest in the family, I was not allowed to attend school until she (the younger) was old enough to go.*' Now the rivalry becomes evident: 'My sister held me back! She was younger, but I was forced to wait for her. She limited my opportunities!' If this is really the meaning of the memory, we would expect this girl or boy to feel: 'It is the greatest danger in my life when someone restricts me and prevents my free development.' The writer is probably a girl. It seems less likely that a boy would be held back until a younger sister was ready to go to school.

'*Accordingly, we began on the same day.*' We would not regard this as the best kind of upbringing for a girl in her position. It might well give her the impression that, because she is older, she must stay behind. In any case, we can see that this particular girl has interpreted it in this sense. She feels that she is neglected in favour of her sister. She will blame someone for this neglect. That someone will probably be her mother. We should not be surprised if she leaned more towards her father, and tried to make herself his favourite.

'I recall distinctly that mother told everyone how lonely she was on our first day at school. She said, "I ran out to the gate several times that afternoon and looked for the girls. It seemed to me they would never come home."' This is a description of the mother, and one that does not show her behaving in a very intelligent way. It is the girl's portrait of her mother. 'It seemed to her we would never come home' – the mother was obviously affectionate, and the girls were aware of her affection, but at the same time she was anxious and tense. If we could speak to this girl, she could tell us more of the mother's preference for the younger sister. Such a preference would not astonish us, for the youngest child is almost always pampered. I would conclude from this memory that the elder of the two sisters felt hindered by her rivalry with the younger. In later life we would expect to find signs of jealousy and fear of competition. It would not surprise us to find her disliking women younger than herself. Some people feel too old all through their lives, and many jealous women feel inferior to members of their own sex who are younger than they are.

2. 'My earliest recollection is of my grandfather's funeral, when I was three years old.' This is a girl writing. Death has made a deep impression on her. What does this mean? She viewed death as the greatest insecurity of her life, the greatest danger. From the events that happened to her in her childhood she deduced the moral, 'Grandfather can die'. We will probably find that she was her grandfather's favourite and that he spoilt her. Grandparents nearly always spoil their grandchildren. They have less responsibility towards them than parents, and often wish to attach the children to themselves and show that they can still gain affection. Our culture does not make it easy for older people to feel assured of

their worth and sometimes they seek this reassurance through easy means – through querulousness, for example. Here we are inclined to believe that the grandfather spoilt this girl when she was a baby and that it was his pampering that fixed him so deeply in her memory. When he died, it was a great blow to her. A servant and ally had been taken away.

'*I remember so vividly seeing him in his coffin, lying there so still and white.*' I am not sure that it is a good idea to let a child of three see a dead person, especially if they have not been prepared beforehand. Many children have told me that they had been deeply impressed by the sight of someone who had died, and could never forget it. This girl has not forgotten it. Such children strive to diminish or overcome the threat of death. Often their ambition is to become a doctor. They feel that a doctor is better trained than others to fight against death. If a doctor is asked his first memory, it will often include some remembrance of death. 'Lying in the coffin so still and white' – a memory of something seen. This girl is probably a visual type, interested in looking at the world.

'*Then at the grave, as the coffin was lowered, I recall those straps being pulled out from underneath the rough box.*' Again she tells us what she saw, which confirms our guess that she is a visual type. '*This experience seems to have left me feeling fearful at any mention of one of my relations, friends or acquaintances who have passed to the other life beyond.*'

Again we can see the deep impression that death made on her. If I had the opportunity to speak to her, I would ask, 'What would you like to be when you grow up?' and perhaps she would answer, 'A doctor'. If she made no answer or avoided the question, then I would suggest, 'Wouldn't you like to be a doctor or a nurse?' When she mentions 'the other life beyond', we can see one type of compensation for the fear of death. What we have learned from her memory as a whole is that her grandfather was friendly to her, that she is a visual type, and that death plays a great role in her mind. The meaning she has drawn from life is, 'We must all die'. This is undoubtedly true, but not everybody has this preoccupation. There are other interests we can occupy ourselves with.

3. '*When I was three years old, my father . . .*' Right at the beginning
her father crops up. We can assume that this girl was more
interested in her father than her mother. An interest in the father
is always a second phase of development. At first a child is more
interested in the mother, since in the first year or two co-
operation with the mother is very close. The child needs the
mother and is attached to her; all the child's psychic strivings are
bound up with the mother. If the child turns to the father, the
mother has lost the game. This child is not satisfied with her
situation. This is generally the result of the birth of a younger
child. If we hear in this recollection that there is a younger child,
our guess will be confirmed.

'*My father bought a pair of ponies for us.*' There is more than one
child, and we are interested to hear about the other. '*He brought
them by their halters to the house. My sister, who is three years older
than me . . .*' We must revise our interpretation. We had expected
this girl to be the older sister, and she proves to be the younger.
Perhaps the older sister was the mother's favourite, and this is why
the girl mentions her father and the present of the two ponies.

'*My sister took one rope and led her pony proudly down the street.*'
Here is a triumph for the older sister. '*My own pony, hurrying after
the other, went too fast for me*' – these are the consequences when
her sister takes the lead! – '*and dragged me face downward in the
dirt.*' It was an ignominious end to an experience that had been
gloriously anticipated. The sister has conquered, she has scored a
point. We can be quite sure that this girl means, 'If I am not
careful, my older sister will always win. I am always being
defeated, I am always in the dirt. The only way to be safe is to be
first.' We can understand, also, that the older sister had triumphed
with the mother; and that this was the reason why the younger
sister turned to her father.

'*The fact that I later became a better rider than my sister never
softened this disappointment in the least.*' All our suppositions are
now confirmed. We can see the race that took place between the
two sisters. The younger felt, 'I am always behind, I must try to get
ahead. I must pass the others.' This is a type I have previously
described, which is very common among second or youngest

children. Such children always have an older brother or sister as a pacemaker, and are always striving to overtake them. This girl's memory reinforces her attitude. It says to her, 'If anyone is ahead of me I am threatened. I must always be in the lead.'

4. '*My earliest recollections are of being taken to parties and other social events by my older sister, who was about eighteen when I was born.*' This girl remembers herself as a part of society; perhaps we shall find in this memory a higher degree of co-operation than in the others. Her sister, eighteen years older, must have been like a mother to her, the member of the family who spoilt her most; but she seems to have broadened the child's interest in a very intelligent fashion.

'*Since until my arrival, my sister was the only girl in a family of four boys, she was naturally pleased to show me off.*' This does not sound nearly so good as we thought. When a child is 'shown off', it may become interested only in being appreciated by society, instead of contributing to it. '*She therefore took me about when I was comparatively young. The only thing I can remember about these parties is that I was continually urged to say something: "Tell the lady your name", and so on.*' A mistaken method of education – we should not be surprised to find that this girl stammered or had speech difficulties. When children stammer, it is generally because too great an emphasis was placed on their speech. Instead of communicating with others naturally and without stress, they were taught to be self-conscious and to look for appreciation.

'*I can also remember that I would say nothing and was invariably scolded when I returned home, so that I came to hate going out and meeting people.*' Our interpretation must be completely revised. We can see now that the meaning behind her first memory is, 'I was brought into contact with other people, but I found it unpleasant. Because of these experiences, I have hated such co-operation and interaction ever since.' We should expect, therefore, that she dislikes meeting people even now. We should expect to find her embarrassed and self-conscious with others, believing that she is expected to shine, and feeling that it is too much to ask of her.

She has developed away from a sense of ease and equality among her fellow human beings.

5. *'One big event stands out in my early childhood. When I was about four years old my great-grandmother came to visit us.'* We have noticed that a grandmother usually spoils her grandchildren, but we have not yet seen how a great-grandmother treats them. *'While she was visiting us we had a four-generation picture taken.'* This girl is very interested in her family tree. Because she remembers so vividly her great-grandmother's visit and the picture that was taken, we can probably conclude that she is very much bound up in her family. If we are right, we shall discover that her ability to co-operate does not go beyond the limits of her family circle.

'I clearly remember being driven to another town and having my dress changed for a white embroidered one after we arrived at the photographer's.' Perhaps this girl, too, is a visual type. *'Before having the four-generation picture taken, my brother and I had ours taken.'* Again we come across interest in the family. Her brother is a part of the family and we shall probably hear more of her relationship with him. *'He was placed beside me on the arm of the chair and was given a bright red ball to hold.'* Now we see the main striving of this girl. She says to herself that her brother is preferred to her. We might guess that she was not pleased when her younger brother came along and took away her position of being the youngest and most pampered. *'We were told to smile.'* She means, 'They tried to make me smile, but what did I have to smile about? They put my brother on a throne and gave him a bright red ball, but what did they give me?'

'Then came the four-generation picture. Everybody tried to look their best except me. I refused to smile.' She is aggressive towards her family because her family is not kind enough to her. In this first memory she has not forgotten to inform us how her family treated her. *'My brother smiled so nicely when asked to smile. He was so cute. To this day I detest having my picture taken.'* Such memories give us a good insight into the way most of us meet life. We take one impression and use it to justify a whole series of actions. We draw conclusions from it and act as if they were indisputable

facts. She clearly had a disagreeable time when this photograph was taken. She still detests having her picture taken. We generally find that anyone who dislikes something as much as this tries to justify their dislike and selects something from their experiences to bear the whole burden of explanation. This first memory has given us two main clues to the personality of the writer. First, she is a visual type; second, and even more important, she is very bound up with her family. The sole action of her first memory is placed within the family circle. She is probably not well adapted to social life.

6. '*One of my earliest recollections, if not the earliest, is an incident that happened when I was about three and a half years old. A girl who worked for my parents had taken my cousin and me down to the cellar and given us a taste of cider. We liked it very much.*' It is an interesting experience to discover that one has cellars with cider in them. This was a journey of exploration. If we had to draw our conclusions at this stage, we might guess one of two things. Perhaps this girl enjoys new experiences and is courageous in her approach to life. Perhaps, on the other hand, she means that there are people with stronger wills who can beguile us and lead us astray. The rest of the memory will help us to decide. '*A little later we decided that we would like another taste, so we proceeded to help ourselves.*' This is a courageous girl. She wants to be independent. '*In due course my legs gave way, and the cellar was rather damp as we had allowed all of the cider to run out on the floor.*' Here we see the making of a prohibitionist!

'*I do not know if this incident has anything to do with my dislike for cider and other intoxicating drinks.*' One small incident is again made the reason for a whole attitude to life. If we look at it in a matter-of-fact way, the incident does not appear sufficiently important to lead to such a far-reaching conclusion. This girl, however, has secretly taken it as sufficient reason to dislike intoxicating drinks. We shall probably find that she is a person who knows how to learn from her mistakes. Probably she is very independent and likes to correct herself if she is in the wrong. This trait may characterize her whole life. It is as if she said, 'I make mistakes, but when I see they *are* mistakes I correct them'. If this is so, she will be of very good character: active, courageous in her striving, always eager to improve herself and her situation, and to lead a good and useful life.

In all these instances, all we are doing is training ourselves in the art of intelligent guesswork; and before we could be sure that our conclusions were accurate we would need to look at a person's other personality traits. Let us now take some case studies, where the coherence of the personality in all its expressions can be seen.

A man of thirty-five came to me suffering from anxiety neurosis. He felt anxious only when he was away from home. From time to time he was compelled to get a job; but as soon as he was put in an office he would moan and cry all day, stopping only when he came back at night and sat at home with his mother. When asked for his first memory, he said, 'I remember at four years of age sitting at home close by the window, looking out on to the street and watching the people working there with great interest'. He wants to see others work; he himself wants only to sit by the window and watch them. If his condition is to be changed, we can do it only by freeing him from the belief that he cannot co-operate in the work of others. So far he has thought that the only way to live was to be supported by others. We must change his whole outlook. We cannot do any good by reproaching him, nor can we convince him with medicines or hormones. His first memory, however, makes it easier for us to suggest work that will interest him. His main interest is in looking. We find out that he has suffered from short-sightedness and, because of this disadvantage, he gave more attention to visible things. When he became old enough to start work he wanted to continue looking on, not to work. The two are not necessarily contradictions, however. When he was cured, he found a career that lay along the lines of this main interest. He opened an art shop and was thus able to contribute in his own way to society and the division of labour.

A man of thirty-two came for treatment, suffering from hysterical aphasia. He could not speak above a whisper. This condition had lasted for two years. It began one day when he slipped on a banana skin and fell against the window of a taxi. He vomited for two days and had migraine afterwards. No doubt he had concussion but since there were no organic changes in the throat, the initial concussion was not enough to explain why he was unable to speak. For eight weeks he was completely speechless. His accident is now a court matter, but the case is difficult. He attributes the accident entirely to the taxi driver and is suing the company for compensation. We can appreciate that he is in a much stronger position with his lawsuit if he can show some disability. We need not say that he is dishonest, but he has no great incentive to speak properly. Perhaps he really did find it difficult to speak after the shock of his accident and he has not seen a reason to change.

The patient had seen a throat specialist but the specialist found nothing wrong. Asked for his first memory, he tells us, 'I was hanging in a cradle, lying on my back. I remember seeing the hook come out. The cradle fell and I was badly hurt.' Nobody likes to fall, but this man overemphasizes falling, and concentrates on its dangers. It is his chief interest. 'The door opened when I fell and my mother came in and was horrified.' He had gained his mother's attention by his fall; but the memory is also a reproach – 'She did not take enough care of me.' In the same way, the taxi driver was at fault and the company who owned the taxi too. None of them took sufficient care of him. This is the life style of a spoilt child: he tries to make others responsible.

His next memory tells the same story. 'At the age of five I fell twenty feet with a heavy board on top of me. For five or more minutes I was unable to speak.' This man is very adept at losing his speech. He is trained for it and makes falling a reason for refusing to speak. We cannot regard it as a valid reason, but he seems to see it that way. He is experienced in this method and now, if he falls, it follows automatically that he is unable to speak. He can only be cured if he understands that this is a mistake, that there is no connection between falling and loss of speech, and especially if he sees that after an accident he need not go about whispering for two years.

In this memory, however, he shows us why it is difficult for him to understand. 'My mother came out', he continues, 'and looked very excited.' On both occasions his fall horrified his mother and drew her attention to him. He was a child who wanted to be made a fuss of, to be the centre of attention. We can understand how he wants to be compensated for his misfortunes. Other spoilt children might do the same in similar circumstances. They might not, however, hit on the device of developing a speech defect. This is the trademark of our patient; it is part of the life style he has built up out of his experiences.

A man of twenty-six came to me complaining that he could not find a satisfactory occupation. Eight years ago he had been put in the brokerage business by his father, but he never liked it and had recently given it up. He had tried to find other work, but he had not been successful. He also complained of sleeplessness and frequently thought of suicide. When he gave up his work in the brokerage business, he ran away from home and found a job in another town, but a letter brought news that his mother was ill and he returned to live with the family.

From this history we could already suspect that he had been pampered by his mother and that his father had tried to exert authority over him. We should probably find that his life was a revolt against the strictness of his father. When he was asked about his position in the family, he replied that he was the youngest child and the only boy. He had two sisters; the elder one always tried to boss him about and the younger was not much different. His father nagged him continually and he felt very deeply that he was dominated by all the family. His mother was his only friend.

He went to school until he was fourteen. Afterwards, his father sent him to an agricultural school, so that he would be able to help him on a farm he was planning to buy. The boy got along fairly well at school, but decided that he did not wish to be a farmer. It was his father who got him the position in the brokerage firm. It is rather surprising that he stuck with it for eight years, but his reason was that he wanted to do as much as possible for his mother.

As a child he was untidy and timid, afraid of the dark and of being left alone. When we hear of untidy children, we must always look for someone who tidies up after them. When we hear of children who are afraid of the dark and do not like to be left alone, we must always look for someone whose attention they can attract and who will console them. With this youth, it was his mother. He had not found it easy to make friends, but he felt sociable enough among strangers. He had never been in love; he was not interested in love and had no wish to get married. He looked on the marriage of his parents as unhappy, which helps us understand why he rejected marriage for himself.

His father still brings pressure on him to continue in the brokerage business. He himself would rather go in for advertising, but he is convinced that his family would not give him the money to train for this career. At every point we can see that the purpose of his actions is to antagonize his father. While he was in the brokerage firm, it did not occur to him, although he was self-supporting, to use his money to train in advertising. He only thinks of it now, as a new demand on his father.

His first memory clearly reveals the protest of a pampered child against a strict father. He remembers how he worked in his father's restaurant. He liked washing the dishes and changing them from one table to another. The way he meddled with them angered his father, who slapped him in front of the customers. He uses his early experience as a proof that his father is an enemy and his whole life has been a fight against him. He still has no real wish to work. He would be completely satisfied only if he could hurt his father.

His ideas of suicide are easy to explain. Every suicide is a reproach, and by thinking of suicide he is saying, 'It's all my father's fault.' His dissatisfaction with his work is also directed against his father. Every plan that the father proposes, the son rejects; but he is a pampered child and he cannot be independent in his career. He does not really want to work. He would rather play, but he still retains some co-operation with his mother. But how does his fight with his father help to explain his insomnia?

If he has had a sleepless night, the next day he is ill-equipped for work. His father expects him to work, but the boy is tired and feels incapable of working. Of course, he could say, 'I don't want to work, and I won't be forced', but he is concerned for his mother and the financial circumstances of the family. If he simply refuses to work, his family will think he is a hopeless case and refuse to support him. He must have an excuse. This is supplied by an apparently undeserved misfortune – sleeplessness.

At first he says that he never dreams. Later, however, he remembers a dream that recurs often. He dreams that somebody is throwing a ball against a wall and the ball always bounces away. This seems a trivial dream. Can we find a connection between the dream and his way of life?

We ask him, 'What happens then?' He tells us, 'Whenever the ball bounces away I wake up'. Now he has revealed the whole structure of his sleeplessness. He uses the dream as an alarm clock to wake him up. He imagines that everybody wishes to push him forward, to drive him and compel him to do things that he does not wish to do. He dreams that somebody is throwing a ball against the wall. At this point he always wakes up. Consequently he is tired the next day, and when he is tired he cannot work. His father is very anxious for him to work, and so, by this roundabout method, he has defeated his father. If we were to look only at his fight with his father, we would think him very intelligent to discover such weapons. His life style, however, is not very satisfactory, either for himself or for others, and we must help him to change it.

When I explain his dream to him, he stops dreaming it, but tells me he still wakes up sometimes in the night. He no longer has the courage to continue with his dream, because he realizes its purpose, but he still tires himself out for the next day. What can we do to help him? The only possible way would be to reconcile him with his father. As long as all his efforts are focused on irritating and defeating his father, nothing will be resolved. I begin as we must always begin, by admitting that there is justification for the patient's attitude.

'Your father seems to be completely wrong', I say. 'It is very unwise of him to try to exert his authority over you the whole time. Perhaps he is a sick man and needs treatment. But what can you do? You cannot expect to change him. Suppose it rains; what can you do? You can take an umbrella or a taxi, but there is no use trying to fight the rain or overpower it. At present you are spending your time fighting the rain. You believe this shows your strength, and that you are getting the better of it. But in reality you are damaging yourself more than anyone else.'

I show him the underlying coherence of all his problems – his uncertainty over his career, his thoughts of suicide, his running away from home, his sleeplessness, and I show him how in all of them he is punishing himself to punish his father. I also give him a piece of advice: 'When you go to sleep tonight, imagine that you want to wake yourself up from time to time, so that you can be tired tomorrow. Imagine that tomorrow you are too tired to go to work and your father explodes into a fit of temper.' I want him to face the truth: his main interest is to annoy and hurt his father. As long as we fail to stop this fight, any treatment will be useless. He is a spoilt child. We can all see it, and now he can see it himself.

The situation closely resembles the so-called Oedipus complex. This youth is preoccupied with damaging his father and is very attached to his mother. It is not a sexual affair, however. His mother has indulged him, and his father has been unsympathetic. He has suffered from an incorrect upbringing and a mistaken interpretation of his position. Heredity plays no part in his trouble. He has not derived it as an instinct from savages who killed and consumed the head man of the tribe. He has created it himself out of his own experiences. Attitudes like this could be provoked anew in every child. We need only give children a mother who indulges them, as this mother did, and a father who is harsh, as this father was. If children revolt against their father, and fail to proceed independently in solving their own problems, we can understand how easy it is to adopt a life style like this.

5

DREAMS

Almost every human being dreams, but very few understand their dreams: an astonishing state of affairs. Dreaming is, after all, a universal activity of the human mind. People have always been interested in dreams and have always been anxious to know what they mean. Many people believe their dreams to be deeply significant, strange and momentous. We can trace this interest back to the earliest ages of mankind. Yet on the whole, people still have no conception of what they are doing when they dream, or why they dream at all. As far as I know, there are only two theories of dream interpretation that attempt to be both comprehensive and scientific. These are the Freudian school of psychoanalysis and the school of Individual Psychology. Of these two, perhaps only Individual Psychologists can claim to have taken a commonsense approach.

DREAM INTERPRETATION IN THE PAST
Previous attempts to understand dreams were not, of course, scientific, but they deserve consideration. At least they will reveal how people have regarded their dreams and what their attitude towards dreaming has been. Dreams are a product of the mind's creative activity, and if we examine the way people have understood the role of dreams in the past, we shall come very close to seeing their purpose. From the beginning of our investigation we find that it has always been taken for granted that dreams have some bearing on the future. People often felt that some master spirit, god or ancestor would take control of their minds in their dreams, while others used their dreams for guidance when in difficulties.

Ancient dream books offered explanations of dreams and how they predicted the future of the dreamer. Primitive peoples looked for omens and prophecies in their dreams. The Greeks and the Egyptians went to their temples in the hope of dreaming a sacred dream that would influence their future lives. Such dreams were looked on as curative, as removing physical or mental difficulties. By purification, fasting and sweat baths, the American Indians took great pains to induce dreams, and based their conduct on the interpretation they gave them. In the Old Testament dreams are always interpreted as revealing something of future events. Even today there are individuals who insist that they have had dreams that later came true. They believe that in dreams they are clairvoyant, and that the dream can somehow be prophetic.

From a scientific standpoint, such views seem ridiculous. From the time I first attempted to solve the problem of dreams, it seemed clear to me that people who are dreaming are in a worse position to foretell the future than those who are awake and in better possession of all their faculties. It seemed unlikely that dreams would be more intelligent and prophetic than everyday thinking, but rather more confused and confusing. Yet this tradition must exist for a reason, and perhaps it is possible to find some truth in it. If we see it in its proper context, it may provide us with the very clue we are looking for.

We have already seen that people have regarded dreams as offering solutions to their problems. We may conclude that the purpose of individuals in dreaming is to seek guidance for the future, and to seek a solution to their problems. This is very far from committing us to a prophetic view of dreams. We still have to consider what sort of solution is required and where it is to be found. It seems obvious that any solution offered by a dream would be less adequate than a solution arrived at after a commonsense examination of the whole situation. Indeed, it is not too much to say that in dreaming individuals are hoping to solve their problems in their sleep.

THE FREUDIAN VIEW
The Freudian approach attempts to treat the dream as having a meaning that can be scientifically understood. On several points,

however, Freudian interpretation has taken the dream out of the realm of science. It presupposes, for example, a difference between the workings of the mind during the day and its workings at night. 'Conscious' and 'unconscious' are placed in opposition to each other, and the dream is given its own special laws which are contradictory to the laws of everyday thinking. Wherever we see such contradictions, we must detect an unscientific attitude. In the thinking of primitive peoples and of ancient philosophers, we always come across this desire to treat concepts as strong antitheses, to regard them as opposites. This antithetic or binary thinking can be illustrated very clearly among neurotic people. People often believe that left and right are contradictions, that man and woman, hot and cold, light and heavy, strong and weak are contradictions. From a scientific standpoint, they are not contradictions, but variations. They are points on a scale, arranged in accordance with their approximation to some fictional ideal. Good and bad, normal and abnormal, are not really contradictions either. Any theory that treats sleeping and waking, dream-thoughts and day-thoughts as contradictory is by nature unscientific.

Another problem with the original Freudian view is that dreams were set against the background of sexuality. This, too, separated them from people's ordinary strivings and activities. If it were true, dreams would have a meaning as an expression not of the whole personality, but only of a part of the personality. The Freudians themselves found a purely sexual interpretation of dreams inadequate, and Freud suggested that it was also possible to see in dreams the expression of an unconscious desire to die. Perhaps we can find a sense in which this is true. Dreams, as we have noticed, are an attempt to grasp an easy solution to problems, and they reveal the individual's lack of courage. The Freudian term, however, is highly metaphorical, and it does not bring us any closer to discovering how the whole personality is reflected in dreams. Once again, the dream-life seems rigorously separated from the waking-life. In the Freudian theories, we are given many interesting and valuable hints. Especially useful, for example, is the hint that it is not the dream itself that is important, but the underlying thoughts of the dream. In Individual Psychology we arrive at a somewhat similar conclusion. What is missing from Freudian psychoanalysis is the first prerequisite for a science of psychology – a recognition of the coherence of the personality and the unity of individuals in all their thoughts, words and deeds.

This deficiency can be observed in the Freudian answer to the crucial questions of dream interpretation, 'What is the purpose of dreams? Why do we dream at all?' The psychoanalyst answers, 'To satisfy the individual's unfulfilled desires'. But this view would by no means explain everything. Where, for example, is the satisfaction if the dream is lost, if the individual forgets it, or cannot understand it? All humankind dreams, yet few people understand their dreams. What pleasure can we get from dreaming? If the dream-life is separated from the day-life, and the satisfaction given by the dream takes place in the former, we could perhaps understand the purpose of dreams for the dreamer. But with this explanation we have lost the coherence of the personality. Dreams would no longer have any purpose for the waking person.

From a scientific point of view, the dreamer and the waking person are the same individual, and the purpose of dreams must be applicable to this one coherent personality. It is true that in one type of human being, we could connect the striving for wish-fulfilment in dreams with the whole personality. This type is the pampered child, the individual who is always asking, 'How can I get what I want? What does life offer me?' Such individuals might look for gratification in their dreams, just as they do in all their behaviour. And indeed, if we look closely, we shall find that Freudian theory is the consistent psychology of pampered children, who feel that their instincts must never be denied, who regard it as unfair that other people should exist, who always ask, 'Why should I love my neighbour? Does my neighbour love me?'

Psychoanalysis is based on the premise of a pampered child, and elaborates on this premise in the most thorough detail. But the striving for gratification is only one of the million manifestations of the striving for superiority, and we cannot accept it as the central motive of all expressions of the personality. If we really discover the purpose of dreams, moreover, this will also help us to see what purpose it serves to forget dreams or to fail to understand them.

THE APPROACH OF INDIVIDUAL PSYCHOLOGY
This was the thorniest problem that faced me when I began, some quarter of a century ago, to investigate the meaning of dreams. I could see that the dream-life is not a contradiction to waking-life; it always parallels the other movements and expressions of life. If by day we are engaged in striving towards the goal of superiority, we must be occupied with the same problem at night. Everyone has the same underlying goals in their dreams as they have in waking-life, as if they have to strive towards superiority in their dreams as well. The dream must therefore be a product of their life style, and consistent with it.

Reinforcing the life style
The following consideration immediately helps to clarify the purpose of dreams. We dream, and in the morning we generally forget our dreams. Nothing seems to be left. But is this true? Is nothing left at all? Something remains: we are left with the feelings our dreams have aroused. None of the pictures persist, no understanding of the dream is left – only the lingering feelings. The purpose of dreams must lie in the feelings they arouse. The dream is only the means, the instrument, to stir up feelings. The aim of the dream is the feelings it leaves behind.

The feelings individuals create must always be consistent with their life style. The difference between dream-thought and day-thought is not absolute; there is no rigid division between the two. To put the difference into a few words, in dreaming we are less in touch with reality than when awake, but there is no actual break with reality. If during the day we are troubled by certain problems, our sleep is troubled too. The fact that during our sleep we can stop ourselves from falling out of bed shows that connections with reality are still present. Parents can sleep through the loudest noises in the street and yet waken at the slightest movement of their child. Even in sleep we remain in touch with the world outside us; however, sensory perceptions, though not absent, are diminished and our contact with reality is lessened. When we dream we are alone. The demands of society do not press so urgently on us. In our dream-thought we are not obliged to deal so honestly with the situation around us.

Our sleep can be undisturbed only if we are free from tension and sure of a solution to our problems. Dreaming is one disturbance of calm and tranquil sleep. We can conclude that we dream only if we are not sure of a solution to our problems, only if reality is pressing in on us even in our sleep and showing us the difficulties with which we are confronted and to which we must find a solution.

Now we can examine how our minds confront problems in our sleep. Since we are not dealing with the whole situation, the problems will appear easier, and the solution offered will demand the least possible adjustment from us. The purpose of the dream will be to support and reinforce the dreamer's life style, to arouse the feelings best suited to it. But why does the life style need support? What can possibly threaten it? It is vulnerable to attack from reality and common sense. The purpose of dreams, therefore, is to defend the life style against the demands of common sense. This gives us an interesting insight. If individuals are confronted by a problem that they do not wish to solve according to common sense, they can confirm their attitude by the feelings that are aroused in their dreams.

At first this may seem a contradiction to our waking-life, but in reality there is no contradiction. We may stir up feelings in precisely the same way when we are awake. If individuals come up against a difficulty and prefer not to tackle it by using their common sense, but rather to pursue their old life style, then they will do everything they can to justify their life style and make it seem satisfactory. For example a person's goal may be to get money easily, without struggling and working for it, without making a contribution to others. Gambling occurs to them as a possibility. They know that many people have lost their money and suffered disaster through gambling, but they want an easy time, they want to get rich quick. What will they do? They picture themselves making money through speculation, then buying a car, living in luxury, being known to everyone as wealthy. Through these images they stir up feelings to prompt themselves into action. Eventually they turn away from common sense and begin to gamble.

The same thing happens in more commonplace circumstances. If we are at work and someone tells us of a play they have seen and enjoyed, we begin to feel like downing tools and going off to the theatre. If someone is in love, they picture the future for them and if they are really smitten they will picture the future as pleasant. Sometimes, if they feel pessimistic, they will have gloomy pictures of the future, but in any case they will be stirring up their feelings, and we can always tell what sort of person they are by noticing the kinds of feelings they arouse in themselves.

But if nothing remains after a dream except feelings, what has happened to common sense? Dreaming and common sense are arch enemies. We shall probably find that people who do not like to be deluded by their feelings, who prefer to proceed in a scientific way, do not dream often or do not dream at all. Others do not want to solve their problems by normal and useful means, or to apply commonsense solutions to them. Common sense is an aspect of co-operation, and people who are not well trained for co-operation dislike common sense. Such people have very frequent dreams. They are anxious that their life style should prevail and be justified; they wish to avoid the challenge of reality. We conclude that dreams are an attempt to make a bridge between an individual's life style and their present problems, so avoiding any adjustments to their life style. The life style is the author, producer and director of our dreams. It will always arouse the feelings that the individual needs. We can find nothing in a dream that we shall not find in all the other characteristics and behaviour of the individual. We would approach problems in the same way whether we dreamed or not, but the dream offers support and justification for our life style.

If this is true, we come to a new and very important step in understanding dreams: in dreams we are fooling ourselves. Every dream is an auto-intoxication, a self-hypnosis. Its whole purpose is to produce the mood in which we are best prepared to meet a particular situation. We should be able to see in a dream exactly the same personality that we find in everyday life, but we should see that personality, as it were, in the workshop of the mind, preparing the feelings to be utilized during the day. If we are right, we will be able to see self-deception even in the construction of a dream, in the means it employs.

What do we find? First of all, we find a certain choice of pictures, incidents and occurrences. We have mentioned these selections before. When individuals look back on their past they compile an anthology of pictures and incidents. We have found that their selections are tendentious, that they select from their collection of memories only those incidents that support their personal goal of superiority. It is their goal that rules their memory. In the same way, in the construction of a dream we pick out only those incidents that reinforce our life style and reveal what our life style demands of us when confronted by particular problems. This selection of incidents thus signifies the meaning of the life style in relation to our present difficulties. In a dream the life style is demanding its own way. To meet those difficulties realistically would call for common sense, but the life style refuses to give way.

Symbols and metaphors

What other resources does a dream draw on? From the earliest times it has been observed, and in our own day Freud has especially emphasized, that dreams are mainly built up out of metaphors and symbols. As one psychologist says, 'We are poets in our dreams'. Why do dreams speak in the language of poetry and metaphor? The answer is simple. If we speak plainly, without metaphors or symbols, we cannot escape common sense. Metaphors and symbols can be abused. They can combine different meanings, they can say two things at the same time, one of which is perhaps quite false. Illogical conclusions can be drawn from them. They can stir up feelings. We also use them in everyday life. If we wish to correct someone we might say, 'Don't be such a baby!' Something irrelevant, something addressed merely to the emotions, always creeps in when we use metaphors.

Perhaps a large man is angry with a small man and says, 'He is a worm. He ought to be trodden on.' He is justifying his anger by his metaphor.

Metaphors are wonderful instruments of expression, but we can use them to deceive ourselves. When Homer describes the army of the Greeks overrunning the fields like lions, he gives us a magnificent image. Do we believe that he wished to describe accurately how some poor, dirty soldiers crept over those fields? No – he wanted us to think of them as lions. We know that they are not really lions, but if the poet had described how the soldiers panted and sweated, how they tried to pluck up courage or to avoid danger, how old their armour was, and a thousand such details, we would not be so impressed. Metaphors are used for beauty, for imagination and fantasy. We must insist, however, that the use of metaphors and symbols is always dangerous in the hands of an individual who has a mistaken life style.

A student is faced with an examination. The problem is straightforward and he should approach it with courage and common sense. But if it is part of his life style to want to run away, he may dream that he is fighting in a war. He pictures this straightforward problem metaphorically and so feels far more justified in being afraid. Or he dreams that he is standing on the edge of an abyss and that he must run back to avoid falling in. He has to generate such feelings as an avoidance tactic, a form of escapism, and he fools himself by identifying the examination with the abyss. Similarly, we can identify another ploy that is often used in dreams. It is to take a problem and to reduce it and boil it down until only the essence of the original problem is left. The remainder is then expressed in a metaphor and treated as if it were the same as the original problem.

Another student, for example, with greater courage and a more long-term view of life, wishes to complete her task and go through with her is examination. She still needs support, however, and wants to reassure herself – her life style demands it. The night before the examination she dreams that she is standing on top of a mountain. The picture of her situation is very much simplified. Only the smallest part of all the circumstances of her life is represented. The problem of the examination is a great one to her, but by excluding many aspects of it and concentrating on her prospect of success, she stirs up feelings to help herself. Next morning she gets up feeling happier, fresher and braver than before. She has succeeded in minimizing the difficulties she must face. But in spite of the fact that she has reassured herself, she has really been fooling herself. She has not faced up to the whole problem in a commonsense way, but has merely stirred up a mood of confidence.

This deliberate stirring up of the feelings is nothing unusual. A man who wants to jump over a stream will perhaps count to three before he jumps. Is it really so important that he should count to three? Is there a necessary connection between jumping and counting to three? There is not the slightest connection. He counts to three, however, to stir up his feelings and to summon up all his powers. We have all the mental resources necessary to elaborate a life style, to fix it and to reinforce it, and one of our most important resources is the ability to stir up our own feelings. We are engaged in this work every night and every day, but it comes out more clearly, perhaps, in dreams.

Let me use a dream of my own to illustrate the way in which we fool ourselves. During the war I was the head of a hospital for shell-shocked soldiers. When I saw soldiers who were unable to cope with war, I tried to help them as much as I could by giving them easy tasks. This relieved a lot of their tension and was often quite a success. One day a soldier came to me, one of the best built and strongest men I have ever seen. He was very depressed and as I examined him I wondered what I could do for him. I would have liked, of course, to send all these troubled soldiers home, but each of my recommendations had to be passed by a superior officer and my benevolence had to be kept within bounds. This soldier's case was a difficult one, but when the time came I said, 'You are shell-shocked, but you are very strong and healthy. I will give you easier work to do so that you need not go to the front.'

The soldier was most distressed to find he was not to be sent home and answered, 'I am a poor student and I have to support my old father and mother by giving lessons. If I cannot give lessons they will starve. They will both die if I cannot help them.'

I wished I could send him home to work in an office, but I was afraid that if this was my recommendation my superior officer would be angry and would send him to the front. In the end I decided to do the utmost I honestly could. I would certify him as fit only for guard duty. When I went home that night and slept I had a terrible dream. I dreamed that I was a murderer and was running round in the dark, narrow streets trying to think who it was that I had murdered. I could not remember who my victim was, but I felt, 'I have committed murder, and because of that I am done for. My life is over. Everything is finished.'

My first thought when I awoke was, 'Whom have I murdered?' Then it occurred to me, 'If I don't give this young soldier a job in an office, perhaps he will be sent to the front and killed. Then I would be the murderer.' You see how I had stirred up my feelings to deceive myself. I had not murdered anyone, and even if the disaster I foresaw really occurred, I would not be guilty. But my life style would not permit me to run the risk. I am a doctor; I am there to save life, not to endanger it. I reminded myself that if I gave him an easier job my superior might send him to the front and the position would be no better. It occurred to me that if I wanted to help him the only thing to do was to follow rules of common sense and not bother about my own life style. I therefore certified him as fit for guard duty.

Later events confirmed the fact that it is always better to follow common sense. My superior read my recommendation and crossed it out. I thought, 'Now he is going to send him to the front. I should have given him office service after all.' My superior wrote, 'Six months' office service.' It turned out that this officer had been bribed to let the soldier off lightly. The youth had never given a lesson in his life and not a word of what he told me had been true. He had told his story only so that I would give him an easier task and enable the superior officer, whom he had bribed, to sign my recommendation. Since that day I have thought it better to give up dreaming.

The fact that dreams are designed to fool and deceive us accounts for the fact that they are so rarely understood. If we understood our dreams they would no longer have the power to arouse our feelings and emotions and they could not deceive us. We would prefer to proceed in commonsense ways, and we would refuse to follow the promptings of our dreams. Consequently, if dreams were understood, they would lose their purpose.

The dream is a bridge between the present real problem and our life style, but our life style should not need any reinforcement. It should be in direct contact with reality. There are many varieties of dream and every dream reveals the points where individuals feel their life style needs reinforcement in relation to the particular situation that confronts them. The interpretation of dreams is therefore always unique to the individual. It is thus impossible to interpret symbols and metaphors by formulae; the dream is a creation of the life style, drawn from the individual's own interpretation of their own particular circumstances. If I describe briefly some of the more typical forms of dreams, I am not doing so to provide a literal guide to interpretation, but only to help towards a general understanding of dreams and their meanings.

COMMON DREAMS

Many people have experienced dreams of flying. The key to these dreams, as to all others, lies in the feelings they arouse. They leave behind them a mood of buoyancy and courage. They lead from below to above. They depict the overcoming of difficulties and the striving for superiority becoming easy and effortless. They allow us to imagine ourselves as courageous, forward-looking and ambitious, as people who cannot free themselves from their ambition, even when asleep. Such dreams involve the problem, 'Should I go on or not?', and the answer suggested is, 'There are no obstacles in my way'.

There are very few people who have not experienced dreams of falling. This is very remarkable; it shows that the human mind is more occupied with self-preservation and the fear of defeat than with attempting to overcome difficulties. This becomes understandable when we remember that traditionally we warn children and put them on their guard. Children are always admonished, 'Don't climb on that chair! Leave the scissors alone! Keep away from the fire!' They are always surrounded by fictitious dangers too. But to make individuals cowardly will never help them to cope with real danger.

When people have recurring dreams of being paralysed or missing a train, the meaning is generally, 'I would be glad if this problem would pass by without any need for interference on my part. I must make a detour, I must arrive too late, so as to avoid having to confront the problem. I must let the train go by.'

Many people dream of examinations. Sometimes they are astonished to find themselves taking an examination so late in life, or having to pass an examination on a subject they already succeeded in long before. With some individuals the meaning would be, 'You are not prepared to face the problem before you'. With others it would mean, 'You have passed this examination before and you will pass the test that you are facing at present'. One individual's symbols are never the same as another's. What we must consider chiefly in the dream is the mood it leaves behind and the way it fits in with the whole life style.

SOME CASE STUDIES

Once a neurotic patient, thirty-two years old, came for treatment. She was a second child and, like most second children, very ambitious. She always wanted to be the first and to solve all her problems in an irreproachable manner. She came to me with a nervous breakdown. She had had a love affair with a married man older than herself, who had failed in his business. She had wanted to marry him, but he was unable to get a divorce. She dreamed that a man, to whom she had rented her apartment while she was in the country, married shortly after he moved in but had no money to pay the rent. He was not an honest or hard-working man and she was compelled to evict him. We can see at once that this dream has some connection with her present problem. She was considering whether she should marry a man who had failed in business. Her lover was poor and unable to support her. What especially strengthened the comparison is that he had invited her out to dinner without having any money. The effect of the dream is to stir up her feelings against marriage. She is an ambitious woman, and she does not wish to be connected with a poor man.

She uses a metaphor and asks herself, 'If he had rented my apartment and could not pay for it, what would I do with such a tenant?' The answer is, 'He would have to leave'.

This married man, however, is not her tenant and he cannot properly be identified with him. A husband who cannot support a family is not the same as a tenant who cannot pay the rent. To solve her problem, and to follow her life style with more assurance, she gives herself the feeling, 'I must not marry him'. Thus she avoids approaching the whole problem in a commonsense way and elects only to deal with a small part of it. At the same time she minimizes the whole problem of love and marriage as if it could be sufficiently expressed by the metaphor, 'A man rents my apartment. If he cannot pay he must be thrown out.'

As the technique of Individual Psychological treatment is always directed towards increasing the individual's courage in facing up to the problems of life, it is obvious that dreams will change in the course of treatment and reveal a more confident attitude. The last dream of a melancholic patient before her discharge was as follows: 'I was sitting all alone on a bench. Suddenly a heavy snowstorm came on. Fortunately I escaped it, since I hurried indoors to my husband. Then I helped him to look for a suitable job in the advertisement columns of a newspaper.' The patient was able to interpret the dream for herself. It shows clearly her feeling of reconciliation with her husband. At first she had hated him and had complained bitterly of his weakness and lack of enterprise in failing to earn a good living. The meaning of the dream is, 'It is better to stay with my husband than expose myself to dangers alone'. Though we may agree with the patient in her conclusions, the way she reconciles herself to her husband and her marriage has shades of the advice anxious relatives customarily give. The dangers of being alone are overemphasized and she is still not quite ready to co-operate with courage and independence.

A boy of ten was brought to the clinic. His teacher at school complained that he was mean and vicious with other children. He stole things at school and put them in other boys' desks to pin the blame on them. Such behaviour only occurs where a child feels the need to humiliate other people, to prove that *they* are mean and vicious, not he. If this is his approach, we can guess that he must have learned it in the family circle, that there must be someone at home in whom he wished to instil guilt. This ten-year-old boy threw stones at a pregnant woman in the street and rightly got into trouble for it. At his age he probably knew about pregnancy. We can suspect that he does not like the idea, and we must see if there is a younger brother or sister whose arrival did not please him. On the teacher's report he is called 'the pest of the neighbourhood'; he bothers the other children, calls them names and tells tales about them. He also chases and hits little girls. This indicates that it is probably a younger sister with whom he is in competition.

We learn that he is in fact the elder of two children, with a four-year-old younger sister. His mother says that he loves his younger sister and is always good to her. This strains our credulity to the limit – it is impossible for such a boy to love his younger sister. We shall see later on that our scepticism is justified. The mother also claims that the relationship between herself and her husband is perfect. This is unfortunate for the child. Obviously his parents are not responsible for any of his faults; they must come from his own wicked nature, from fate, or perhaps from some remote ancestor!

We often hear in our case studies of these ideal marriages: such excellent parents and such a horrid child! Teachers, psychologists, lawyers and judges all bear witness to these mishaps. And indeed an 'ideal' marriage may pose great problems for a boy like this: if he sees that his mother is devoted to his father, it may irritate him. He wants to monopolize his mother's attention and he may resent any display of affection to anyone else. What are we to do, then, if happy marriages are bad for children and unhappy marriages are worse? We must make the child co-operative from the first. We must avoid letting him cling to one parent only. This particular boy is a spoilt child; he wants to keep his mother's attention and he is deliberately setting out to cause trouble whenever he feels that he is not given enough attention.

Here again we find confirmation of our suspicions immediately. The mother never punishes the child herself; she waits for the father to come home and punish him. She probably thinks she is too weak, and feels that only a man can order and command, and is strong enough to punish. Perhaps she wishes to keep the boy attached to her and is afraid of losing his affection. In either case she is steering the boy away from interest in and co-operation with his father, and friction is bound to develop between the two. We hear that the father is devoted to his wife and family, but he dreads coming home after work because of the boy. He punishes him very severely and frequently beats him. The boy has no dislike for his father, we are told. This, again, is impossible – the boy is not feeble-minded. He has simply learned to be very skilful in hiding his feelings.

He loves his sister, but he does not play nicely with her and often slaps or kicks her. He sleeps in the dining-room on a day bed; his sister sleeps in a cot in her parents' room. Now if we can identify ourselves with this boy, if we can empathize with him, this cot in the parents' room will bother us. We are trying to think, feel and see through the boy's mind. He wants to be the centre of his mother's attention. At night his sister is so much closer to his mother. He must fight to bring her nearer. The boy's health is very good; his birth was normal and he was breast-fed for seven months. When he was first placed on the bottle he vomited, and his vomiting spells continued till he was three years old. In all probability he had a weak stomach. He is now well fed and well nourished, but his preoccupation with his stomach has persisted. He considers it a weak point. We can understand a little better now why he threw stones at a pregnant woman. He is very finicky about his food. If he does not fancy what is set before him, his mother gives him money and he goes out and buys what he likes. Nevertheless he goes around to the neighbours and complains that his parents do not give him enough to eat. This is a trick he has honed to perfection. It is always the same: his way to recover his feeling of superiority is to slander somebody else.

We are now in a position to understand a dream he described when he came to the clinic. 'I was a cowboy in the West', he said. 'They sent me to Mexico and I had to fight my way through to the United States. When one Mexican came against me I kicked him in the stomach.' The feeling of the dream is, 'I am surrounded by enemies. I must struggle and fight.' In America cowboys are looked on as heroes; he thinks that chasing little girls and kicking people in the stomach is heroic. We have already seen that the stomach plays a great role in his life – he sees it as the most vulnerable point. He himself suffered from a weak stomach and his father has a nervous stomach problem of which he is always complaining. The stomach has been elevated in this family to a position of the highest importance. The boy's aim is to hit people at their weakest point.

His dream and his actions show exactly the same life style. He is living in a dream, and if we are not able to waken him from it, he will go on living in the same way. He will not only fight his father, his sister, little children and girls especially, but he will want to fight the doctor who tries to stop his fighting. His dream impulse will stimulate him to go on, to be a hero, to conquer others; and unless he can see how he is fooling himself, no treatment can help him.

His dream is explained to him at the clinic. He feels he is living in hostile territory and everybody who wants to punish him and hold him back is a Mexican; they are all his enemies. Next time he comes to the clinic we ask him, 'What has happened since we saw each other last?'

'I've been a bad boy', he answers.

'What did you do?'

'I chased a little girl.'

Now this is far more than a confession; it is a boast and an attack. This is a clinic where people are trying to improve him and he insists that he has been a bad boy. He is saying, 'Don't hope for any improvement. I will kick you in the stomach too.' What are we to do with him? He is still dreaming, he is still playing the hero. We must diminish the satisfaction he gets from his role.

'Do you believe', we ask him, 'that this hero of yours would really chase a little girl? Isn't that a rather poor kind of heroism? If you are going to be a hero, you should chase a big, strong girl. Or perhaps you shouldn't chase a girl at all.' This is one side of the treatment. We must open his eyes and make him less eager to continue his life style. We must 'spit in his soup', as the old German proverb says. After this, he will not like this soup of his any longer. The other side of the treatment is to give him courage to co-operate, to seek significance in a socially beneficial way. Nobody adopts antisocial behaviour unless they fear that they will fail if they remain on the social side of life.

A woman of twenty-four, living alone and doing secretarial work, complains that her boss makes life intolerable for her with his bullying manner. She also feels unable to make friends and keep them. Experience would lead us to believe that if individuals cannot keep friends it is because they wish to dominate others; they are really interested only in themselves, and their goal is to show their personal superiority. Probably this woman's boss is the same sort of person. They both wish to rule others. When two such people meet, there are bound to be difficulties. The woman is the youngest of seven children, the pet of the family. She was nicknamed 'Tom' because she always wanted to be a boy. This increases our suspicion that she has identified her goal of superiority with personal domination; to be masculine, she thinks, is to be the master, to control others and not to be controlled herself.

She is pretty, but she thinks that people only like her because of her pleasant face and she is afraid of being disfigured or hurt. Attractive people find it easier in our society to impress and control others, and this woman is well aware of this. She wants to be a boy, however, and to dominate in a masculine way. Consequently, she is not particularly interested in her own prettiness.

Her earliest memory is of being frightened by a man, and she confesses that she still fears becoming the victim of burglars and attackers. It might appear odd that a girl who wanted to be masculine would be afraid of burglars and attackers; but it is not really so strange. It is her feeling of weakness that dictates her goal. She wants to be in circumstances where she can rule and subjugate, and she would like to exclude all other situations. Burglars and attackers cannot be controlled and she would like to destroy them all. She wishes to be masculine in an easy way and to have resort to

extenuating circumstances if she fails. This very widespread dissatisfaction with the feminine role, the 'masculine protest' as I have
called it, is always accompanied by feelings of tension – 'I am a man
fighting against the disadvantages of being a woman.'

Let us see whether we can trace the same feeling in her
dreams. Frequently she dreams of being left alone. She was a spoilt
child; her dream means, 'I must be watched. It isn't safe to leave
me alone. Others could attack and subjugate me.' Another dream
she frequently experiences is that she has lost her purse. 'Take
care', she is saying, 'You are in danger of losing something.' She
does not want to lose anything at all; in particular, she does not
want to lose her power to control others. She chooses one
incident in her life, the loss of a purse, to stand for the whole. We
have here another illustration of how dreams reinforce the life
style by creating feelings. She has not lost her purse, but she
dreams she has lost it, and the feeling remains behind.

A longer dream helps us to see her attitude even more
clearly. 'I had gone to a swimming pool where there were a lot of
people', she says. 'Somebody noticed that I was standing on the
heads of the people there. It seemed to me that someone
screamed at the sight of me standing on their heads, and I was in
great danger of falling down.' If I were a sculptor, I would carve
her in just this way, standing on the heads of others, using others
as her pedestal. This is her life style, these are the feelings she
likes to arouse. She sees her position, however, as precarious, and
she thinks that others ought to recognize her danger too. Others
ought to watch her and take care, so that she can continue to
stand on their heads! She does not feel safe swimming in the
water, and this is the whole story of her life. 'To be a man in
spite of being a girl' has become her psychological goal. She is
very ambitious, as most youngest children are, but she wants to
seem superior, rather than to respond adequately to her situation,
and she is constantly pursued by the fear of defeat. If we are to
help her, we must find the way to reconcile her to her feminine
role, to take away her fear and overestimation of the other sex,
and to help her to feel friendly and equal among her fellow
human beings.

A girl whose younger brother had been killed in an accident when she was thirteen gave as her earliest recollection: 'When my brother was a baby and was learning to walk, he grabbed hold of a chair to pull himself up and the chair fell on him.' Here is another accident and we can see that she is deeply impressed by the dangers of the world. 'My most frequent dream', she related, 'is very strange. I am usually walking along the street where there is a hole that I do not see. Walking along, I fall into the hole. It is filled with water, and as I touch the water I wake with a start, with my heart beating terribly fast.'

We shall not find the dream as strange as she finds it herself; but if she is to continue to alarm herself with it, she must think it mysterious and fail to understand it. The dream says to her, 'Be cautious. There are dangers that you know nothing of.' It tells us more than this, however. You cannot fall if you are already down. If she is in danger of falling, she must imagine that she is above the others. As in the last example, she is saying, 'I am superior, but I must always take care not to fall'.

In another case we shall see if we can find the same life style at work in a first memory and a dream. A girl tells us, 'I remember being very interested in seeing a block of flats being built.' We can guess that she is co-operative. A small girl cannot be expected to participate in building a house, but by her interest she can show her enjoyment in sharing tasks with others. 'I was a little tot, and I was standing by a very tall window, and the panes of glass are as clear to me as if it were yesterday.' If she notices that it is tall, she must have a contrast in her mind between tall and small. She means, 'The window was big and I was little'. I would not be surprised to hear that she is undersized, and it is this that interests her so much in comparative sizes. Her mentioning that she remembers it so clearly is a sort of boast.

Now let us turn to her dream. 'Several other people were riding with me in a car.' She is co-operative, as we thought; she likes to be with others. 'We drove until we stopped in front of a wood. Everyone got out and ran into the woods. Most of them were bigger than me.' Again she notices the difference in size. 'But I managed to arrive in time to get into an elevator, and it went down into a mine-shaft about ten feet deep. We thought that if we stepped out, the air would poison us.' She pictures a danger now. Most people are afraid of certain dangers; humankind is not very courageous. She continues, however, 'We stepped out perfectly safe'. You can see the optimism here. If individuals are co-operative, they are always courageous and optimistic. 'We stayed there a minute, then came up again and ran quickly to the car.' I am convinced that this girl is always co-operative, but she has the impression that she would like to be larger and taller. We shall find some tension here, as if she were standing on tiptoe, but it will be offset by her liking for others and her interest in shared achievements.

6

FAMILY INFLUENCES

THE ROLE OF THE MOTHER

From the moment of birth babies seek to bond with their mother. This is the purpose of all their behaviour. For many months their mother plays by far the most important role in their lives: they are almost completely dependent upon them. It is in this situation that the ability to co-operate first develops. A mother gives babies their first contact with another human being, their first interest in someone other than themselves. She is their first bridge to social life; a baby who could not make any bond at all with his or her mother, or with some other human being who took her place, would inevitably perish.

The fact that this bond is so intimate and far-reaching means that in later years we can never identify any characteristic as the effect of heredity. Every tendency that might have been inherited has been adapted, trained, educated and remoulded by the mother. Her skill, or lack of skill, has influenced all the child's potentialities. By a mother's skill we mean simply her ability to co-operate with her child and to persuade the child to co-operate with her. This ability cannot be taught as a set of rules. New situations arise every day. There are thousands of points in which she must apply her insight and understanding to the child's needs. She can only acquire these skills if she is interested in her child and concerned with winning his affection and securing his welfare.

We can see the mother's attitude in all her activities. Whenever she picks the baby up, carries him, speaks to him, baths him or feeds him, she has opportunities to bond with him. If she is not skilled in her tasks or not interested in them, she will be clumsy and the baby will resist. If she has never learned how to bath a child, he will find bath-time an unpleasant experience. Instead of bonding with her, he will try to get rid of her. She must be skilful in the way she puts her baby to bed, in all her movements and in the noises she makes. She must be skilful in watching him and in leaving him alone. She must consider his whole environment – fresh air, the temperature of the room, nutrition, sleeping times, physical habits and cleanliness. On every occasion she is providing an opportunity for the child to like her or dislike her, to co-operate or reject co-operation.

There is no special secret to the skill of motherhood. All skill is the result of interest and training. Preparation for motherhood begins very early in life. The first steps can be seen in a girl's attitude to younger children, her interest in babies and in her future tasks. It is never advisable to educate boys and girls as if they had precisely the same tasks ahead of them. If we are to have skilful mothers, girls must be educated for motherhood and educated in such a way that they like the prospect of being a mother, consider it a creative activity, and are not disappointed by their role when they come to it in later life.

Unfortunately our western culture does not regard motherhood highly. If boys are preferred to girls – if their role in society is assumed to be superior – it is natural for girls to dislike their future tasks. No one can be content with a subordinate position. When such girls marry and face the prospect of having children of their own, they show their resistance in one way or another. They are not willing or prepared to have children; they do not look forward to it; nor do they regard it as a creative and interesting activity.

This is perhaps the greatest problem of our society and little effort is made to confront it. The whole of human society is bound up with the attitude of women to motherhood. Almost everywhere the woman's part in life is undervalued and treated as secondary. Even in childhood we find boys looking at housework as if it were a job for servants, as if it were beneath their dignity to lift a finger to help with it. Running a house and home-making are too often regarded not as careers open to women, but as drudgery they are relegated to.

If a woman can really see housework and home-making as an art in which she can be interested and through which she can lighten and enrich the lives of others, she can make it a task equal to any other in the world. If, on the other hand, it is regarded as work too menial for a man, is it surprising that some women resist their tasks, revolt against them, and set out to prove what should be obvious from the first – that they are the equals of men and no less entitled to consideration and to the opportunity to develop their potential to the full? However, potential can only be fully developed through social feeling, and social feeling will point women in the right direction, provided no extraneous limits and restrictions are placed on their development.

Where the woman's role is undervalued, all the harmony of married life is destroyed. No woman who considers that caring for children is an inferior task can apply herself properly to developing the skill, care, understanding and sympathy that are so necessary if children are to be given a favourable start in life. A woman who is dissatisfied with her role has a goal in life that prevents her from bonding properly with her children. Her goal is not like other women's; she is often preoccupied with proving her personal superiority; and from this point of view the children can only be a nuisance and a distraction. If we trace back the causes of failure in life, we almost always discover that a mother did not fulfil her functions properly: she did not give her child a favourable start. If mothers fail, if they are dissatisfied with their tasks and take insufficient interest in them, the whole of humankind is endangered.

We cannot regard the mother as guilty, however, because of her failures. There is no guilt. Perhaps the mother herself was not trained for co-operation. Perhaps she is repressed and unhappy in her married life. She may be confused and worried by her circumstances; and may even succumb to a sense of hopelessness and despair. There are many hindrances to the development of good family life. If the mother is ill she may want to co-operate with the children but feels too exhausted when she comes home. If economic conditions are difficult, food, clothing and temperature may all be wrong for the children. Moreover, it is not the children's experiences that dictate their actions; it is the conclusions they draw from their experiences. When we investigate the background of problem children, we often find difficulties in the relationship between them and their mothers, but we can see the same difficulties among other children who have dealt with them more successfully. Here we come back to the fundamental view of Individual Psychology: there are no fixed causes in the development of character, but children can make use of experiences to attain their goal and turn them into reasons for their outlook on life. We cannot say, for example, that if children are badly nourished they will become criminals. We must see what conclusions they have drawn from their experiences.

It is clear, however, that if a woman is dissatisfied with her role as a mother, both she and her children will encounter difficulties and stress. But we know how strong the mothering instinct is. Investigations have made it clear that a mother's tendency to protect her children is stronger than all other tendencies. Among animals, among rats and apes, for instance, the mothering instinct has been shown to be stronger than the drives of sex or hunger, so that if they must choose between following one drive or another, it is the mothering instinct that prevails.

The foundation of this striving is not sexual. It derives from the goal of co-operation. A mother often regards her children as a part of herself. Through her children she is connected with the whole of life. She feels she has the power of life and death. In every mother we can find, to some degree, the feeling that through her children she has actually created something. She feels, we might almost say, that she has created in the way God creates – out of nothing she has brought forth a living being. The desire for motherhood is really one aspect of the human striving for superiority, the human goal of god-likeness. It gives us one of the clearest examples of how this goal can be used for the sake of humankind and the interest of others in accordance with the deepest social feeling.

Any mother, of course, may exaggerate her feeling that her children are a part of herself and press them into the service of her goal of personal superiority. She may try to make the children wholly dependent upon her and control their lives so that they will always remain bound to her. Let me quote the case of a seventy-year-old peasant woman. Her son, at the age of fifty, was still living with her. Both of them contracted pneumonia at the same time. The mother survived, but the son was taken to hospital and died. When the mother was told of his death, she said, 'I always knew that I would never bring the boy up safely'. She felt responsible for the whole life of her child. She had never tried to make him a full member of society. We can begin to understand how mistaken a mother is in failing to widen the connection she has made with her children and lead them to co-operate on equal terms with the rest of their environment.

The relationships of a mother are not simple and even her connection with her children must not be overstressed. This is true for their sake as well as for hers. Where one problem is over-stressed all other problems suffer from neglect, and even the single problem we are focused on cannot be tackled as effectively if we attach too much importance to it. A mother relates to her children, to her partner, and to the whole of society around her. These three ties must be given equal attention: all three must be faced calmly and with common sense. If a mother only considers her tie with her children, she will be unable to avoid pampering and spoiling them. She will make it hard for them to develop independence and the ability to co-operate with others. After she has succeeded in bonding with her children, her next task is to extend their interest to include their father. This task will prove almost impossible if she herself is not interested in the father. She must also turn the children's interest to their social environment: to the other children in the family, to friends, relatives and fellow human beings in general. Her task is thus twofold. She must give the children their first experience of a trustworthy human being, and she must then be prepared to extend this trust and friendship until it includes the whole of human society.

If the mother is only concerned with interesting the children in herself, later on they will resent all attempts to interest them in others. They will always look for support from their mother and feel hostile to anyone they regard as competing for her attention.

Any interest she shows in her partner or in other children in the family will be felt as a deprivation, and each child will develop the view, 'My mother belongs to me and to no one else'.

For the most part, modern psychologists have misunderstood the situation. In the Freudian theory of the Oedipus complex, for example, it is supposed that boys have a tendency to fall in love with their mothers and wish to marry them, and to hate their fathers and wish to kill them. Such a mistake could never arise if we understood the development of children. The Oedipus complex would appear openly in a child who wished to be the centre of his mother's attention and to get rid of everyone else. Such a desire is not sexual. It is a desire to subjugate the mother, to have complete control of her and to make her into a servant. It can only occur with children who have been pampered by their mothers and whose feeling of fellowship has never included the rest of the world. There have been isolated cases where a boy who always related only to his mother also made her the centre of his attempts to solve the problem of love and marriage; but the meaning of such an attitude would be that he could not conceive of co-operation with anyone except his mother. No other woman could be trusted to be as subservient as she was. An Oedipus complex would thus always be an artificial product of a mistaken upbringing. We have no reason to presume the existence of inherited incestuous instincts, or indeed to imagine that such an aberration has its origin in sexuality.

When children whose mother has bound them only to herself are placed in a situation where they can no longer be close to her, there is always trouble. When they go to school, for example, or play with children in the park, their goal will always be to remain close to their mother. They will bitterly resent any separation from her. They wish always to drag their mother along with them, to occupy their thoughts and to make them pay attention to them. There are many courses of action at their disposal. They may become a mother's darling, always feeble and affectionate and pleading for sympathy. They may weep or fall sick every time things go against them, to show how much they need to be looked after. On the other hand, they may have outbursts of temper; they may be disobedient or argue with their mother in order to be noticed. Among problem children we find thousands of varieties of spoilt children, struggling for the attention of their mothers and resisting every demand from their wider environment.

It is ridiculous to imagine that the best way to remedy the mistakes that mothers make would be to take all children from the care of their mothers and hand them over to nurses or to institutions. Whenever we try to find a substitute for a mother, we are looking for someone who will play a mother's part – who will interest the child in herself just as a mother does. It is much easier to train the child's own mother to do this. Children who grow up in orphanages often show a lack of interest in others: there was no one who could make the personal bridge between them and their fellow human beings.

Experiments have been tried on children in such institutions who were not developing well. A nurse or a sister has given the children individual care, or they have been fostered with a family where the mother could look after them as well as her own children. The result has always been a great improvement, provided the foster-mothers were well chosen. The best way of bringing up such children is to find a substitute for a mother and father and for a family life, and all we would be doing if we took children from their parents would be hunting around for other people who could fulfil the requirements of parents. The importance of a mother's affection and interest can be seen also from the fact that so many problem children are orphans, illegitimate or unwanted children and the children of broken marriages.

The role of a stepmother is notoriously difficult, and the children of the first mother often fight her. The problem is not insoluble and I have seen some very successful stepmothers. Too often, however, the woman does not fully understand the situation. Perhaps, if the children lost their mother, they turned to the father for attention and were pampered by him. Now they feel deprived of his attention and attack their stepmother. She feels that she must fight back and the children now have a real grievance. She has challenged them and they fight more than ever. A battle with children is always a losing battle: they can never be beaten or won over to co-operation by fighting. In these struggles the weakest always triumphs. Something is demanded of them that they refuse to give, something that can never be gained by such means. An incalculable amount of stress and useless effort would be spared in this world if we realized that co-operation and love can never be won by force.

THE ROLE OF THE FATHER

The father's role in family life is every bit as important as the mother's. At first his relationship with children is less intimate. It is later on that his influence has its effect. We have already described some of the dangers that arise if a mother is unable to extend the children's interest to include their father. The child ren suffer a serious block in the development of their social interest. Where the marriage is unhappy, the situation is full of danger for the children. Their mother may feel unable to include the father in the family life; she may wish to keep the children entirely to herself. Perhaps both parents use the children as a pawn in their personal war. Each wishes to bind the children to them, to be more loved than the partner.

If children see dissension between their parents they are very skilful in playing them off against each other. Thus a competition may arise to see who can control the children better or spoil them more. It is impossible to train children in co-operation with such an atmosphere around them. Their first experience of co-operation among other people is the co-operation between his parents, and if their own co-operation is poor, they cannot hope to teach their children to be co-operative. Moreover, it is from the marriage of their parents that children gain their first idea of marriage and the partnership of the sexes. The children of unhappy marriages, unless their first impression is corrected, will grow up with a pessimistic view of marriage. Even when they become adults they will feel that marriage is bound to turn out badly. They will try to avoid the other sex or they will be sure that they will fail in their approach. Children are thus severely handicapped if their parents' marriage is not a co-operative part of social life, a product of social life and a preparation for it. Marriage should be a partnership of two people for their mutual welfare, for the welfare of their children and for the welfare of society. If it fails in any of these respects it cannot satisfy the demands of life.

Since marriage is a partnership, no one member should be supreme. This point needs much closer consideration than we are accustomed to giving it. In the whole conduct of family life there is no need for the use of authority, and it is unfortunate if one member is especially prominent or valued more greatly than the others. If the father is quick-tempered and tries to dominate the rest of the family, his sons will get a false view of what is expected from a man. His daughters will suffer still more. In later life they will picture men as tyrants. To them marriage will seem to be a kind of subjugation and slavery. Sometimes in adult life they may seek to protect themselves against men by cultivating a sexual interest in other women.

If the mother is domineering and nags the other members of the family, the position is reversed. The girls will probably imitate her and become sharp and critical themselves. The boys will always be on the defensive, afraid of criticism and keeping watch for attempts to subjugate them. Sometimes it is not only the mother who is tyrannical; sisters and aunts may all join in to keep a boy in his place. He becomes reserved and is never willing to come forward and join in social life. He is afraid that all women will have the same nagging, censorious attitude and he wishes to avoid the whole sex. Nobody likes to be criticized, but if an individual makes escaping criticism his main interest in life, all his relations with society are affected. He looks at every event and judges it only in accordance with his scheme of things: 'Am I the conqueror or the conquered?' No comradeship is possible for those who look at all relations with others as situations of potential defeat or victory.

The task of a father can be summed up in a few words. He must prove himself a good companion to his partner, to his children and in society. He must deal properly with the three problems of life – work, friendship and love – and he must co-operate on an equal footing with his partner in the care and protection of the family. He should not forget that the woman's role in family life can never be upstaged. It is not his task to dethrone the mother, but to work with her. It is especially important to emphasize that even if the financial support of the family does come through him, it is still a matter of sharing. He should never make it appear that he does all the giving and the others all the receiving. In a good marriage the fact that he earns the money is only a result of the division of labour in the family. Many fathers use their economic position as a means of ruling the household. There should be no ruler in the family, and every occasion that might create feelings of inequality should be avoided.

Every father should be aware of the fact that our culture has overemphasized the privileged position of the man, and that in consequence, when he married his wife, she was probably to some extent afraid of being dominated and put in an inferior position. He should know that his wife is not on a lower level merely because she is a woman and might not support the family in the same way that he might support it. Regardless of the wife's financial contribution to the support of the family, if family life is a genuinely co-operative affair, there will be no question of who makes the money and who it belongs to.

The father's influence on his children is so important that many of them look on him, throughout their lives, either as their ideal or as their greatest enemy. Punishment, especially corporal punishment, is always harmful to children. Any teaching that cannot be given in a spirit of friendship is wrong teaching. Unfortunately it is frequently the case that the father of the family is given the task of punishing the children. There are many reasons why this is unfortunate. First of all, it reveals a conviction on the mother's part that women are not really able to bring up their children, that they are weak creatures who need a strong arm to help them. If a mother tells her children, 'Just wait till your father comes home', she is preparing them to regard men as the final authorities and the real powers in life. Second, it disturbs the children's relationship with their father and makes them fear him, instead of regarding him as a good friend. Perhaps some women are afraid of losing their hold over their children's affections if they mete out punishment themselves; but the solution is not to delegate punishment to the father. The children will not reproach their mother any the less because she has summoned an avenger to her aid. Many women still use the threat of 'telling Father' as a means of compelling their children's obedience. What sort of conclusion will the children draw about the man's role in life?

If the father is meeting the three problems of life in a useful way he will be an integral part of the family, a good husband and a good father. He must be at ease with others and able to make friends. If he makes friends he is already making his family a part of the wider society around him. He will not be isolated and bound to traditional ideas. Influences from outside the home will find their way into it and he will show his children the way to social interest and co-operation.

There is a real danger, however, if the husband and wife have separate friends. They should live in the same group in society and avoid being separated through friendships. I do not mean, of course, that they should cling together and never go out by themselves, but there should be no obstacles to their being together. Such a difficulty occurs, for example, if the husband does not want to introduce his wife into his circle of friends. The centre of his social life, in that case, is outside the family. It is very valuable in the development of children that they learn that the family is a unit of a larger society and that there are trustworthy people outside the family too.

It is a favourable sign of his ability to co-operate if the father is on good terms with his own parents, sisters and brothers. Of course, he must leave his family and become independent, but this does not imply that he should dislike his closest relatives and break with them. Sometimes two people will marry when they are still dependent on their parents and will exaggerate the connection that binds them to their families. When they speak of 'home' they will refer to the home of their parents. If they still regard their parents as the centre of the family, they will not be able to establish a real family of their own. Here it is a question of the co-operative ability of everybody concerned.

Sometimes a man's parents are jealous. They want to know everything about their son's life and often make difficulties in the new family. His wife feels that she is not sufficiently appreciated and is angry at the interference of her husband's parents. This is particularly likely to occur where a man marries against the wishes of his parents. His parents may or may not have been wrong. Before their son marries they can oppose his choice, if they are dissatisfied, but after he has married they have only one course open to them – they must do everything they can to ensure the success of the marriage. If family differences cannot be avoided, the husband should understand the difficulties and not worry about them. He should look on his parents' opposition as a mistake on their part and do his best to prove that it was he, the son, who was right. There is no need for the husband and wife to submit to the wishes of their parents, but it is obviously easier if there is co-operation and the wife feels that her husband's parents are thinking of her welfare and advantage, not of their own.

The one function that is most expected of a father is a solution to the problem of work. He must be trained for a career and must be able to support himself and the family. His wife may help in this and later on, perhaps, his children, but in our western culture economic responsibility has historically fallen mainly on the man. To solve this problem, he must work and be courageous, he must understand his profession and know its advantages and disadvantages, and he must be able to co-operate with others in his profession and be respected by them.

It means even more than this. By his own attitude he is setting an example to his children in how to face the problems of work. He should therefore examine what is necessary for him to successfully tackle this problem – to find work that is useful to the whole of humankind and contributes to its welfare. It does not matter so much whether he himself considers his work useful; what is important is that it should actually *be* useful. We do not need to listen to his words. If he is boastful and egotistical, that is a pity; but if at the same time the work he is doing contributes to the common good, no great harm is done.

Let us now deal with the solution of the problem of love – with marriage and the building of a happy and useful family life. The chief demand upon the husband is that he should be interested in his partner, and it is very easy to see whether one person is interested in another or not. If he is interested, he interests himself in the same things as his partner and makes her welfare his own spontaneous aim. It is not only affection that proves interest; there are too many kinds of affection for us to regard it as sufficient evidence that all is well. He must also be a companion to his wife, and he must take pleasure in pleasing her. It is only when both partners place their joint welfare higher than their individual welfare that true co-operation can take place. Each partner must be more interested in the other than in himself.

A husband should not show his affection for his wife too openly in front of the children. It is true that the love of a husband and wife is not to be compared with their love for their children. They are quite different things and neither can diminish the other. But sometimes children feel, if the parents are too demonstrative in their affection for each other, that their own situation is threatened. They become jealous and wish to cause trouble between the parents.

The sexual partnership should not be taken lightly. It is also important that when giving explanations of sexual matters, parents should be careful not to volunteer information, but to explain only as much as children wish to know and can understand at their current stage of development. I believe that in our own time there is a tendency to explain to children far more than they can fully grasp. This can arouse interests and feelings for which the children are not prepared. In this way, sexual matters are trivialized. This fashion is not much better than the old fashion of being dishonest with children and concealing all sexual information from them. It is best to find out what children wish to know and give them that information, not force on them what in our opinion should be common knowledge. We must preserve their trust and their feeling that we are co-operating with them and are interested in helping them find solutions to their problems. If we do this we cannot go far wrong.

Money should not be overemphasized or made the subject of quarrelling. Women who are not earning money themselves may be much more sensitive than their husbands generally realize, and may feel deeply hurt if they are accused of extravagance. Financial affairs should be settled in a co-operative way, within the financial capabilities of the family. There is no excuse for the wife or children to use their influence to make the father pay out more than he can afford; an agreement on expenses should be made from the beginning so that no one feels dependent or badly treated.

A father should not think that he can assure the future of his children by money alone. I once read an interesting pamphlet written by an American, in which he described how a man who had been born into a very poor family and later became rich wished to protect his descendants from poverty. He went to a lawyer and asked him how it could be done. The lawyer asked him how many generations would satisfy him. The rich man replied that he wanted to provide for ten generations.

'Yes, you can do it', said the lawyer. 'But do you realize that every member of this tenth generation will have more than five hundred ancestors with as much part in producing him as you have? Five hundred other families will be able to lay claim to him. Is he your descendant any longer?'

We can see here another example of the fact that whatever we do for our own descendants we are doing for the whole community. We cannot escape this bond with our fellow human beings.

Authority is unnecessary in the family but there must be real co-operation. Father and mother must work together and agree together on everything concerning the education of their children. It is of the utmost importance that neither the father nor the mother should show any favouritism among their children. The dangers of favouritism cannot be over-stressed. Almost every discouragement in childhood springs from the feeling that someone else is preferred. Sometimes the feeling is not at all justified, but where there is true equality there should be no occasion for it to develop. Where boys are preferred to girls, inferiority complexes amongst the girls are almost inevitable. Children are very sensitive and even a very good child can take an entirely wrong direction in life through the suspicion that others are preferred.

Sometimes one of the children develops faster, or in a more acceptable way than the others, and it is difficult not to show more affection for this child. Parents should be experienced enough and skilful enough to avoid showing any such preferences. Otherwise the child who develops better will overshadow and discourage all the other children; they will become envious of him or her and doubtful of their own abilities, and their ability to co-operate will be frustrated. It is not enough for parents to say that they have no such preference; they must be on the alert for any suspicion of such a preference in the minds of any of their children.

ATTENTION AND NEGLECT

Children quickly become expert at finding ways to gain attention. Pampered children, for example, are often afraid of being left alone in the dark. It is not the dark itself that they are afraid of. They make use of fear in their attempt to bring their mothers closer to them. One such pampered child always cried in the dark. One night, when his mother came in response to his cries, she asked him, 'Why are you afraid?' 'Because it is so dark', he answered. But his mother had now recognized the purpose of his behaviour. 'And after I have come', she said, 'is it any less dark?' The darkness itself is unimportant – his fear of darkness only meant that he disliked being separated from his mother. All his emotions, all his strength and all his mental powers were engaged in setting up a situation in which his mother had to come to him and be close to him again. He strove to bring her near by crying, calling out, being unable to sleep or by making a nuisance of himself in some other way.

One feeling that has long attracted the attention of educators and psychologists is fear. In Individual Psychology we no longer concern ourselves with finding out causes of fear, but rather with identifying its purpose. All pampered children suffer from fear: it is by means of their fears that they can attract attention, and they build this emotion into their life style. They make use of it to secure their goal of staying close to their mother. A child who is timid is a child who has been pampered and wants to be indulged again.

Sometimes these spoilt children have nightmares and cry out in their sleep. This is a well-known symptom; but as long as sleep was thought to be the opposite of waking it was impossible to understand. This was a mistake, however. Sleep and waking are not opposites but variations of the same thing. In their dreams children behave in much the same way as during the day. Their goal of changing the situation to their advantage influences their whole body and mind, and after some training and experience they discover the most successful means of achieving their goal. Even in their sleep, thoughts, pictures and memories come into their mind which are appropriate to their purposes. Pampered children, after a few experiences, discover how to make use of nightmare-inducing thoughts to bring their mother close to them again. Even when they grow up, spoilt children often keep their anxiety dreams. To be afraid in dreams was a tried and tested device for gaining attention which has crystallized into a habit.

This use of anxiety is so obvious that we should be very surprised to hear of a pampered child who never caused any trouble during the night. The repertoire of tricks to attract attention is very large. Some children will find the bedclothes uncomfortable or call for a drink of water. Others will be afraid of burglars or monsters. Some are unable to go to sleep unless their parents sit by their bedsides. Some dream, some fall out of the bed and some wet it. One pampered child I treated seemed to give no trouble at all at night. Her mother said that she slept soundly without dreaming or waking up and caused no trouble at all. It was only during the day that she made trouble. I found this very surprising. I suggested all the tricks that could serve to attract the attention of the mother and draw her closer; this girl used none of them. At last the explanation occurred to me.

'Where does she sleep?' I asked the mother.

'In my bed', she replied.

Sickness is often a refuge for pampered children, for when they are sick they are indulged more than ever. It often happens that such children begin to show signs of being problem children shortly after an illness. It appears at first that it is the illness that has made them problem children. The fact is, however, that when they are well again they remember the fuss that was made over them when they were ill. Their mother can no longer pamper them as they were pampered then, and they take their revenge by becoming problem children. Sometimes children who notice how others, through being sick, became the centre of attention, will wish to fall sick themselves and will even kiss the sick children in the hope of catching their disease.

One girl had been in hospital for four years and had been very spoilt by the doctors and nurses. At first, when she returned home, she was spoilt by her parents too, but after a few weeks their attention decreased. If ever she was denied something she wanted, she would put her finger in her mouth and say, 'I have been in hospital'. She continually reminded others she had been ill and she tried to recreate the favourable situation in which she had found herself. We can find the same behaviour in adults, who often like to speak of their diseases or the operations they have undergone. On the other hand, children who have been a problem to their parents often change after an illness and no longer bother them. We have already seen that physical imperfections are an additional burden to children, but we have also seen that they are not sufficient to explain bad traits of character. We doubt therefore, whether curing the physical problem has, in itself, anything to do with the change.

One boy, the second boy in a family, gave a great deal of trouble by lying, stealing, playing truant and being cruel and disobedient. His teacher did not know what to do with him and urged that he should be put in a reform school. At this time the boy fell ill. He suffered tuberculosis of the hip and spent six months lying in a plaster cast. When he recovered he became the best-behaved boy in the family. We cannot believe that his illness had this effect on him, and it soon became very clear that the change was due to a recognition of his previous mistakes. He had always thought that his parents preferred his brother and had always felt rejected. During his illness he found himself the centre of attention, taken care of and helped by everybody, and he was intelligent enough to put aside the idea that he was always neglected.

EQUALITY BETWEEN SIBLINGS

Now we come to an equally important part of family co-operation, the co-operation of the children among themselves. Unless children feel equal, humankind will never be well grounded in social feeling. Unless girls and boys feel equal to one another, relationships between the two sexes will continue to pose the greatest problems. Many people ask, 'Why do children in the same family often differ so widely?' Some scientists have attempted to explain it as the result of differing genetic make-up; but we have seen that this is mere superstition. Let us compare the growth of children with the growth of young trees. If a group of trees are growing up together, each one of them is really in a quite different situation. If one grows faster because it is more favoured by sun and soil, its development has more and more influence over the growth of all the others. It overshadows them; its roots stretch out and take away their nourishment. The others are dwarfed and stunted. The same is true of a family in which one member is too prominent.

We have seen that neither father nor mother should assume a dominant position in the family. Often, if the father is very successful or very talented, the children feel that they can never equal his achievements. They grow discouraged: their interest in life is diminished. This is why the children of famous men and women are sometimes a disappointment to their parents and to the rest of society. The children have seen no possibility of equalling the achievements of their father or mother. Consequently, if parents are very successful in their professions, they should never make too much of their success within the family, or their children's development will be hindered.

The same holds good for the children themselves. If one child develops especially well, it is quite likely that he or she will receive most attention and favour. It is a pleasant situation for the child concerned, but the other children feel the difference and resent it. It is not possible for a human being to endure, without resentment and irritation, the experience of being held in lower esteem than someone else. A prominent child can damage all the others, and it is not putting it too strongly to say that the others will all grow up suffering from lack of mental stimulation. They will not stop striving for superiority, for this striving is never-ending. It will be channelled, however, in other directions, which may well be unrealistic or less socially useful.

THE FAMILY CONSTELLATION

Individual Psychology has opened up a very wide field for research work by inquiring into the relative advantages and disadvantages experienced by children according to their position in the family. To enable us to consider this issue in its simplest form, let us suppose that the parents are co-operating well and doing their best in bringing up the children. The position of each child in the family still exerts a big influence, and each child will still grow up in a completely different situation from the others. We must reiterate that the situation is never the same for two children in a family, and the life style of each child will reflect their attempts to adapt themselves to their own particular circumstances.

The eldest child

All eldest children have experienced a certain period of being an only child and have suddenly been compelled to adapt themselves to a new situation at the birth of the next child. Firstborn children are generally given a good deal of attention and spoiling. They have often been accustomed to being the centre of the family. All too often they find themselves quite suddenly and abruptly ousted from their position. Another child is born and they are no longer unique. Now they must share their parents' attention with a rival. Such a change always makes a great impact and there are many problem children, neurotic people, criminals, alcoholics and deviants whose difficulties began in such circumstances. They were the eldest children who felt the arrival of another child very deeply, and whose sense of deprivation then moulded their whole life style.

Simplistic – sweeping statement

Subsequent children may lose their position in the same way, but they will probably feel it less strongly. They have already experienced co-operation with another child; they have never been the sole object of care and attention. To eldest children this represents a complete change. If they are in fact neglected on the arrival of the new baby, we cannot expect them to accept the situation easily. If they bear a grudge, we cannot hold it against them. Of course, if their parents have allowed them to feel sure of their affection, if they know that their position is secure and, above all, if they are carefully prepared for the arrival of a younger child and have been trained to co-operate in its care, the crisis will pass without ill effects. But generally they are not prepared. The new baby does indeed take attention, love and appreciation away from them. They begin trying to draw their mother back to them and thinking up ways of regaining her attention. Sometimes we can see a mother being pulled this way and that by her two children, each struggling to occupy her more than the other.

Eldest children are better able to use force and to think up new tricks. We can well imagine what they will do in these circumstances. They will do exactly as we would if we were in their shoes and were pursuing their aim. We would try to worry the mother, and fight her, and behave in such a way that she could not possibly overlook us. Eldest children will do the same. In the end they exhaust their mother's patience. They use everything at their disposal, fighting a desperate battle. Their mother tires of the trouble they cause her, and now they really begin to experience what it is like to be no longer loved. They were fighting for their mother's love, but as a result they lose it. They felt pushed into the background but because of their actions they really *are* pushed into the background. They feel justified. 'I knew it', they say. The others are wrong and they are right. It is as if they were in a trap: the more they struggle, the worse their position becomes. All the time their view of their situation is being confirmed. How can they give up the fight when all their instincts tell them that they are in the right?

In all such fights, we must inquire into the individual circumstances. If the mother fights back, these children will become quick-tempered, uncontrollable, critical and disobedient. When they turn against their mother, the father often offers them a chance to renew their former favourable position. They become more interested in their father and try to win his attention and affection. Eldest children frequently prefer their fathers and lean towards them. We can be sure wherever children prefer their father, this is a secondary phase: at first they were attached to their mother, but now she has lost their affection and they have transferred it to their father as a reproach against her. If children prefer their father, we know that they have previously suffered a setback; they have felt rejected and left out of things; they cannot forget it and their whole life style is built around this sense of rejection.

Fights like these last a long time; sometimes a whole lifetime. These children have trained themselves to fight and resist and they go on fighting in all situations. Perhaps there is no one whose interest they can engage. They then lose hope and imagine they can never win anyone's affection. They become peevish, reserved and unable to join in with others. They train themselves for isolation. All the actions and expressions of such children are directed towards the past, the bygone times when they were the centre of attention.

For this reason, eldest children generally show, in one way or another, an interest in the past. They like to look back and to speak of the past. They are admirers of the past and pessimistic about the future. Sometimes such children who have lost their power, the small kingdom they rule, understand better than others the importance of power and authority. When they grow up, they like to take part in the exercise of authority and they exaggerate the importance of rules and laws. Everything should be done according to rules and no rule should ever be changed. Power should always be preserved in the hands of those who are entitled to it. We can understand that influences like these in childhood give a strong tendency towards conservatism. If such people establish a good position for themselves, they are always suspicious that other people are coming up behind them with the intention of taking their place and dethroning them.

The position of eldest children offers a special problem, but it is one that can be used and turned to advantage. If firstborn children have already been trained for co-operation when a younger child is born, they suffer no harm. Among such eldest children we find individuals who develop a wish to protect others and help them. They train to imitate their fathers or mothers; often they play the part of a father or mother with the younger children, looking after them, teaching them and feeling responsible for their welfare. Sometimes they develop a great talent for organization. These are the favourable cases, though even a striving to protect others may be exaggerated into a desire to prolong their dependence and to rule over them.

In my own experience in Europe and America I have found that the greatest proportion of problem children are eldest children, with youngest children a close second. It is interesting that these extreme positions provide the greatest problems. Our educational methods have not yet been successful in solving the difficulties of eldest children.

The second child

The second child is in quite a different position, a situation that cannot be compared with that of the other children. From the time they are born, they share attention with another child, and they are therefore a little closer to co-operation than eldest children. They have a larger circle of human beings around them, and provided the eldest child is not fighting against them and pushing them back, they are very well situated. The most significant fact of their position, however, is that throughout their childhood they have a pacemaker. There is always a child ahead of them in age and development and they are constantly stimulated to exert themselves in order to catch up. Typical second children are very easy to recognize: they behave as if they were in a race, as if someone were a step or two in front and they had to hurry to get ahead of them. They are going full steam ahead all the time. They train continually to surpass their older sibling and conquer them.

The Bible contains many marvellous psychological insights and the typical second child is beautifully portrayed in the story of

Jacob. He wanted to be first, to take away Esau's position, to beat Esau and surpass him. Second children are irritated by the feeling that they are lagging behind and struggle hard to overtake others. They frequently succeed. Second children are often more talented and successful than the firstborns. Here we cannot suggest that heredity has any part in this development. If they go ahead faster, it is because they worked harder at it. Even when they are grown up and outside the family circle, they often make use of a pacemaker; they compare themselves with someone whom they think more advantageously placed and try to outdo them.

It is not only in our waking life that we see these characteristics. They leave their marks on all expressions of the personality and they are easily found in dreams. Eldest children, for example, often have dreams of falling. They are on top, but they are not sure that they can keep their superiority. Second children, on the other hand, often picture themselves in races. They run after trains and ride in bicycle races. Sometimes these busy, hurrying dreams are so marked that we can easily guess that the dreamer is a second child.

We must say, however, that there are no hard and fast rules. You do not need to be an eldest child to behave like one. The situation counts, not the order of birth. In a large family a later child is sometimes in the same situation as an eldest child. Perhaps there were two children born close together, then after a long interval a third was born, and then two others followed. The third child may show all the features of an eldest child. So, too, with a second child; a typical 'second child' may appear after four or five children have been born. Wherever two children grow up close together and are separated from the others they will show the characteristics of an eldest and a second child.

Sometimes the eldest is beaten in this race; you will then find that the eldest child develops problems. Sometimes they can keep their position and push back the younger; it is then the second child who gives trouble. It is a very difficult position for the eldest child when he is a boy and the second is a girl. He runs the risk of being beaten by a girl, which, in our contemporary society, he will probably consider a serious disgrace. The rivalry between a boy and a girl is more intense than the rivalry between two boys or two girls.

In this struggle the girl is favoured by nature; until her sixteenth year she develops more quickly, physically and mentally, than a boy. It frequently happens that the older boy gives up the fight, and becomes lazy and discouraged. He seeks to gain supremacy by underhand means, through boasting or lying, for example. We can almost guarantee that in such a case the girl will win. We shall see the boy taking to all kinds of mistaken paths, while the girl solves her problems with ease and makes astonishing progress. Such difficulties can be avoided, but the danger must be recognized beforehand and steps taken before any damage has been done. Bad consequences can be avoided only in a family which is a unity of equal and co-operative members, where there is no need for rivalry and no grounds for children to feel threatened and spend their time fighting.

The youngest child

Except for the youngest, all children have followers, and thus all can be dethroned. Youngest children, however, can never be dethroned. They have no followers but they have many pacemakers. They are always the baby of the family and probably the most pampered. They face the problems of any spoilt child but, because they are stimulated so much, because they have so much competition, youngest children often develop extraordinarily well, progress faster than the other children and outdistance them all. The position of the youngest has remained unchanged throughout human history. In our most ancient legends we find accounts of how youngest children surpassed their brothers and sisters.

In the Bible it is always the youngest who conquers. Joseph was brought up as the youngest. Although Benjamin came seventeen years after Joseph, he played no part in Joseph's development. Joseph's life style is typical of the life style of a youngest child. He is always asserting his superiority, even in his dreams. The others must bow down before him; he outshines them all. His brothers understood his dreams very well. It was not difficult for them, since they had Joseph with them and his attitude was clear enough. They too had experienced the feelings Joseph aroused in his own dreams. They feared him and wanted to get rid of him. From being the last, however, Joseph became the first. In later days he was the pillar and support of the whole family.

The youngest child is often the pillar of the whole family, and this cannot be accidental. People have always known it and told stories of the power of the youngest. They are, in fact, in a very favourable situation: helped by their parents and siblings, with so much to stimulate their ambition and effort and with no one to attack them from behind or distract their attention.

And yet, as we saw, youngest children make up the second largest group of problem children. The reason for this generally lies in the way in which they are indulged by the whole family. Spoilt children can never be independent. They lack the courage to succeed by their own efforts. Youngest children are always ambitious, but the most ambitious children of all are lazy children. Laziness is a sign of ambition combined with discouragement: ambition so strong that the individual sees no hope of realizing it. Sometimes youngest children will not admit to any single ambition, but this is because they wish to excel in everything, they wish to be unlimited and unique. It is clear, also, how much youngest children can suffer from inferiority feelings. Everyone around them is older, stronger and more experienced.

The only child

Only children have their own special problems. They have a rival, but this rival is not a brother or a sister. Their feelings of competition are directed against their father. Only children are indulged by their mother. She is afraid of losing them and wants to keep them under her wing. They develop what is called a 'mother complex'; they are tied to their mother's apron strings and wish to push their father out of the family picture. This, too, can be prevented only if the father and mother work together and let the child be interested in both of them; but in most cases the father has less to do with the child than the mother. Eldest children are occasionally very similar to only children: they want to get the better of their father and they enjoy the company of people who are older than themselves.

Often only children are scared to death of having brothers and sisters following them. Friends of the family say, 'You ought to have a little brother or sister', and they dislike the prospect intensely. They want to be the centre of attention all the time. They really feel that this is their right and feel extremely hard done by if their position is challenged. In later life, when they are no longer the centre of attention, they have many difficulties. Another situation that may endanger their development is if they are born into a timid environment. If, for medical reasons, the parents cannot have any more children, we can do no more than apply ourselves to solving the problems of the only child. But we often find these only children in a family where there could have been more children. The parents are timid and pessimistic. They feel they will not be able to provide financially for more than one child. The whole atmosphere is full of anxiety and the child suffers badly.

If there is a long interval between the children in a family, each child will have some of the characteristics of an only child. The situation is not very favourable. I am often asked, 'What do you think would be the best spacing for a family?' 'Should children be born very close together or should there be a longer interval between them?' From my experience I should say that the best interval is about three years. At the age of three children can co-operate if a younger child is born. They are old enough to understand that there can be more than one child in a family. If they are only one and a half or two, we cannot discuss it with them; they cannot understand our arguments. We shall not be able, therefore, to prepare them properly for the event.

An only boy brought up in a family of girls has a hard time ahead of him. He is in a wholly feminine environment if the father is absent for most of the day. He sees only his mother, his sisters and perhaps home helps. He feels different and grows up isolated. This is especially true when the women gang up on him. They think they must all have a hand in his upbringing or they want to prove that he has no reason to be conceited. There is a

may become more well rounded?!

All Children Should Socialise with other Children

good deal of antagonism and rivalry. If he is in the middle, he is probably in the worst place of all – attacked from both sides. If he is the eldest, he is in danger of being followed by a girl who is a very keen competitor. If he is the youngest, he is spoilt.

The situation of an only boy among girls is not well liked, but the problem can be solved if they have an active social life in which they can meet other children. Otherwise, surrounded by girls, they may behave like girls. A feminine environment is quite different from a mixed environment. If the home is not just standardized but furnished according to the taste of the people in it, you may be sure that a home where women live will be neat and tidy, that the colours will be chosen with care and that attention will have been paid to a thousand details. If there are men and boys about, it is not nearly so neat; there is much more roughness and noise and broken furniture. A single boy among girls is apt to grow up with feminine tastes and a feminine outlook on life.

On the other hand, he may fight back strongly against this atmosphere and lay great stress on his masculinity. He will then always be on the defensive, determined not to be dominated by women. He will feel that he must assert his individuality and superiority, but there will always be a certain amount of tension. His development will proceed by extremes: he will train himself to be either very strong or very weak. In a rather similar way, an only girl among boys is apt to develop either very feminine or very masculine qualities. Frequently, she is pursued through life by feelings of insecurity and helplessness. This is a situation that deserves study and inquiry. We do not come across it every day, and before we say much about it we must examine more cases.

Wherever I have studied adults, I have found impressions that were made on them in their early childhood and have lasted ever since. The position in the family leaves an indelible stamp upon the individual's life style. Every difficulty with development is caused by rivalry and lack of co-operation in the family. If we look around at our social life, or indeed at the world as a whole, and ask why rivalry and competition is its most obvious aspect, then we must recognize that people everywhere are pursuing the goal of being a conqueror, of overcoming and surpassing others. This goal is the result of experiences in early childhood, of the rivalries and competitive striving of children who have not felt equal as members of their family. We can get rid of these disadvantages only by training children in co-operation.

7

SCHOOL INFLUENCES

THE CHANGING FACE OF EDUCATION

The school is an extension of the family. If all parents were able to undertake the education of their children and equip them adequately for solving the problems of life, there would be no need for schools. In the past child were often trained almost entirely within the family. A craftsman would bring up his sons in his own craft and teach them the skills he had acquired from his own father and from practical experience. Our present-day culture, however, makes more complex demands on us, and schools are needed to lighten the workload of parents and build on what they have begun. Social integration demands a higher level of education from young people than we can give them in the home.

In America, schools have not gone through all the phases of development that have taken place in Europe, but sometimes we can still see relics of an authoritarian tradition there. At first, in the history of European education, only princes and aristocrats received any formal schooling. They were the only members of society on whom a value was placed: others were expected to get on with their work without aspiring to anything higher. Later on, the range of people considered valuable to society was enlarged. Education was taken over by religious institutions where a few selected individuals could be trained in theology, the arts, the sciences and professional disciplines.

As technology developed, the old forms of education became quite inadequate. The struggle for a wider education was a long, drawn-out affair. Schoolteachers in the villages and towns were often the local cobblers and tailors. They taught with a stick in their hands and the results were very poor. Only the religious schools and the universities gave instruction in the arts and sciences, and sometimes even emperors did not learn to read or write. With the industrial revolution, however, it became necessary for workers to read and write, do sums and draw, and the state schools as we know them were founded.

These schools, however, were always established in accordance with the needs of the government, and the governments of the time required educated, obedient subjects, trained for the benefit of the upper classes and capable of being turned into soldiers. The curriculum in the schools was adapted to this end. I myself can remember a time in Austria when these conditions, in part, survived; when the training for the least privileged classes was designed to make them obedient and fit them for tasks appropriate to their status. Increasingly, however, the failings of this type of education were revealed. Freedom blossomed; the working classes grew stronger and more demanding. The state schools adapted to these demands, and now it is the prevailing ideal of education that children should be taught to think for themselves, should be given the opportunity to familiarize themselves with literature, the arts and sciences, and should grow up able to share in our whole human culture and contribute to it. We no longer wish to train children only to make a living or to perform a task in a factory. We want people who will work together for the common good.

THE ROLE OF TEACHERS

Whether we know it or not, everyone who proposes school reform is seeking a way to increase the degree of co-operation in social life. This is the purpose, for example, behind the demand for character training, and if we understand it in this light, the justification for the demand becomes obvious. On the whole, however, the aims and techniques of education are not yet thoroughly understood. We must find teachers who can train children not only to earn their living but also to work in ways beneficial to humankind. They must be conscious of the importance of this task and they must be trained to fulfil it.

The importance of character training

The effectiveness of character-training is still on trial. We must ignore the legal system, since there has been no serious and organized attempt at corrective character-training there. However, even in schools, the results are not very satisfactory. Children come to school having already been failures in family life, and they go on making the same mistakes, in spite of all the lectures and exhortations they receive. There is nothing for it, therefore, but to improve the training of teachers in understanding and helping the development of children in school.

I have done much of my own work in schools, and I believe that many of the schools in Vienna lead the world. Elsewhere there are psychiatrists who see the children and give advice on their care, but what use are they unless the teachers agree with their advice and understand how to carry it out? Psychiatrists see children once or twice a week – perhaps even once a day – but they do not really know the influences from the environment, from the family, from outside the family, from the school itself. They write a note that children should be better nourished or should have thyroid treatment. Perhaps they give a teacher hints for the personal treatment of a child. Teachers, however, do not know why the psychiatrist has prescribed the treatment and are not experienced in avoiding mistakes. They can do nothing unless they themselves understand the character of a child. We need the closest co-operation between psychiatrists and teachers. Teachers must know everything psychiatrists know, so that after discussing the child's problem they can proceed on their own, without further help. If any unexpected problem turns up, they should understand what to do, just as psychiatrists would if they were present. The most practical method seems to be the Advisory Council, such as we established in Vienna. I shall describe this method towards the end of the chapter.

When children first go to school, they face a new test in their social life, a test that will reveal any short comings in their development. They must now co-operate in a wider field than before. If they have been pampered at home, they may be unwilling to leave their sheltered life and join in with the other

children. Thus we can see on their very first day at school the
limits of a pampered child's social feeling. They may cry and want
to be taken home. They will not be interested in schoolwork or in
their teachers. They will not listen to what is said, because they
are thinking of themselves all the time. It is easy to see that if they
continue in this self-interested way, they will not make good
progress at school. Often parents tell us how problem children are
no trouble at home. and that problems only arise when they are at
school. We can suspect, however, that the children feel that they
are in an especially favourable situation in the family. No tests are
set for them there, and the mistakes in their development are not
apparent. At school, however, they are no longer indulged and
consequently experience their situation as a defeat.

One child, from his first day at school, did nothing but laugh
at everything the teacher said. He showed no interest in any of
the schoolwork and the staff thought that he must be mentally
retarded. When I saw him, I said to him, 'Everybody wonders why
you are always laughing at school.'

He replied, 'School is a joke made up by parents. They send
children to school to fool them.'

He had been teased at home and was convinced that every
new situation was a yet another joke against him. I was able to
show him that he overemphasized the need to preserve his dignity,
and that not everybody was trying to make a fool of him. As a
result, he began to take an interest in his schoolwork and made
good progress.

The teacher–child relationship

It is the task of teachers to notice children's difficulties and to
correct parents' mistakes. They will find some of their pupils
prepared for this wider social life; these children have already been
trained in their families to take an interest in other people. Some
are not prepared, and whenever individuals are not prepared for a
problem, they hesitate or withdraw. All children who seem slow
but are not actually retarded are balking at the problem of
adjustment to social life, and teachers are in the best position to
help them to meet what is in fact a new situation for them.

But how can teachers help them? They must do exactly what a mother should do – bond with the children and gain their attention. The children's whole future adjustment depends on first capturing their interest. Nobody can do this through severity or punishment. If children come to school and find it difficult to relate to their teachers and fellow pupils, the worst possible thing to do is to criticize and scold them. This approach would only confirm that they were right to dislike school. It seems to me that if I were a child who was always scolded and reproached at school, I would withdraw my interest from my teachers as far as possible. I would look for ways of getting out of the situation and avoiding school altogether.

It is mainly the children for whom school is made an artificially unpleasant environment who play truant, perform poorly and appear stupid or difficult to handle. They are not really stupid; they often display great ingenuity in making up excuses for not attending school or in forging letters from their parents. Outside the school, however, they find other children who have played truant before them. From these companions they gain far more appreciation than they get at school. The circle in which they feel involved and where they feel valued is not the school class but the gang. We can see, in this situation, how children who are not accepted into the class as an equal member are provoked to turn towards a criminal career.

Interesting children in learning

If teachers are to attract the interest of children, they must discover what the children's interests have previously been and convince them that they can make a success of these interests and of others. When children feel confident about one subject it is easier to stimulate their interest in others. From the first, therefore, we should find out how children look at the world and which sense organ has been used most and trained to the highest degree. Some children are most interested in seeing, some in listening, some in moving. Children of a visual type will be easier to interest in subjects in which they have to use their eyes, such as geography or drawing. If the teacher gives lectures, they will not listen; they are less accustomed to auditory attention. If such

children have no opportunity to learn through their eyes, they
will be slow learners. It may be taken for granted that they have
no abilities or talents, and the blame will be put on heredity.

If anyone is to blame for educational failures, it is the teachers
and parents who have not found the right way to interest the
children. I am not proposing that children's education should
encourage early specialization, but any interests that children have
developed should be used to motivate them towards other interests
also. There are some schools nowadays where subjects are taught to
children in a way that appeals to all the senses. Exercises in
modelling or drawing, for example, are combined with traditional
lessons. This tendency should be encouraged and developed
further. The best way to teach any subject is in the context of the
rest of life, so that the children can see the purpose of the
instruction and the practical value of what they are learning. The
question is often raised as to whether it is better to teach children
to absorb facts or to teach them to think for themselves. It seems
to me that this need not be an either/or issue: the two approaches
can be combined. It is a great advantage, for example, to teach
children mathematics in connection with the building of houses,
and let them find out how much wood is needed, how many people
will live there, and so forth.

Some subjects can easily be taught together, and many
teachers are expert at linking one aspect of life with another.
Teachers can, for example, take a walk with the children and find
out what they are most interested in. At the same time they can
teach them to understand plants and plant structure, the growth
and uses of the plant, the influences of climate, the physical
features of the landscape, the agricultural history of humankind
and indeed any aspect of life. We must presuppose, of course, that
such teachers are really interested in the children they teach, but
there is no hope for education if this is not the case.

CO-OPERATION AND COMPETITION IN THE CLASSROOM

Under our present system we generally find that when children
first come to school they are better prepared for competition than

for co-operation, and the training in competition continues throughout their school days. This is a disaster for children, and it is just as much a disaster if they surge ahead and strain to beat other children as it is if they fall behind and give up the struggle. In both cases they will be interested primarily in themselves. Their primary objective will not be to contribute and help, but to secure what they can for themselves. As the family should be a unit, with each member an equal part of the whole, so, too, should the class. When they are trained in this way, children are really interested in one another, and enjoy co-operation.

I have seen many 'difficult' children whose attitude was entirely changed through the interest and co-operation of their classmates. I would like to mention one child in particular. He came from a home where he felt that everyone was hostile to him and he expected everyone to be hostile to him at school too. His work at school had been bad, and when his parents heard of it, they punished him at home. This situation occurs all too often: children get a bad report at school and are scolded for it there; they take it home and are punished again. One such experience is discouraging enough; to double the punishment is cruel. No wonder this child under-achieved and was a disruptive influence in class. Eventually he found a teacher who understood his circumstances and who explained to the other children how this boy believed that everyone was his enemy. He enlisted the children's help in convincing him that they were his friends, and the whole conduct and progress of the boy improved beyond belief.

Some people doubt whether children can really be trained to understand and help one another in this way, but it is my experience that children often understand these things better than their elders. A mother once brought her two children, a girl of two and a boy of three, into my room. The little girl climbed up on a table and her mother was petrified. She was too scared to move, but cried out, 'Come down! Come down!' The little girl paid no attention to her. The three-year-old boy said, 'Stay there!' and the girl immediately climbed down safely. He understood her better than her mother and knew what to do in the circumstances.

One frequent suggestion for developing unity and co-operation in a class is to make the children self-governing, but we must proceed carefully in such matters, under the guidance of teachers, and assure ourselves that the children are properly prepared. Otherwise we shall find that the children are not very serious about their self-government: they look on it as a kind of game. In consequence, they are much more strict and severe than teachers would be, or they use their meetings to gain a personal advantage, to air quarrels, to score off one another, or to achieve a position of superiority. In the beginning, therefore, it is important for teachers to watch and advise.

ASSESSING CHILDREN'S DEVELOPMENT

We cannot avoid tests of one kind or another if we are to obtain an up-to-date picture of a child's standard of intellectual development, character and social behaviour. Sometimes, indeed, a test such as an intelligence test can be the salvation of a child. One boy has bad school reports, for example, and the teacher wishes to put him in a lower class. He is given an intelligence test and it is discovered that he could really cope in a higher class. We must realize, however, that we can never predict the limits of a child's future growth. The Intelligence Quotient should only be used to throw light on a child's difficulties, so that we can find a way to overcome them. In so far as my own experience goes, an IQ test result, when it does not reveal actual mental retardation, can always be changed if we discover the right method. I have found that where children are allowed to play with intelligence tests, become familiar with them, find out how they work and increase their experience of them, their IQ score improves. Above all the Intelligence Quotient should not be regarded as fixing a limit, set by fate or heredity, on the child's future achievements.

Nor should the children themselves or their parents be told her IQ score. They do not know the purpose of the tests and they may think they represent a final judgement. The greatest problem in education is posed, not by the limitations of children, but by what they think their limitations are. If children know that their IQ score is low, they may lose hope and believe that success is beyond them. In education we should direct our energies towards increasing the confidence and interest of children and in removing the limits which, through their interpretation of life, they have set on their own powers.

Much the same is true of school reports. If teachers give children bad reports, they probably believe that they are stimulating them to try harder. If the children have had a strict upbringing, however, they will be afraid to take their report home with them. They may stay away from home or alter the report. Some children have even committed suicide in such circumstances. Teachers should consider, therefore, what the repercussions may be. They are not responsible for the home life of children and its effects on them, but they must take it into consideration.

If the parents are ambitious, there are probably scenes and reproaches when children come home with a bad report. If the teacher had been a little kinder and more lenient, the children might have been encouraged to forge ahead and succeed. When children always have a bad school report and everyone else thinks they are the worst pupil in the class, they come to believe it themselves, and to believe that it is an unalterable fact. Even the worst pupil can improve, however, and there are sufficient examples, among the most eminent people, to show that children who are backward at school may recover their confidence and interest and go on to great achievements.

It is very interesting to note that children themselves, without any help from reports, generally have quite a sound judgement of one another's abilities. They know who is best at arithmetic, spelling, drawing and games, and know everyone's position in the pecking order. Their most common mistake, however, is to believe that they could never do better. They see others ahead of them and believe that they could never catch up. If children are very firmly fixed in this attitude, the chances are that they will allow it to dog them throughout their life. Even as an adult they will calculate their position in relation to others and assume that they will always lag behind.

The great majority of children at school occupy more or less the same position in all the classes they pass through. They are always near the top, in the middle or at the bottom. We should not look at this fact as if it showed that they were more or less gifted by birth. It shows the limits they have set for themselves, the degree of their optimism and the field of their activity. It is not uncommon for children who have been at the bottom of their class to change dramatically and begin to make surprising progress. Children should understand the mistake involved in self-limitation, and both teachers and children must rid themselves of the myth that the progress of children of normal intelligence is linked to their heredity.

NATURE VERSUS NURTURE

Of all the mistakes made in education, the belief in hereditary limits to development is the worst. It gives teachers and parents an opportunity to explain away their errors and relax their efforts, and conveniently frees them from the responsibility of their influence over the children. Every attempt to avoid responsibility should be opposed. If educators really attributed the whole development of character and intelligence to heredity, I do not see how they could possibly hope to accomplish anything in their profession. If, on the other hand, they recognize that their own attitude and exertions influence the children, they cannot escape their responsibilities.

I am not referring here to physical heredity. The inheritance of physical disadvantages is beyond question. The importance of such inherited problems on the development of the mind is only understood, I believe, in Individual Psychology. Children are conscious of their physical disability, and they limit their own development in accordance with their judgement of that disability. It is not the disability itself that affects the mind, but the children's attitude to their disability, and their consequent development. If children suffer, therefore, from a physical disability, it is especially important for them to understand that they are not necessarily lacking in either intelligence or character. We have seen in a previous chapter that the same physical disability may be taken either as a stimulus for even greater effort and success or as an obstacle that is bound to hinder development.

When I first advanced this idea, many people accused me of being unscientific and of putting forward private beliefs of my own that did not agree with the facts. It was from my personal experiences, however, that I had formulated my conclusion, and the evidence in its favour has been steadily accumulating. Now, many other psychiatrists and psychologists have come round to the same point of view, and the belief in inherited traits of character may be called a superstition. It is of course a superstition that has existed for thousands of years. Whenever people have wished to avoid responsibility and have taken a fatalistic view of human conduct, the theory that character traits were inherited was almost bound to come up. In its simplest form it is the belief at birth that a child is already good or bad. In this form it can easily be shown to be nonsense, and only a very strong desire to escape responsibility could allow it to persist.

'Good' and 'bad', like other expressions of character, have meaning only in a social context; they are the result of training in a social environment, among our fellow human beings, and they imply a judgement that a person's behaviour is 'conducive to the welfare of others', or 'opposed to the welfare of others'. Before children are born, they have no social environment in this sense. At birth they have the potential to develop in either direction. The path they choose to follow will depend on the impressions and sensations they receive from their environment and from their own body, and on the way they interpret these impressions and sensations. Above all, it will depend on their education.

It is the same with the inheritance of intellectual ability, although the evidence for this is perhaps less clear. The strongest factor in the development of intellectual ability is *interest*, and we have seen how interest is blocked, not through heredity, but through discouragement and the fear of defeat. It is doubtless true that the actual structure of the brain is to some degree inherited, but the brain is the instrument, not the origin, of the mind, and provided any defect is not too severe for us to overcome it with our present knowledge, the brain can be trained to compensate for it. Behind very exceptional degrees of ability we shall find, not an exceptional inheritance, but sustained interest and training.

Even where we find families that have contributed many gifted members to society in more than one generation, we need not assume that hereditary influence has been at work. We may suppose, rather, that the success of one member of the family acted as a stimulus to the others, and that family traditions and expectations enabled the children to follow their interests and train themselves through exercise and practice. So when we learn, for example, that the great chemist, Liebig, was the son of a drugstore proprietor, we have no need to assume that his ability in chemistry was inherited. On closer investigation we can discover that his environment allowed him to pursue his interest, and that at an age when most children understand nothing at all of chemistry he had already familiarized himself with a great deal of his subject.

Mozart's parents were interested in music, but Mozart's talent was not inherited. His parents wished him to be interested in music and provided him with every encouragement. His whole environment was musical from the earliest age. We generally find this fact of an 'early start' among outstanding people: they played the piano at the age of four, or they wrote stories for the other members of the family when they were still very young. Their interest was long and sustained, and their training was spontaneous and widespread. They did not lose their courage, nor did they hesitate or hang back.

No teacher can succeed in removing the limits children have set to their own development if he or she believes that these limits are fixed. It may make the life of teachers easier if they can say to a child, 'You have no gift for mathematics', but it can only discourage the child. I myself have had some personal experience of this. For several years I was the mathematical dunce of my class, quite convinced of my total lack of talent for mathematics. Fortunately I found myself one day, much to my astonishment, able to complete a problem that had stumped my teacher. The unexpected success changed my whole attitude towards mathematics. Where previously I had withdrawn my interest from the whole subject, I now began to enjoy it and to use every opportunity to increase my ability. In consequence I became one of the best mathematicians in my school. The experience helped me, I think, to see the fallacy of theories of special talents or inborn capacities.

RECOGNIZING PERSONALITY TYPES

For anyone who is trained in the understanding of children, it is easy to distinguish different characters and life styles. The degree of co-operation of children can be seen in their posture, in the way they look and listen, in the distance they keep from other children, in the ease with which they make friends, in their capacity for attention and concentration. If they forget their tasks or lose their schoolbooks, we can infer that they are not interested in their work. We must find the reason why school is so distasteful to them. If they do not join in the other children's games, we can recognize a feeling of isolation and self-absorption. If they are always asking for help with their work, we can see a lack of independence and a desire to be supported by others.

Some children only work if they are praised and appreciated. Many pampered children do very well in their schoolwork so long as they can gain the attention of their teachers. If they lose this position of special consideration, trouble begins. They cannot function unless they have an audience; if there is no one to watch them they lose interest. Often mathematics presents great difficulties for such children. While they are only asked to memorize a few rules or sentences, they acquit themselves admirably, but as soon as they have to solve a problem by themselves they are quite at a loss.

This may seem a small failing, but it is children who always claim the support and attention of others who represent the greatest danger to the welfare of others. If this attitude remains unchanged, they will continue to need and demand the support of others throughout adult life. Whenever a problem confronts them, they will respond in a way calculated to force others to solve it for them. They will go through life making no contribution to the welfare of others but as a permanent liability to their fellow human beings.

A different type of child who wants to be the centre of attention will, if the position is not accorded to them, try to gain it by mischief-making, by disturbing the whole class, by leading the other children astray, and by being a general nuisance. Reproaches and punishments will have no effect on them; they revel in them. They would rather be punished than overlooked; and the unpleasantness their bad behaviour brings upon them seems to them a fair price to pay for the attention they gain. Many children see punishment only as a personal challenge. They regard it as a contest or game to see who can hold out longest; and they can always win, because the outcome is in their own hands. So children who are fighting with their parents or teachers will sometimes train themselves to laugh when they are punished, instead of crying.

Lazy children, unless their laziness is a direct attack on their parents and teachers, are almost always ambitious children who are afraid of defeat. Success is a word that everyone understands differently, and it can be astonishing to find out what it is that children regard as a defeat. There are many people who think themselves defeated unless they are ahead of everyone else. Even if they are successful, they consider it a defeat if someone else has done better still. Lazy children never experience any true feeling of defeat because they never face a real test. They avoid problems and postpone the decision on whether to compete with others. Everybody else is fairly sure that if they were less lazy they could overcome their difficulties. They take refuge in that blissful daydream, 'If only I tried, I could accomplish anything'. Whenever they fail, they can diminish the importance of their failure and keep their self-esteem by saying to themselves, 'It is only laziness, not lack of ability.'

Sometimes teachers will say to lazy pupils, 'If you worked harder, you could be the brightest pupil in the class.' If they can gain such a reputation by doing nothing, why should they risk it by working? Perhaps if they stopped being lazy, their reputation for hidden brilliance would come to an end. They would be judged on actual accomplishments, not on what they might have achieved. Another personal advantage for lazy children is that if they do the least bit of work, they are praised for it. Everyone hopes they are at last starting to mend their ways, and is eager to encourage further improvement, even though the same piece of work from industrious children would not even have been noticed. In this way, lazy children live on the expectations of other people. They are spoilt children who have trained themselves from babyhood to expect everything to come to them through the efforts of others.

Another type of child, always easy to recognize, is the child who takes the lead amongst his or her peers. Humankind has a real need for leaders, but only for those who lead in the best interests of everyone else, and such leadership is rare. Most children who take the lead are interested only in situations where they can rule and dominate others, and they will join in with their fellows only on those conditions. The future for such children, therefore, is not bright. Difficulties are bound to occur in later life. Often two such people meet in marriage, in business or in social relations, with tragic or comic results. Each seeks an opportunity of dominating the other and establishing their own superiority. Sometimes the older members of a family are amused to see spoilt children try to boss them and tyrannize over them. They laugh at them and egg them on. Teachers, however, can soon see that this is not a character-development conducive to a useful life in society.

Naturally there will always be wide variations among children, and it is most definitely not our aim to try to cut them all to the same pattern or cast them all in the same mould. What we want to do, however, is to prevent the development of habits that obviously lead towards defeat and difficulty, and these developments are comparatively easy to correct or prevent in childhood. Where such habits have not been corrected, the social consequences in adult life are severe and damaging. There is a direct link between childhood mistakes and adult failures. In extreme cases, children who have not learned to co-operate may become the neurotic, alcoholic, criminal or suicide cases of later years.

As a child, the anxiety-neurotic was terrified of the dark, or of strange people, or of new situations. The melancholic was a cry-baby. We cannot, in our present society, hope to reach all parents and help them to avoid mistakes, especially since the parents who most need advice are often the ones who never ask for it. We can hope, however, to reach all the teachers. Through them we can reach all the children and try to correct the mistakes that have already been made and to train the children for an independent, courageous and co-operative life. This is where the greatest promise for the future welfare of humankind lies.

SOME OBSERVATIONS ON TEACHING

Even in a large class we can observe the differences between the children, and we can handle them better if we understand their characters than if they remain an undistinguished mass. Large classes, however, are certainly a disadvantage. The problems of some of the children are concealed and it is difficult to treat them properly. Teachers should know all of their pupils intimately or they will not be able to engage their interest and co-operation. I think it is a great help if the children have the same teacher for several years. In some schools teachers change every six months or so. No teacher is given sufficient opportunity to mix with the children, to see their problems and follow their development. If teachers stayed with the same children for three or four years, they would be in a better position to find out and remedy mistakes in a child's life style, and it would also be easier to help the class develop into a co-operative unit.

It is not usually an advantage for children to skip a year; they are generally burdened with expectations that they do not fulfil. Perhaps promoting children to a higher class could be considered if they are too old for their classmates or if they develop quicker than the other children in their class. If the class is a unit, however, as we have suggested that it should be, the successes of one member are an advantage to the others. Where there are brilliant children in a class, the progress of the whole class can be accelerated and heightened, and it is unfair to the other members to deprive them of such a stimulus. I would prefer to recommend that unusually bright pupils should be given other activities and interests – painting, for example – in addition to the ordinary tasks of the class. Their successes in these activities would also widen the interests of the other children and encourage them to surge ahead too.

It is even more unfortunate for children to repeat a year. Every schoolteacher will agree that children who repeat classes are generally a problem in school and at home, although this is not always the case. A small minority can repeat a class without giving us any problems at all. The great majority of children who repeat classes, however, always remain backward and troublesome. They are not well thought of by their fellow pupils and they have a pessimistic view of their own capabilities. This is a difficult question and with our present school structure it is not easy to avoid some children repeating classes. Some teachers have managed to make it unnecessary for backward children to repeat classes by making use of the holidays to train them to recognize the mistakes in their life styles. When their mistakes have been recognized, the children can progress through the next class with every success. Indeed, this is the only way in which we can really help backward children: by letting them see the mistakes they have made in their estimation of their own capabilities, we can set them free to progress by their own efforts.

Wherever I have seen children divided into brighter and slower pupils and put into different streams, I have noticed one outstanding fact, although I should note that my experience has been mainly in Europe and I cannot tell whether the same observation would hold good for America. In the slower streams I have found mentally retarded children lumped together with children who came from poor homes. In the brighter streams I have found mainly children of richer parents. This fact seems understandable enough. In poorer homes children are less well prepared for school. The parents are confronted with too many difficulties; they cannot spare as much time to prepare their children and perhaps they are not well enough educated themselves to help them.

I do not think, however, that children who are not well prepared for school should be placed in slower streams. A well-trained teacher will know how to correct their lack of preparation and they will gain from association with children who are better prepared. If they are placed in slower streams they are generally quite aware of the fact, and the children in the brighter streams know it too, and look down on the others. This constitutes fertile ground for discouragement and misdirected strivings for personal superiority.

In principle, co-education deserves every support. It is an excellent means for boys and girls to get to know each other better and learn to co-operate with the other sex. Those who believe that co-education solves all problems, however, are making a great mistake. Co-education provides special problems of its own, and unless those special problems are recognized and dealt with, the estrangement between the sexes is greater in mixed schools than in single-sex ones.

One of the difficulties, for example, is that girls develop faster than boys until their sixteenth year. If the boys do not understand this, it is difficult for them to preserve their self-esteem. They see themselves outdistanced by the girls and become disheartened. In later life they are afraid of competing with the other sex, because they remember their defeat. Teachers who are in favour of co-education and understand its problems can accomplish a great deal through it, but if they do not wholly approve of it and are not interested in it, they will fail. Another difficulty is that unless the children are properly trained and supervised, sexual problems are bound to arise.

The question of sex education in school is a very complex one. The classroom is not the right place for sex education: if teachers speak to the whole class they have no means of knowing that each child understands them properly. They may thus arouse interests without knowing whether the children are prepared for them or how they will adapt them to their own life style. Of course, if children wish to know more and ask questions in private, teachers should give truthful and straightforward answers. They then have the opportunity of judging what the children really want to know and setting them on the right path to a correct solution. It is a disadvantage, however, if there are repeated discussions about sex in class. Some of the children are sure to misunderstand, and it is not useful to treat sex as if it were a matter of no great importance.

THE WORK OF ADVISORY COUNCILS
It was with the aim of reaching teachers and establishing a programme of school counselling services that I started to develop,

some fifteen years ago, the Advisory Councils in Individual Psychology that proved so valuable in Vienna and in many other cities in Europe. It is all very well having lofty ideals and high hopes, but unless a method of realizing them is found, ideals prove worthless. After the experiences of these fifteen years, I think I may say that these Advisory Councils have proved a complete success and offer us the best instrument we possess for dealing with the problems of childhood and the education of children to be responsible citizens. Naturally, I am convinced that Advisory Councils will succeed best if they are grounded in Individual Psychology, but I can see no reason why they should not cooperate with psychologists of other schools. Indeed, I have always advocated that Advisory Councils should be established in connection with the different schools of psychology, and a comparison made of the results obtained by each one.

In the procedure established by the Advisory Council, well-trained psychologists who are experienced in the problems faced by teachers, parents and children join with the teachers of a school and discuss with them the problem that have arisen in their work. When they visit the school, one or other of the teachers describes the case of a child and the problems he or she has: the child is lazy, perhaps, or quarrelsome, plays truant, steals, or is behind in their work. The psychologists contribute their own experiences and a discussion follows. The family life and character development of the child are described, as are the circumstances in which the problem first occurred. The teachers and the psychologists discuss possible reasons for the problem and how to deal with it. Because they are experienced, they soon agree on a solution.

On the day of a psychologist's visit, the children and their parents are in attendance. After it has been decided between the psychologist and teachers how best to speak to the parents and how to influence them and show them the reason for the children's failure, they are called in. The parents have more information to contribute, and a discussion begins between the psychologist and the parents, in which the psychologist suggests what can be done to help the children. Generally the parents are very glad of the opportunity for consultation and are prepared to co-operate, but if they resist, the psychologist or the teachers can discuss similar cases and draw conclusions from them that can be applied to the children in question. The children then come into the room and the psychologist speaks to them, not about their mistakes, but about their problems. The psychologist looks for the opinions and judgements in the children that prevented them from developing well, for a belief that they are slighted and other children are preferred, and so on. He or she does not reproach the children, but carries on a friendly conversation with them in order to understand their point of view. If the psychologist mentions the children's particular mistake, it is put as a hypothetical case and the children's opinion is invited. Anyone not experienced in this work would be surprised to see how well the children understand and how quickly their whole attitude can change.

All the teachers I have trained in this work are happy in it and would not give it up on any account. It makes their whole contact with their work more interesting and all their efforts more successful. None of them feels it is an added burden, for often, in half an hour or less, they can solve a problem that would have dogged them for years. The spirit of co-operation in the whole school is heightened and, after a short time, there are no more major problems and only minor ones are referred for treatment. The teachers themselves become psychologists too. They learn to understand the unity of the personality and the coherence of all its aspects and expressions, and if any problem crops up in the course of the day, they can settle it themselves. Indeed, it would be our hope, if all teachers could be trained in psychology, that psychologists would become redundant.

So, for example, if teachers have a lazy child in the class, they will suggest to the children that they have a discussion about laziness. The teachers initiate the discussion by asking, 'Where does laziness come from?' 'Why are some people lazy?' 'Why doesn't a lazy child change?' and 'What is it that should be changed?' The children will talk about the problem and reach a conclusion. The lazy children themselves do not know that they are the subject of the discussion, but the problem is their own, so they are interested in it and learn a great deal from the discussion. If they were to be attacked, she would learn nothing; but if she can listen to a calm discussion, she will think about the question and perhaps change her opinions.

No one can understand the minds of children as well as teachers who work and play with them. They see so many types of children and, if they are skilful, establish a relationship with each one of them. It rests with them as to whether the children's early mistakes are allowed to continue or are corrected; like a parent, they are the guardian of the future of humankind, and the service they can render is incalculable.

8

ADOLESENCE

WHAT IS ADOLESCENCE?

There are whole libraries of books on adolescence, and almost all of them treat the subject as if it represented a dangerous crisis that threatened to transform the whole character of an individual. There are many dangers in adolescence, but it is not true that they can change a person's character. Adolescence confronts growing children with new situations and new tests; they feel that they are approaching the front line of life. Hitherto unobserved mistakes in their life style may reveal themselves, but a practised eye could always have seen them. With adolescence, they loom large and can no longer be overlooked.

The psychological dimension

For almost all young people, adolescence means one thing above all else: they must prove that they are no longer children. We might persuade them, perhaps, that they can take this for granted; and, if we could do that, a great deal of stress would be removed from the situation. But if they feel they must prove their maturity, they will inevitably overstress this point.

Much of adolescent behaviour is the outcome of a desire to show independence, equality with adults, and the attainment of manhood or womanhood. The direction this behaviour takes will depend on the meaning children have attributed to being 'grown up'. If to be 'grown up' has meant to be free from constraints, children will fight against all restrictions. It is common for children to do this at this stage. Many adolescents begin to smoke, to swear and to stay out late at night. Some of them reveal an unexpected opposition to their parents, who may be at a loss to know how such obedient children can suddenly have become so disobedient. But it is not really a change of attitude; apparently obedient children always were in opposition to their parents, but it is only now, when they have more freedom and strength, that they feel able to declare that opposition openly. One boy, who had always been bullied by his father and had to all appearances been a quiet and submissive child, was only biding his time while awaiting an opportunity for revenge. As soon as he felt strong enough, he challenged his father to a fight, thrashed him and left home.

Frequently children are given more freedom and independence during their adolescence. The parents no longer feel they have a right to watch over them and guard them all the time. If parents do try to continue their supervision, however, children will make still more strenuous efforts to escape their control. The more their parents try to prove that they are still children, the more they will fight to prove the opposite. Out of this struggle an antagonistic attitude develops, and we are then presented with the typical picture of 'adolescent revolt.'

The physical dimension

We cannot place strict limits on the period of adolescence. It generally runs from about fourteen years of age to about twenty, but sometimes children are already adolescent at ten or eleven years of age. All the organs of the body are growing and developing at this time and sometimes children have difficulties with co-ordination. Children grow taller, their hands and feet grow larger, perhaps they are less active and dextrous. They need to work to improve their co-ordination, but if, in the process, they are laughed at and criticized, they will come to believe they are naturally awkward. If children's movements are laughed at, they will become clumsy.

The endocrine glands are also contributing to the child's development. In adolescence they increase their activity. It is not a complete change – the endocrine glands were active even in infancy – but now their secretions are greater and the secondary sex characteristics become more apparent. A boy's beard will begin to grow and his voice to break. A girl's figure fills out and is more obviously feminine. These too are facts that an adolescent can misunderstand.

THE CHALLENGE OF ADULTHOOD

Sometimes children, inadequately prepared for adult life, panic at the approach of the adult challenges of career-building, friendship, and love and marriage. They lose all hope of ever being able to cope with them. In company, they are bashful and reserved, preferring to isolate themselves and stay at home. In the world of work, they can find nothing that attracts them and are sure that they would be a failure at everything. With regard to love and marriage, they are embarrassed in the company of the other sex and frightened to meet them. If they are spoken to, they blush; they cannot find words to reply. Every day they slip into deeper and deeper despair.

In extreme cases such individuals are completely unable to cope with any of the problems of life, and no one can understand them any longer. They do not look at others, speak to them or listen to them; they do not work or study; they retreat into a world of fantasy. Only a shabby remainder of sexual activity is left. This is the condition of schizophrenia, a condition that basically arises from a mistake. If it is possible to encourage such children, to show them that they have taken a wrong turning and to point out a better path to them, they can be cured. It is not easy, for their whole upbringing must be corrected. The meaning of their past, present and future must be seen in an objective, more scientific light, not in the light of their private logic.

All the dangers of adolescence are caused by inadequate training to cope with the three tasks of life. If children fear or are pessimistic about the future, it is natural enough for them to try to tackle it using the methods that call for the least effort. These easy ways, however, are ineffective, and the more such children are ordered about, exhorted and criticized, the stronger their impression becomes that they are standing on the edge of an abyss. The more we push them, the more they try to draw back. Unless we can encourage them, every effort to help them will be a mistake and will damage them still further. While they are so pessimistic and so frightened, we cannot expect them to feel he capable of additional efforts.

SOME ADOLESCENT PROBLEMS

The pampered child

A great many 'failures' in adolescence were spoilt as children, and it is easy to see that the approach of adult responsibilities is a special strain on children who have become accustomed to having everything done for them by their parents. They still want to be pampered, but as they grow older they find that they are no longer the centre of attention, and they feel that life has deceived and failed them. They have been brought up in an artificially warm atmosphere and the air outside feels bitterly cold.

Clinging to childhood

During this period a few young people betray a wish to remain children. They may even speak in baby talk, play with children younger than themselves and pretend that they can remain childish forever. The vast majority, however, make some attempt to behave in an adult fashion. If they are not really courageous, they offer a sort of caricature of the adult: boys imitate the supposed actions of men; perhaps they will spend money freely, strike up flirtations and have love affairs.

Petty crime

In more difficult cases, where children do not see their way clear to coping with the problems of life, yet remain outgoing and active, they embark on a criminal career. This is especially likely if they have already committed misdemeanours without being found out and think they are clever enough to avoid detection again. Crime is one of the easy escapes from the problems of life, and especially from the problem of making a living. So it happens that between the ages of fourteen and twenty there is a great increase in the occurrence of delinquency. Here again, we are not facing a new development, but greater pressure has revealed the flaws already present in a child's life style.

Neurotic behaviour

In less active and outgoing children, the easy way of escape is neurosis, and it is in adolescence that many children begin to suffer from functional disorders and nervous diseases. Every neurotic symptom is designed to provide a justification for a refusal to solve the problems of life, without lowering the sense of personal superiority. Neurotic symptoms appear when an individuals are confronted by social problems that they are not prepared to face in a social way. The difficulty creates a great deal of stress. During adolescence, the physical constitution is especially responsive to such tensions; all the organs can be irritated and the whole nervous system affected. This can provide yet another excuse for hesitation and failure. Individuals in such a situation now begin to regard themselves, both privately and with others, as relieved of responsibility because of their suffering; and the structure of a neurosis is complete.

Every neurotic person professes the best of intentions. They are convinced of the necessity for social feeling and for facing the problems of life. It is only in their own case that there is an exception to this universal demand. What excuses them is the neurosis itself. Their whole attitude says, 'I am anxious to solve all my problems, but unfortunately I am prevented from doing so.' In this they differ from the criminal, whose professions of bad intentions are often quite open and whose social feeling is concealed and suppressed. It is difficult to decide which does the most harm to human welfare: neurotic individuals whose motives are so good, but whose actions seem spiteful, selfish and designed to hinder the co-operation of their fellow human beings; or criminals, whose hostility is so much more open and who takes pains to subdue the remnants of their social feeling.

Contradicting expectations

At this time we find apparent reversals in established trends. The children of whom most was expected begin to fail in their studies and their work, while children who had previously seemed less gifted begin to overtake them and to reveal unsuspected abilities. This does not contradict previous events. Perhaps children who were very promising become anxious about disappointing the expectations with which they have been burdened. As long as they were supported and appreciated, they could move forward; but when the time comes to make an effort on their own, their courage fail and they retreat. Others may be encouraged by their new-found freedom. They see clearly before them the road towards the fulfilment of their ambitions. They are full of new ideas and new projects. Their creativity is intensified and their interest in all aspects of human life becomes more vivid and enthusiastic. These are the children who have kept their courage, and to whom independence means not difficulty and the risk of defeat, but wider opportunities for achievements and contributions.

Seeking praise and approval

Children who earlier felt slighted and neglected will perhaps now, when they have established better relationships with their fellow human beings, begin to hope that they will at last be appreciated. Many of them become completely obsessed with this craving for appreciation. While it is dangerous enough for a boy to focus so much on seeking praise; many girls are even more lacking in self-confidence and see in the approval and appreciation of others their only means of proving their worth. Such girls are easy prey for men who know how to flatter them. I have come across many girls who, feeling unappreciated at home, begin to have sexual relations, not merely to prove that they are grown-up, but out of the vain hope of finally achieving a situation in which they are appreciated and become the centre of attention.

Let me take one example, a girl of fifteen who came from a very poor family. She had an older brother who, during her childhood, was always sickly. The mother was forced to devote a good deal of care to him, and could not give her daughter much attention. In addition, during her early childhood, the father was ill, and his sickness further limited the time that the mother could give her.

Thus the girl was in a position to notice and understand what it means to be cared for; it was always her desire to achieve this position, but she could not find it in her family. A younger sister was born, and at this time the father recovered and the mother was free to devote herself to the baby. Consequently, the girl felt that she was the only one who did not receive love and affection. But she persevered; she behaved well at home and was the best pupil in her school. Because of her success, it was proposed that she should continue her studies, and she was sent to a high school where the teacher did not know her. At first, she could not understand the methods of instruction at the new school. Her work began to fall off, her teacher criticized her and she became steadily discouraged. She was too eager for quick appreciation. When she found she was not appreciated either at home or at school, what was left?

She looked around for a man who would appreciate her. After a few experiences, she went away and lived with a man for a fortnight. The family were very worried about her and tried to find her, but predictably she soon discovered that she was still not appreciated for herself alone and began to regret the episode.

Suicide was her next thought, and the girl sent a note home saying, 'Do not worry. I have taken poison. I am quite happy.' In fact, she had not taken poison, and we can understand why. She knew that in reality her parents cared about her and she felt that she could still attract their sympathy. So she did not commit suicide, but waited until her mother came, found her and took her home. If the girl had known what we know, that all her efforts were directed to gaining appreciation, these difficulties would not have arisen. If the teacher at the high school had understood her, this would also have prevented problems. In the past the girl's school reports had always been excellent, and if the teacher had noticed that the girl was sensitive on this point and needed more careful treatment, she would not have become discouraged.

In another case, a girl was born into a family where both father and mother were weak personalities. The mother had always wanted sons and was disappointed at the arrival of a girl. She undervalued the role of women and her daughter was bound to feel it. More than once she overheard her mother say to her father, 'The girl is not at all attractive. No one will like her when she grows up', or 'Whatever shall we do with her when she is older?' After about ten years of this poisonous atmosphere she found a letter from one of her mother's friends, consoling her for having had only a daughter and saying that she was still young and there was still time to have a son.

It is not difficult to imagine how the girl felt. A few months later she went to the country to visit an uncle. While she was there, she met a country boy of low intelligence and became his sweetheart. He left her, but she persisted in the same line of behaviour. When I saw her, she already had a long list of lovers, but she had not felt properly appreciated in any of her relationships. She came to me because she was now suffering from anxiety-neurosis and could not leave the house by herself. Dissatisfied with one way of gaining appreciation, she had tried another. She began to tyrannize over the family with her pain and suffering; no one could do anything without her permission; she would weep and threaten to commit suicide. It was hard work to make the girl appreciate her position and to convince her that in her adolescence she had overemphasized the need to escape the feeling of rejection.

ADOLESCENT SEXUALITY
Both girls and boys tend to overvalue and exaggerate sexual relations in their adolescence, out of a desire to prove that they are grown up. If a girl, for example, is rebelling against her mother and always believes that she is being suppressed, she may, in protest, be promiscuous in her sexual relations. She does not care if her mother finds out or not; in fact she is happiest of all if she can cause her mother anxiety. It is not uncommon that a girl, after prolonged quarrels with her mother, and perhaps with her father too, runs quickly into a sexual relationship. These were girls who were always thought to be good girls, well brought up, the last people we would have expected to behave like this. However, the girls are not really guilty. They have not been properly prepared for life; they have felt neglected and inferior, and this seems the only way open to them of achieving a stronger position.

The masculine protest

Many girls who have been pampered find it difficult to adjust themselves to their feminine role. Our culture still frequently gives the impression that men are superior to women, and as a result these girls dislike the thought of being women. Now they reveal what I have called the 'masculine protest'. The masculine protest can express itself in a wide variety of behaviour. Sometimes only a dislike and avoidance of men is manifested. Sometimes such women like men well enough, but are embarrassed in their company and cannot speak to them, are reluctant to join gatherings where men are present, and feel generally ill at ease with sexual matters. Often they insist that they are eager to marry when they are older, but they make no approach to members of the other sex and form no friendships with them.

Sometimes a dislike of the feminine role may be expressed more actively in adolescence. Girls will behave more boyishly than before, trying to imitate boys and especially their vices: smoking, drinking, swearing, joining gangs and generally displaying their sexual freedom. Often they argue that boys would not be interested in them if they behaved in any other way.

Where the dislike of the feminine role is still further developed, we find the appearance of sexual deviance or prostitution. From early childhood all prostitutes have held a firm conviction that nobody likes them. They believe that they were born to an inferior role and that they could never win the real affection or interest of any man. We can understand how, in these circumstances, they are inclined to throw themselves away, to belittle their sexual role and to regard it only as a means for making money. This dislike of the feminine role does not originate in adolescence. Rather we would find that from a very young age the girl had always disliked being female, although in her childhood she had had neither the same need to express her dislike nor the opportunity to do so.

It is not only girls who suffer from a 'masculine protest'. All children who overvalue the importance of being masculine see masculinity as an ideal and are doubtful whether they are strong enough to achieve it. In this way, the stress put upon masculinity in our culture can be as difficult for boys as for girls, especially if they are not entirely confident about their sexual identity. Many children live for several years with the vague belief that at some time or other their gender can be changed, and it is important that from the age of two all children should know quite definitely whether they are boys or girls.

Often a boy who has a rather girlish appearance has a particularly difficult time. Strangers will sometimes mistake his gender, and even friends of the family will say to him, 'You really ought to have been a girl'. Such children are very likely to take their appearance as a sign of inadequacy and to regard the problem of love and marriage as too severe a test. Boys who are not sure that they can acquit themselves well in their sexual role have a tendency, during adolescence, to imitate girls. They behave in an effeminate manner and take on the vain, coquettish, capricious ways of girls who have been over-indulged.

Our formative years

The preparation for a person's attitude to the other sex has its roots in the first four or five years of life. The sex drive is evident in the first weeks of babyhood, but nothing should be done to stimulate it before it can be given an appropriate outlet. If the sex drive is not stimulated, its manifestations will be natural and need cause us no alarm. We should not be worried, for example, if we see babies in their first year of life investigating their bodies and perhaps touching themselves; but we should use our influence to co-operate and interest the children less in their own bodies and more in the world around them.

It is another matter if these attempts at self-gratification cannot be stopped. Then we can be sure that the children have a mind of their own: they are not the victim of their sex drive but rather are making use of it for their own purposes. Generally, the aim of little children is to gain attention. They sense that their parents are worried and horrified and they know how to play on these feelings. Consequently, if their habit no longer serves the children's purpose of attracting attention, they will give it up.

Care must be taken when touching children. There is nothing wrong with affectionate hugs and kisses between parents and children, provided that there is no inappropriate stimulation of children's physical responses. Furthermore, children have often told me, as have adults recalling their childhood, of the feelings that were aroused when they discovered some erotic book in their parents' library or saw an explicit film. It is better to protect children from exposure to such books and films. If we do not stimulate children erotically, we can avoid such difficulties.

Another form of stimulation, to which we referred earlier, is the insistence on giving children quite unnecessary and inappropriate information about sex. Many adults seem to have an absolute passion for imparting sex education and are horribly afraid of the danger of someone growing up in ignorance. If we look at our own experience and that of others, we will not find the catastrophes they expect. It is better to wait until children become curious and want to know something. If the parents are attentive, they will understand the children's curiosity even if they do not voice it. If the children have a good, friendly relationship with their parents, they will ask; and they should be answered in such a way that they can understand and assimilate the information.

It is also advisable for parents to avoid excessive displays of physical affection for each other in front of the children. If possible, children should not sleep in the same room as their parents, let alone in the same bed; and it is also preferable that a girl should not sleep in the same room as her brother. Parents must be attentive to their children's development and should not deceive themselves. If they are not acquainted with the characters and development of their children, they will never know what influences their children are being subjected to.

ANTICIPATING ADOLESCENCE

It is common for the phases of human development to be given a heightened private meaning and viewed as if they were definitive turning-points. There is an almost universal superstition, for example, that adolescence is a very special and peculiar time. Menopause is regarded in a similar way. These phases do not bring radical change, however; they are merely a continuation of life and their phenomena have no critical importance. What is important is what individuals expect to find in such phases, the meaning they ascribe to it and the way they have taught themselves to face it.

Children are often startled when adolescence begins, and act as if they have been visited by a ghost. If we understand this reaction properly, we shall see that the children are not at all concerned about the physical facts of adolescence, except in so far as social conditions call for a new adaptation of their life style. Often, however, the problem is that they believe adolescence is the end of everything; all their worth and value is lost. They no longer have any right to co-operate and contribute: nobody wants them any more. All the difficulties of adolescence develop from these sorts of feelings and concerns.

If children have been trained to regard themselves as equal members of society and to understand their task of contributing to the community, and especially if they have been trained to regard members of the other sex as companions and equals, adolescence will simply give them an opportunity to begin devising their own creative and independent solution to the problems of adult life. If they feel inferior to other people, if they suffer from a mistaken view of their circumstances, they will appear ill-prepared for freedom in adolescence. If someone is always present to compel them to do what is necessary, they can accomplish it. If they are left to themselves they hesitate and fail. Such children would be well adapted for servitude, but in freedom they are at a loss.

9

CRIME AND ITS PREVENTION

UNDERSTANDING THE CRIMINAL MIND

Individual Psychology can help us recognize all the various types of human beings and understand that, despite this variation, human beings are not remarkably different from one another. We find, for example, the same kind of failures exhibited in the behaviour of criminals as in that of problem children, neurotics, psychotics, suicides, alcoholics and sexual deviants. They all fail in their approach to the problems of life; and, in one very definite and noticeable area, they fail in precisely the same way: every one of them fails in social interest; they are not concerned with their fellow human beings. Even here, however, we cannot distinguish them from other people. No one can be held up as an example of perfect co-operation or perfect social feeling, and criminals only differ from the common run in the severity of their failure.

The human striving for superiority

One issue is particularly important for the understanding of criminals, although we will find that in this regard they are just like the rest of us: we all wish to overcome difficulties; we are all striving to reach a future goal whose attainment will help us to feel strong, superior and complete. This tendency has been referred to, quite rightly, as the striving for security. Others call it the striving for self-preservation, but whatever name we give it, we will always find in all human beings this dominant theme running through their lives – the struggle to rise from an inferior position to a superior position, from defeat to victory, from *below* to *above*. It begins in our earliest childhood and it continues to the end of our lives. Life involves continuing to exist on the crust of this planet, striving to surmount obstacles and overcome difficulties. We should not be surprised, therefore, to discover exactly this philosophy among criminals.

In all the actions and attitudes displayed by criminals, they show that they are struggling to be superior, to solve problems, to overcome difficulties. What distinguishes them is not the fact of their striving but rather the direction it takes. If we recognized that it takes this direction because they have not understood the demands of social life and are not concerned with their fellow human beings, we would immediately find their actions quite intelligible.

Environment, heredity and change

I want to stress this point very strongly, because there are people who think otherwise. They regard criminals as exceptions to the human norm, as totally unlike ordinary people. Some scientists, for example, assert that all criminals are mentally handicapped. Others put great emphasis on heredity; they believe that a criminal is born wicked and cannot help committing crimes. Still others say 'Once a criminal always a criminal!' Considerable evidence can now be brought against all these opinions. More importantly, if we accepted them we would never stand a chance of solving the problem of crime. We want to end this human disaster as soon as possible. History tells us that crime has always been disastrous, but now we are anxious to do something about it; we can never be content to shelve the problem by saying, 'It is all heredity, and nothing much can be done'.

There is no compulsion in either our environment or heredity. Children of the same family and the same environment can develop in entirely different ways. Sometimes criminals come from a family of irreproachable reputation. Sometimes in a thoroughly disreputable family, with frequent experiences of prison and reform school, we find children of good character and behaviour. Moreover, some criminals reform in later life, and criminal psychologists have often had difficulty in explaining how burglars, on reaching the age of thirty, may settle down and become good citizens. If criminal tendencies were an inborn defect, or irrevocably ingrained by a person's childhood environment, this fact would be quite beyond understanding. From our own point of view, however, we have no trouble understanding such a change. Individuals may find themselves in a more favourable situation, perhaps; there are fewer demands on them, and the errors in their life style are no longer brought to the surface. Or perhaps they have already got all they wanted from crime and thus it no longer serves a purpose. Perhaps, finally, they are growing older, less suited to a criminal career; their joints are stiff and they are no longer as nimble as they were: burglary has become too difficult for them.

Childhood influences and the criminal life style

The only way we can reform criminals is to find out what happened to them during their childhood that prevented them from learning to co-operate. Here Individual Psychology has cast some light on a whole dark territory for us. We can see much more clearly. By the age of five years the psyche of children is a unit: the threads of their personality have been drawn together. Heredity and environment contribute something to their development, but we are not so concerned with what children bring into the world, or with the experiences they encounter, as with the way they utilize them, how they turn them to account and what they do with them. It is particularly important to investigate this aspect because we really do not know anything of inherited abilities or disabilities. All we need consider are the potentialities of their situation, and how fully he has made use of them.

The extenuating circumstance for all criminals is that they have a certain ability for co-operation, but not sufficient for the demands of society, and on this point the primary responsibility rests with the parents. They must understand how to broaden the scope of children's interest, how to widen it until it becomes an interest in other people. They must behave in such a way that the children can take an interest in the whole of humankind and their own future life. But perhaps the parents do not want the children to be interested in anyone else. Perhaps the marriage is not happy and the two parents do not get on. Perhaps they are considering divorce, or are jealous of each other. Perhaps, therefore, one parent wishes to keep the children all to themselves. They spoil them and pamper them and will not allow them any independence. It is quite obvious how limited the development of co-operation will be in such circumstances.

Interest in other children is also very important for the development of social interest. Sometimes if one child is one parent's favourite, the others are not very inclined to be friendly to that child and include him or her in their social group. When this circumstance is misunderstood, it can be the starting point of a criminal career. If there is one child of outstanding ability in a family, the next is often a problem child. It may also happen that the second son is more amiable and charming, and his older sibling feels deprived of affection. It is easy for such a child to deceive himself and become obsessed with the feeling that he is neglected. He looks for evidence to prove himself right. His behaviour becomes worse. He is treated with more severity; he thus finds confirmation for his belief that he is thwarted and pushed aside. Because he feels deprived, he begins to steal; he is found out and punished and now he has still more proof that nobody loves him and that everyone is against him.

When parents complain of bad times and difficult circumstances in front of their children, they can cause a block in the development of social interest. The same thing can happen if they are always making accusations about their relatives or neighbours, always criticizing others and showing bad feeling and prejudice. It would hardly be surprising if their children grew up with a distorted view of what their fellow human beings were like; nor should we be surprised if, in the end, they turned against their parents too. Wherever social interest is blocked, only a self-centred attitude is left. Children feel: 'Why should I do anything for other people?', and, as they cannot solve the problems of life in this frame of mind, they are bound to hesitate and look for an easy way out. They find it too difficult to struggle and they do not feel concerned if they hurt others. This is war – and in a war anything goes.

Let me give you a few examples in which you can trace the development of the criminal pattern. In one family, the second son was a problem child. As far as we could see he was quite healthy and had no hereditary disabilities. The eldest boy was the favourite, and the younger brother was always trying to catch up with his achievements, as if he were running a race and trying to overtake the front runner. His social interest was not developed - he depended very much on his mother and wanted to get all he could out of her. He had a difficult task in trying to rival his older brother, who was at the top of his class in school, while he himself was at the bottom.

His desire to rule and dominate was very obvious. He used to give orders to an old maidservant in the house, march her around the room and drill her like a soldier. The maidservant was fond of him and she let him play at being a general even when he was twenty years old. He often became anxious and was over-awed by the tasks he had to accomplish, yet he never actually achieved anything. He could always get money from his mother when he was in difficulty, though he was reproached and criticized for his conduct.

Suddenly he married, which increased all his difficulties. All that mattered to him, however, was the fact that he had married before his elder brother; he looked on this as a great triumph. This shows that his estimate of his own worth was really very low - he wanted to triumph in such ridiculous ways. He was not well prepared for marriage and he and his wife were always quarrelling. When his mother could no longer afford to help him as much as she had done before, he ordered pianos and sold them off without paying for them. This was what brought him to prison. In this case history we can observe the roots of his later career in early childhood. He grew up overshadowed by an elder brother, like a small tree overshadowed by a bigger one. He gained the impression that he was slighted and neglected in comparison with his good-natured elder brother.

Another example I will give is of a girl of twelve, very ambitious and spoilt by both her parents. She had a younger sister of whom she was very jealous and her rivalry showed itself both at home and at school. She was always on the alert for instances in which her younger sister was preferred, given more sweets or more money. One day she stole money from the pockets of her school friends, was found out and punished. Fortunately I was able to explain the whole situation to her and free her from her belief that she could not compete with her younger sister. At the same time, I explained the circumstances to her family and they managed to stop the rivalry and to avoid giving the impression that the younger sister was preferred. This happened twenty years ago. The girl is now a very honest woman, married, with a child of her own, and she has made no great mistakes in her life since that time.

The structure of the criminal personality

In Chapter 1 we looked at situations where the development of children is especially endangered, but I would like to recap briefly at this point. It is important to emphasize them since, if the findings of Individual Psychology are right, it is only by recognizing the effect of such situations on the outlook of criminals that we can really guide them towards co-operative behaviour. The three main types of children with special difficulties are: first, children with physical disabilities; secondly, pampered children; and thirdly, neglected children.

By studying the criminals with whom I have been in contact myself and the descriptions of crime I have read in books and newspapers, I have tried to ascertain the structure of the criminal personality, and I have always found that Individual Psychology is a key to deeper understanding. Let me give a few further illustrations.

1. The case of Conrad K, who murdered his father with the help of another man. The father had neglected the boy, treated him cruelly and mistreated the whole family. Once the boy struck back at him and his father brought him before the courts. The judge said: 'You have a wicked and quarrelsome father and I can see no solution.'

You notice how the judge himself provided the boy with an excuse. The family tried in vain to find a remedy for their troubles; they were in despair. Then the father took a woman of loose morals to live with him and drove his son out of the house. At this time the boy made the acquaintance of a casual labourer who had a passion for putting out hens' eyes. The labourer advised him to kill his father. The boy hesitated because of his mother, but the situation went from bad to worse. After long deliberations, the son came to his decision, and killed the father with the aid of the labourer.

Here we see how the son was not able to extend his social interest even to his father. He was still deeply attached to his mother and held her in high esteem. Before he could break down what remained of his social interest, he needed to have extenuating circumstances suggested to him. It was only when he gained support from the casual labourer, with his passion for cruelty, that he could work himself up to committing the crime.

2. Margaret Zwanziger, otherwise known as 'the famous poisoner'. She was an abandoned child and was small and deformed. This, Individual Psychologists would say, stimulated her to be vain and anxious to attract attention. She was also ingratiatingly polite.

After many adventures, which nearly brought her to despair, she tried three times to poison women in the hope of securing their husbands for herself. She felt deprived and could not think of any other way to 'get her own back'. She also feigned pregnancy and attempted suicide in order to obtain a hold over these men. In her autobiography she gives unconscious testimony to the view of Individual Psychology, but without understanding her own statement: 'Whenever I did anything wicked, I thought, "No one is ever sorry for me: why should I worry if I make others sorry?"'

In these words we can see how she works up to the crime, drives herself on and seeks extenuating circumstances. It is a remark I often hear when I suggest co-operation with and interest in others: 'But other people don't show any interest in me!'

My answer is always: 'Somebody has to start. If the others are not co-operative it is not your affair. My advice is that you should begin, without worrying if the others are co-operative or not.'

3. NL, eldest son, badly brought up, lame in one foot, who took

on the role of father to his younger brother. We can recognize this relationship, too, as a goal of superiority, probably a beneficial one at first. Perhaps, however, it was always a matter of personal pride and a desire to show off. Later, he drove his mother out of the house to beg, saying, 'Get out of here, you old hag.'

We should pity this boy: he is not interested even in his mother. If we had known him as a child we could have seen how he was developing towards a criminal career. For a long time he was out of work. He had no money. He contracted a venereal disease. One day, on his way home from a futile search for work, he killed his younger brother in order to gain control of his small income. Here we see the limits of his willingness to co-operate – he had no work, no money, a venereal disease. There are always limits beyond which the individual feels incapable of proceeding.

4. A child who was orphaned early in life was handed over to a foster mother who indulged him beyond belief. As a result he was a pampered child who developed badly in later years. He was very astute in business, constantly trying to impress everybody, always wanting to be the best. His foster mother encouraged him in his ambition and fell under his spell. He became a liar and a swindler, getting money wherever he could. His foster parents belonged to the minor nobility: he put on aristocratic airs, squandered all their money and drove them out of their own house.

Bad training and pampering have spoilt him for honest work. He sees it as his task in life to get the better of everyone by lying and cheating. His foster mother preferred him to her own children and to her husband. This treatment gave him the feeling that he had a right to everything, but his low estimation of his own self-worth is shown in the fact that he does not feel capable of succeeding by normal means.

Crime, insanity and cowardice

Before I go any further I wish to dismiss the idea that all criminals are insane. There are psychotics who commit crimes, but their crimes are of quite a different nature. We cannot hold them criminally responsible: their crimes are a result of a complete failure in our understanding of them and mistaken methods of treating them.

In the same way we must exclude those whose lack of intelligence makes them mere tools of the true criminals who plan the crime. They are often simple-minded individuals who are exploited by people who paint glowing pictures of prospective gains, who excite their greed or ambitions, only to go into hiding, leaving their gullible victims to carry out the crime and run the risk of punishment. The same thing holds, of course, when younger people are made use of by old and experienced criminals. It is the experienced criminal who plans the crime; children are deluded into carrying it out.

All criminals are also cowards. They are evading problems they do not feel strong enough to solve. We can see their cowardice in the way in which they face life as well as in the crimes they commit. They skulk in dark and isolated places; they take their victims by surprise and draw their weapons before they can defend themselves. Criminals think they are being courageous; but we should not be fooled into agreeing with them. Crime is a coward's imitation of heroism. They are striving for a fictitious goal of personal superiority and they like to believe that they are heroes, but this is again a mistaken view of life, a failure of common sense. We know that they are cowards, and if they realized we knew it, it would be a big shock to them. It swells their vanity and pride to think of themselves as outsmarting the police, and they often think, 'They'll never catch me.'

Unfortunately, a careful investigation of the career of all criminals would reveal, I believe, that they had indeed committed crimes without being found out, and this fact is regrettable. When they *are* found out they think, 'This time I wasn't quite clever enough, but next time I shall outwit them.' And if they do get away with it, they feel they have achieved their goal; they feel superior and they are admired and appreciated by their comrades. It is important to dismantle this common myth of the criminal's courage and cleverness, but where should we begin this process? We can do it in the family, in the school, and in detention centres, and later on I shall describe the best point of attack.

CRIMINAL TYPES

You will find that criminals are divided into two types. There are those who do know that there is fellowship in the world but have never experienced it. Such criminals have a hostile attitude to other people; they have felt excluded and unappreciated. The other type is the pampered child, and I have frequently noticed in the assertions of prisoners the complaint, 'The reason for my criminal career is that my mother indulged me too much.' We should really elaborate on this, but I mention it here just to emphasize that, in various ways, criminals have not been brought up and trained in the right degree of co-operation.

Parents may have wanted to make their children into good members of society, but they did not know how. If they had been dictatorial and severe, they would have had no chance of succeeding. If they had pampered their children and let them take centre stage, they would have taught them to consider themselves important through the mere fact of their existence, without making any effort to deserve the good opinion of others. Such children, therefore, lose the ability for sustained effort; they always want to have notice taken of them and are always expecting something. If they do not find an easy way to gain satisfaction, they blame something or someone else for it.

Some case histories

Now let us examine some cases and see whether we can illustrate these points, in spite of the fact that the descriptions were not written for this purpose. The first case I shall give is from *Five Hundred Criminal Careers* by Sheldon and Eleanor T. Glueck: the case of 'Hard-boiled John'. This boy explains the genesis of his criminal career:

'I never thought I would let myself go. Up to fifteen or sixteen I was more or less like other kids. I liked athletics and took part in sport. I read books from the library, kept sensible hours, and all that. Then my parents took me out of school and put me to work and took all my wages except fifty cents each week.'

Here he is making an accusation. If we questioned him about his relationship with his parents, and if we could gain an impartial view of his whole family situation, we could find out what he *really* experienced. At present we must regard his statement only as an affirmation that his parents were not co-operative.

'I worked about a year, then I began going with a girl who liked a good time.'

We often find this in the careers of criminals: they attach themselves to a girl who has extravagant tastes. Remember what we mentioned before – this is a problem and tests the degree of co-operation. He goes with a girl who wants a good time and he has only fifty cents a week. We could hardly call this a true solution to the problem of love; for one thing, there are other girls. He is not on the right track. In the same circumstances I would have said, 'If all she wants is a good time, she is not the girl for me.' These are different estimates of what is important in life.

'You can't give a girl a good time these days, even in this town, on fifty cents a week. The old man wouldn't give me any more. I was angry and it preyed on my mind: how could I make more money?'

Common sense would say, 'Perhaps you could look around and earn more'; but he wants things to be easy, and if he wishes to have a girlfriend it is for his own pleasure and nothing more.

'One day a man came along and I got acquainted with him.'

When a stranger comes along, it is another test for him. A boy with the right ability for co-operation could not be led astray, but this boy is on a path that makes it possible.

'He was a clever thief, an intelligent, capable fellow who knew the business, and would "divvy" with you and not do you down. We did a lot of jobs in this town and got away with it, and I've been at this game ever since.'

We hear that the parents own their own home. The father is a foreman in a factory and the family are only just able to make ends meet. This boy is one of three children, and up to the time of his misconduct no member of the family had been known to be delinquent. I would be curious to hear how a scientist who believed in heredity would explain this case. The boy admits to having had his first heterosexual experience at the age of fifteen. I am sure some people would say he is over-sexed. But this boy has no interest in other people and all he wants is pleasure. Anybody can be over-sexed. He is, in fact, searching for appreciation in this way – he wants to be a sexual hero.

At sixteen he was arrested with a companion for breaking and entering and larceny. Other points of interest follow and confirm what we have said. He wants to appear successful, to attract the attention of girls, to win them by spending money on them. He wears a wide-brimmed hat, red bandana neckerchief, and a belt with a revolver in it. He assumes the name of a Western outlaw. He is a vain boy: he wants to look like a hero and knows no other way to do it. He admits having committed all the crimes he was accused of, 'and a lot more'. He has no scruples about other people's property rights.

'I don't think life is worth living. For humanity in general, I've nothing but the utmost contempt.'

All these apparently conscious thoughts are really unconscious; he does not understand what they actually mean. He feels that life is a burden, but he does not understand why he is so discouraged.

'I have learned not to trust people. They say thieves won't cheat each other, but they will. I was with a fellow once, treated him fair; and he did the dirty on me.'

'If I had all the money I wanted, I would be just as honest as anybody. That is, if I had enough so that I could do what I wanted without working. I never liked work. I hate it and I never will work.'

We can translate this last point as follows: 'It is repression that is responsible for my criminal career. I am compelled to repress my desires and therefore I am a criminal.' It is a point that deserves a lot of consideration.

'I have never committed a crime just for the sake of it. Of course there is a certain "kick" in driving up to a place in a car, doing your job, and making your getaway.'

He believes he is a hero and does not see his behavior as cowardice.

'When I was caught once before I had fourteen thousand dollars' worth of jewellery, but I stupidly went to see my girl, and cashed in only enough to pay my expenses to go to her, and they caught me.'

These people pay their girls and so gain an easy victory. But they think of it as a real sexual triumph.

'They have schools here in the prison and I am going to get all the education I can get – not to reform myself, but to make myself more dangerous to society.'

This is the expression of a very bitter attitude towards humankind. But he does not want anything to do with humankind. He says:

'If I had a son I would wring his neck. Do you think I would ever be guilty of bringing a human being into the world?'

Now how are we going to reform such a person? There is no other way than to improve his capacity for co-operation and to show him where he has gone wrong in his estimate of life. We can only convince him when we retrace the misunderstandings of his earliest childhood. I do not know what happened in this case. The description of it does not deal with the points I believe to be important. Something happened in his childhood that made him such an enemy of humankind. If I had to guess, I would suggest that he was the eldest boy; made much of at first, as eldest children generally are. Later on, he felt dethroned because another child was born. If I am right, you will find that even small things like this can prevent the development of co-operation.

John remarks further that he was treated roughly at an approved school to which he was committed, and he subsequently left this school with a feeling of intense hatred towards society. I must say something on this point. From the psychological standpoint, all harsh treatment of criminals in prison is open to interpretation as a challenge, a trial of strength. In the same way, when criminals continually hear people saying, 'We must put an end to this crime wave', they take it as a challenge. They want to be heroes, and they are only too happy to have the gauntlet thrown down to them. They feel that society is daring them to continue; and they do so with all the more determination. If someone thinks they are fighting the whole world, what could give them a bigger 'kick' than to be issued with a challenge?

In the education of problem children, too, challenging them is one of the worst errors to make. 'We'll see who is stronger! We'll see who can hold out the longest!' These children, like criminals, are intoxicated with the idea of feeling strong; and they know that they can get away with it if they are clever enough. In prisons and detention centres the staff sometimes challenge the criminals, and this is a very harmful policy.

Now let us examine the case of a murderer who was hanged for his crime. He cruelly murdered two people and before he did it he wrote down his intentions. This will give me an opportunity of describing the kind of planning that goes on in the criminal's mind. No one can commit a crime without planning it, and the planning always contains a justification for the deed. In all the literature of such confessions I have never found an instance where the crime itself was described simply and clearly, and I have never found a case in which the criminal did not try to justify himself.

Here we see the importance of social feeling; even criminals must try to reconcile themselves with it. At the same time they must prepare themselves to kill their social feeling, to break through the wall of social interest before they can commit the crime. Similarly in Dostoevsky's *Crime and Punishment*, Raskolnikov lies in bed for two months, considering whether to commit a murder. He drives himself on with the question: 'Am I Napoleon, or am I a louse?' Criminals deceive themselves and spur themselves on with such imaginings. In reality, all criminals know that they are not leading a useful life and also know what a useful life means. They reject it, however, out of cowardice: and they are cowardly because they lack the ability to be useful: the problems of life demand co-operation and they have not been trained in co-operation. Later in life, criminals want to relieve themselves of their burden; they want, as we have shown, to justify themselves and plead extenuating circumstances: 'He was sick and a layabout', and so forth.

Here are the extracts from the murderer's diary:

'I was disowned by my people, the subject of disgust and contempt [he was born with a deformed nose], almost overwhelmed by my misery. There is nothing to keep me back. I feel I cannot bear it any longer. I might resign myself to my abandoned condition; but the stomach, the empty stomach cannot be gainsaid.'

He produces the extenuating circumstances.

'It was prophesied that I would die on the gallows; but the thought came to me, "What difference does it make whether I die of starvation or on the gallows?"'

In another case the mother of a child had prophesied: 'I am sure that one day you will strangle me.' When he was seventeen he strangled his aunt instead. A prophecy and a challenge act in the same way. The diary continues:

'I am not concerned with the consequences. I have to die in any case. I am nothing, no one will have anything to do with me. The girl I want shrinks from me.'

He wanted to attract this girl, but he had no smart clothes and no money. He looked on the girl as a piece of property – this was his solution to the problems of love and marriage.

'It is all the same. I will find either my salvation or my ruin.'

I will say here, though I wish I had more space for an explanation, that all these people like extremes or antitheses. They are like children. It must be everything or nothing, a choice between two extremes: 'starvation or gallows', 'salvation or ruin.'

'Everything is planned for Thursday. The victim has been chosen. I am awaiting my opportunity. When it comes, it will be something that not everybody can do.'

He is a hero to himself: 'It is dreadful, and not everybody could do it.' He took a knife and killed a man in a surprise attack. Not everybody could do it!

'As the shepherd drives his sheep, the pangs of hunger drive man to the most vicious crime. Maybe I shall not see another day, but I don't care. The worst possible thing is to be tormented by hunger. I am consumed by an incurable sickness. My final ordeal will come when they sit in judgement on me. A man must pay for his crimes, but that is a better death than by starvation. If I die of hunger, no one will take any notice of me. Now people will flock to my execution, and perhaps someone will be sorry for me. I shall have done what I set out to do. No man has ever suffered fear as I have tonight.'

So he is not the hero he believes himself to be! Under cross-examination he said: 'Although I did not stab him to the heart I have committed murder. I know I am destined for the hangman: but the man had such wonderful clothes and I knew I would never have clothes like them.' He no longer says that hunger is his motive; it is now the clothes that have become a fixed idea. 'I did not know what I was doing', he pleaded. You will always find this statement, in one form or another. Sometimes criminals drink themselves insensible before their crimes. All this just goes to prove how hard they must struggle to break through the wall of social interest. I believe that in every description of a criminal career I could show all the points I have brought out here.

THE IMPORTANCE OF CO-OPERATION

Now let us return to the theme I mentioned above: the fact that all criminals – and every other human being – strive to gain a victory, to reach a position of supremacy. However, there is a great deal of variety in these goals, and we find that the goal of criminals is always to be superior in a private and personal sense. What they are striving for contributes nothing to other people. They are not co-operative. Society needs from all its members – and we all need from each other – a contribution to the common good, and an ability to co-operate. The goal of a criminal does not include this usefulness to society, and this is the really significant aspect of every criminal career. We shall see later how this comes about. At this point I want to make clear that the main thing to look for if we want to understand criminals, is the degree and nature of their failure in co-operation.

Criminals differ in their ability to co-operate; some of them fail less seriously than others. Some, for example, confine themselves to petty crime and do not go beyond these limits. Others prefer major crimes. Some are leaders, other followers. In order to understand the variety in criminal careers we must examine the life style of the individual.

Personality, life style and the three tasks

We can find the main characteristics of the life style particular to individuals when they are only four or five. We can assume, therefore, that it is not an easy matter to change it. It is someone's unique personality; it can only be changed by recognizing the mistakes they made in building it up. We can begin to understand, therefore, that many criminals, despite being punished many times, often humiliated and despised and deprived of every good thing that our society can offer, still do not change their ways, but commit the same crime over and over again.

It is not financial hardship that forces them into crime. True, if times are difficult and people are hard-pressed, crimes increase. Statistics show that sometimes the number of crimes increases in line with a rise in the price of wheat. This is no guarantee, however, that it is the economic situation that causes the crime. It is more a sign that many people are limited in their behaviour. There are limits to their capacity for co-operation, and when these limits are reached they can no longer contribute, they lose the last remnant of co-operation and resort to crime. From other facts, too, we discover that there are plenty of people who in favourable situations are not criminals but who, if a problem arises for which they are not prepared, can also turn to crime. It is their life style, their method of facing problems, that is important.

After all the investigations of Individual Psychology, we can at last clarify a very simple point. Criminals are not interested in other people. They can only co-operate to a certain degree. When this is exhausted, they turn to crime. The final straw comes when a problem is too difficult for them. It is interesting to consider the universal problems of life, the problems that criminals cannot succeed in solving. It appears that, ultimately, we have no problems in our lives except social problems; and these problems can only be solved if we are interested in others.

As we noted briefly in Chapter 1, Individual Psychology has taught us to make three broad divisions in the problems of life. First let us take the problem of relationships with other people, the problem of fellowship. Criminals sometimes have friends, but only among their own kind. They can form gangs and they can even show loyalty to one another, but they have clearly narrowed their sphere of activity. They cannot make friends with society at large, with ordinary people. They behave like a group of strangers in a strange land and do not know how to feel at home with other people.

The second group of problems includes all those connected with work. Many criminals, when questioned about these problems, reply, 'You don't know the terrible working conditions around here.' They find work uncongenial, and are not inclined, as others are, to struggle with their difficulties. A useful occupation implies an interest in other people and a contribution to their welfare, but this is exactly what is lacking in the criminal personality. This lack of a spirit of co-operation appears early, and consequently most criminals are ill-prepared to meet the demands of work. The majority of criminals are untrained and unskilled workers. If you look back over their lives you will find that at school, and even before school, there was a block, a switching off of interest, an unwillingness to co-operate. Co-operation is something that must be taught, and these criminals were never trained in co-operation. If they fail to address the problems of work, therefore, we cannot hold them responsible. If we make such demands on them it is like imposing a geography test on a person who has never learned any geography. In such a situation we would receive either a wrong answer or no answer at all.

The third group of problems includes all those associated with love. A good and fruitful love relationship calls in equal measure for interest in the other person and for co-operation. It is revealing to observe that half the criminals who were sent to prisons or detention centres were suffering from venereal disease on admission. This would tend to indicate that they wanted an easy way out of the problems of love. They regard the partner in love merely as a piece of property and we often find them thinking that love can be bought. To such people, sex is a matter of conquest and acquisition; it is a means by which they seek to possess others, rather than a part of a lifelong relationship. 'What is the use of life,' many criminals say, 'if I can't have everything I want?'

This lack of co-operation in all the problems of life is a major defect. We need co-operation every moment of the day, and the degree of our ability to co-operate shows itself in the way we look and speak and listen. If I am right in my observations, criminals look and speak and listen in a different way from other people. They have a different language, and the development of their intelligence is likely to be handicapped by this difference. When we speak we intend everybody to understand us. Understanding is itself a social function; we give words a common interpretation, and we understand them in the same way that anyone else might understand them. With criminals it is different. They have a private logic, a private intelligence; we can observe this in the way they explain their crimes. They are not stupid or mentally handicapped. For the most part they draw quite sensible conclusions, if we grant them their goal of a fictitious personal superiority.

A criminal may say, 'I saw a man who had nice trousers, and I hadn't any, so I had to kill him.' Now if we go along with such criminals in believing that their desires are all-important, and that there is no need for them to make a living in a useful way, their conclusion is sensible enough; but it is not *common* sense. There was a court case in Hungary where a number of women were accused of multiple murders by poison. When one of them was sent to prison she said, 'My boy was sick and a layabout, and I had to poison him.' If she excludes co-operation, what is left for her to do? She is intelligent, but she has a different way of looking at things, a different view of life. We can understand, then, how criminals who see attractive things and want to get hold of them easily will conclude that they must take them from a hostile world, a world in which they have no interest. They are suffering from a misguided outlook on life, a misguided estimate of their own importance and of the importance of other people.

EARLY INFLUENCES ON CO-OPERATION
Here I would like to explore the circumstances in which a failure
in co-operation may occur.

Family environment
Sometimes we must lay the responsibility on the parents. Perhaps
they were not skilful enough to get the children to co-operate
with them. Perhaps they behaved as if they were so infallible that
no one could help them, or they were incapable of co-operation
themselves. It is easy to see that in unhappy or broken marriages
the co-operative spirit is not being properly developed. The first
bond of children is with their mother, and perhaps the mother did
not wish to widen the children's social interest to include the
father and other children or grown-ups.

Or, again, the children may have felt they were the centre of
the family; when they were three or four years old, another child
came along and the first ones felt that they had suffered a setback.
They had been ousted from their position; they refused to co-
operate with their mother or with the younger child. These are all
factors to be considered, and, if you trace back the life story of
criminals, you will almost always find that the trouble began in
their early family experiences. It was not the environment itself
that counted. The children misunderstood their circumstances in
the family and there was no one there by their side to explain
things to them.

It is always difficult for the other children if one child in the
family is especially prominent or gifted. Such a child attracts the
most attention and the others feel discouraged and thwarted.
They do not co-operate: they wish to compete but do not have
enough confidence to do so. We often come across unfortunate
developments in children who have been outshone in this way,
and have not been shown how they could use their own capabilities. Among these people we may find criminals, neurotics or
suicides.

When children who are lacking in co-operation go to school,
this shortcoming can be seen in their behaviour on the very first
day. They cannot make friends with the other children. They do

not like the teacher, they are inattentive and do not listen to the lessons. Moreover, if they are not treated with sensitivity and understanding, they may suffer a new setback. They are often reproached and scolded, instead of being encouraged and taught co-operation. No wonder they find the lessons more distasteful than ever! They cannot be interested in school life if they are always suffering new blows to their courage and self-confidence. You will often find in the career of criminals that around the age of thirteen they were in a slow class and were criticized for stupidity. Their whole later life is thus endangered. They progressively lose interest in others and their striving tends to be directed more and more to the useless side of life, to antisocial or undesirable things.

Poverty

Poverty also offers opportunities for a mistaken interpretation of life. Children who come from a poor home may meet social prejudice outside the home. Their family suffers many deprivations, they have many trials and sorrows. The children may have to go out to work at a very young age to help their parents. Later they come across rich people who lead an easy life and can buy everything they want, and these children feel that these people have no more right to enjoy easy circumstances than they have. It is not hard to understand why the number of criminals is so high in big cities, where there are very noticeable extremes of poverty and luxury. No useful activity ever came from envy, but children in these circumstances can easily misunderstand the situation and think that the way to achieve superiority is to get money without working for it.

Physical disadvantages

The feeling of inferiority can also be centred round a physical handicap. This was one of my own discoveries; and I feel a little guilty, on this point, for having paved the way for theories of heredity in both neurology and psychiatry. But even in the beginning, when I first wrote of organ inferiorities (physical disadvantages) and an individual's mental compensations, I recognized this danger. It is not the handicap that is to blame, but our methods of education. If we followed the right methods, children with physical disadvantages would be interested in others as well as themselves. Children burdened with a physical handicap is self-centred only if nobody is at their side to develop their interest in others.

There are many people suffering from endocrine deficiencies, but I should like to make clear that we can never say, conclusively, what the normal functioning of an endocrine gland should be. The functioning of our endocrine glands can vary enormously without damage to the personality. This factor must therefore be excluded, especially if we want to find the right method of making these children into good members of the community, with a co-operative interest in other people.

Social disadvantages

Among criminals there is a large proportion who were orphaned, and it seems to me a grave indictment of our culture that we did not instil the spirit of co-operation into these orphans. In a similar way there are many who were illegitimate children. No one was around to win their affection and transfer it to their fellow human beings. Unwanted children often take to crime, especially if they know and feel that nobody wanted them. Among criminals, also, we often find unattractive people, and this fact has been used as evidence of the importance of heredity. But think how it feels to be an unattractive child! They are at a great disadvantage. Perhaps they are the children of a particular mixture of ethnic groups that happens to produce unattractive children, or meets with social prejudice. If such children are unattractive, it blights their whole life: they do not possess the thing we all value so much – the charm and freshness of childhood. But all these children, if they were treated in the right way, would develop social feeling.

It is interesting to observe, however, that we sometimes find among criminals unusually good-looking people. While physically unattractive criminals may be regarded as victims of bad hereditary traits, perhaps inherited along with actual physical deficits – deformed hands, for example, or a cleft palate – how might we explain the existence of handsome criminals? In reality, they too have grown up in a situation where it was difficult to develop social interest; they were pampered children.

SOLUTIONS TO THE CRIMINAL PROBLEM

What can we do now? That is the problem. What can we do if I am right, if we can always find in the criminal career the striving for a fictitious superiority by an individual who is lacking in social interest and has not been trained in co-operation? The answer, in the case of criminals, as of neurotic people, is absolutely nothing, unless we can succeed in gaining their co-operation. I cannot stress this point too strongly: success is assured if we interest criminals in human welfare, if we interest them in other human beings, if we can train them for co-operation, if we can set them on the way towards solving the problems of life by co-operative means. If we fail to do this, we can do nothing.

We can see now where we should begin in our treatment of criminals. We must train them to be co-operative. Very little is achieved by just locking them in prison, but letting them loose is a danger to society and under present conditions it cannot even be considered. Society must be safeguarded from criminals – but that is by no means all. We must also think: 'They are not prepared for social life; what can we do to help them?'

The task is not quite as straightforward as it sounds. We cannot win them over by making things easy for them, anymore than by making them hard for them. We cannot win them over by pointing out that they are wrong or by arguing with them. Their mind is made up. They have been looking at the world in this way for years. If we are to change them we must find the root cause of their way of thinking. We must discover where their failures began and the circumstances that provoked them. The main features of their personality had already been decided by the time they were four or five years old: by that time they had already made those mistakes in their estimation of themselves and of the world that we see displayed in their criminal career; and it is these early mistakes that we must understand and correct. We must look for the first development of their attitude to life.

Later on, they turn everything they experience into a justification for this attitude; and if their experiences do not quite fit into their scheme they brood on them and mould them until they are more amenable to it. If someone's attitude to life is, 'Other people humiliate me, and treat me badly', they will find plenty of evidence to confirm them in this view. They will be looking for events to prove them right, and ignore all evidence to the contrary. Criminals are interested only in themselves and their own point of view. They have their own way of looking and listening and frequently pay no attention to things that do not agree with their own interpretation of life. We cannot convince them, therefore, unless we can dig down behind all their interpretations, all their training in their own point of view, and discover the way in which this attitude first began.

The ineffectiveness of corporal punishment

Corporal punishment is ineffective because it only confirms to criminals that society is hostile and impossible to co-operate with. Something of this sort happened to criminals, perhaps, at school. They were not trained to co-operate and so they did their work badly, or misbehaved in class. They were reproached and punished. Now, is that going to encourage them in co-operation? They only feel that the situation is more hopeless than before. They feel that people are against them. Of course they hate school. Would any one of us be fond of a place where we expected to be reproached and punished?

The children lose whatever shreds of confidence they had. They are not interested in their schoolwork, their teachers or their school friends. They begin to play truant and to hide where they cannot be found. In these places they find other children who have had the same experience and have taken the same road. They understand; they do not reproach. On the contrary, they flatter them, play on their ambitions, and give them the hope of making their mark in an antisocial way. Of course, since they are not interested in the social demands of life, they see them as their friends and society in general as their enemy. These people like them and they feel better in their company. It is in this way that thousands of children join criminal gangs, and if in later life we treat them in the same way, this will only bear out their view that we are their enemies and only criminals are their friends.

There is no reason at all why such children should be defeated by the tasks of life. We should never allow them to lose hope and we could prevent this very easily if we organized our schools so that such children were given confidence and courage. We shall deal more fully with this proposal later: we are using this example at present to show how criminals will interpret punishment only as a sign that society is against them, *just as they always thought*.

Corporal punishment is ineffective for other reasons too. Many criminals do not value their lives very highly. Some of them are very near suicide at certain moments of their lives. Corporal or even capital punishment hold no terrors for them. They can be so obsessed with their desire to outdo the police that they do not even feel any pain. This is part of their whole response to what they regard as a challenge. If staff are harsh to criminals, or if they are severely treated, they are put on their mettle to resist. This further increases their feeling of being cleverer than the police.

As we have seen, they interpret everything in this fashion. They see their contact with society as a form of continuous warfare in which they are struggling for supremacy, and if we ourselves treat it in the same way we are only playing into their hands. Even the electric chair can act as a challenge in this sense. Criminals conceive of themselves as battling against fearful odds. The higher the penalty, the greater their desire to show their superior cunning. It is easy to see that many criminals think of their crimes purely in these terms. Criminals who are condemned to death in the electric chair will often spend their last hours considering how they might have avoided detection: 'If only I hadn't left my spectacles behind!'

Training in co-operation

We have pointed out already that there is no reason why any children should suffer from discouragement, this deep conviction that they are inferior and that it is useless to co-operate. No one need be defeated by the problems of life. Criminals have chosen the wrong way of dealing with them; we must show them where they have made the wrong choice and why, and we must develop in them the courage to be interested in others and to co-operate. If this were fully recognized everywhere, the greatest self-justification would be taken away from criminals and no children would choose to train themselves for crime in the future. In all criminal cases, whether they are correctly described or not, we can see the influence of a mistaken childhood life style, a philosophy showing a lack of the ability to co-operate.

I would like to emphasize that this ability to co-operate must be learned. There is no question of its being hereditary. There is a potential for co-operation, and this potential must be regarded as inborn, but it is common to every human being, and to be developed it must be trained and exercised. All other points of view about crime seem to me irrelevant, unless we can produce evidence of people who were trained in co-operation but still became criminals. I have never met such a person, and I have never heard of anybody else who *has* met one. The proper protection against crime would be the proper degree of co-operation. So long as this is not recognized, we cannot hope to avoid the tragedy of crime.

The value of co-operation can be taught in the same way that geography can be taught, for it is a truth and we can always teach the truth. If children, or adults, are tested in geography and they are not prepared, then they fail. If children, or adults, are tested in situations that require a knowledge of co-operation and they are not prepared, then they too fail. All our problems require a knowledge of co-operation.

We have come to the end of our scientific investigation of the problem of crime, and now we must be courageous enough to face the truth. After thousands and thousands of years, humankind has still not found the right method of coping with this problem. All the measures that have been tried seem to have been useless and this disaster is still with us. Our investigation has told us why: the right steps have never been taken to change the criminal life style and to prevent the development of mistaken attitudes to life. Short of this, no measures can be really effective. We know, therefore, exactly what we must do: we must train criminals in co-operation.

We have the knowledge, and by now we have the experience too. I am convinced that Individual Psychology shows us how we could reform every single criminal. But consider what a task it would be to take every single criminal and treat them in such a way as to transform their life style. Unfortunately, in our culture, the majority of people would exhaust their ability to co-operate if their difficulties went beyond a certain point, and we find that in hard times the number of criminals always increases. Therefore, I believe that if we were to be sure of abolishing crime in this way we would have to treat a very large percentage of the human race, and it would not be practicable to have an immediate aim of making every criminal or potential criminal a useful member of society.

Some practical measures

There is plenty that we *can* do, however. If we cannot reform every criminal, we can do something to lighten the burdens of those people who are not strong enough to bear them. With regard to unemployment, for example, and the lack of occupational training and skill, we ought to make it possible for everyone who wants to work to secure a job. This would be the only way to realize the demands of life in our society so that a great part of humankind would not lose the last remnants of their ability to co-operate. There is no question at all that if this were done the number of criminals would go down. Whether the time is ripe for this improvement in our economic conditions I do not know, but we should certainly work for this change.

We should also train children better for their future careers, so that they can face life better prepared and with a wider choice of jobs. Such training can also be given in our prisons. To some extent steps have already been taken in this direction and perhaps all we need to do here is to increase our efforts. While I do not believe it would be possible to give every criminal individual treatment, we could do a great deal of good by treating them en masse. I would propose, for instance, that we should hold discussion groups on social problems with a number of criminals, exactly as we have considered them here, and let them answer. We should enlighten them and awaken them from their lifelong dream; we should free them from the poisonous influence of their private interpretation of the world and their low opinion of their own potential. We should teach them not to limit themselves. We should calm their fear of the situations and social problems they must face. I am very sure that we could achieve great results from such treatment.

We should also avoid in our society everything that can act as a temptation to criminals or to poor and destitute people. If great extremes of poverty and luxury are apparent, it offends those who are badly off and incites them to envy. We should, therefore, cut down on ostentation: it is not necessary to flaunt one's wealth.

We have learned in the treatment of handicapped and delinquent children that it is entirely useless to challenge them to a trial of strength. It is because they think they are at war with their environment that they persist in a negative attitude. The same thing applies to criminals. Throughout the world we can see how police officers, judges and even the laws we make challenge criminals and put them on their mettle. Criminals should never be threatened, and it would be much better if we were more discreet and did not mention the names of criminals or give them so much publicity. Our attitude to crime is a mistaken one. We should not believe that either severity or mildness can change criminals. They can be changed only if they understand their own situation better. Of course we should be humane, and we should not imagine that criminals can be terrified by the prospect of capital punishment. As we have seen, there are times when capital punishment only adds to the excitement of the game, and even when criminals are to be executed they will think only of the fatal mistake they made that led to their capture.

It would be very helpful if we increased our efforts to improve our crime-solving record. As far as I can see, at least forty per cent of criminals, and perhaps far more, escape detection, and this fact is always at the back of every criminal's mind. Almost all criminals have experienced occasions when they committed crimes and were not found out. We have already made progress on some of these points and we are moving in the right direction. It is also important that criminals should not be humiliated or challenged either in the prison itself or after they leave prison. An increase in the number of probation officers would be useful, if the right type of person is appointed; and probation officers themselves should be taught about the problems of society and the importance of co-operation.

A *preventive approach*

We could accomplish a great deal if these suggestions were implemented. However, we would still not be able to reduce the number of crimes as much as we might wish. Fortunately we have another means at our disposal, and it is a very practical and very successful method. If we could train our children to the right degree of co-operation, and if we could develop their social interest, the number of criminals would drop very considerably and the effects would be seen in the near future. These children could not then be incited or lured into crime. Whatever troubles or difficulties they encountered, their interest in others would not be wholly destroyed: their ability to co-operate and to cope satisfactorily with the problems of life would be far more fully developed than in our own generation.

The majority of criminals begin their careers very early. It is generally in adolescence that they start, and crimes are most frequent between the ages of fifteen and twenty-eight. Our success, therefore, would be seen very soon. Moreover, I am sure that if children were taught in the right way they would influence their whole home life. Independent, forward-looking, optimistic and well-developed children are a help and a comfort to their parents. The spirit of co-operation would spread all over the world, and the social development of humankind would be raised to a much higher level. At the same time as we influence the children we should also concentrate on influencing parents and teachers.

The only question that remains is how we can choose the best point of attack, and what method we adopt to teach children to cope with the tasks and problems of later life. Perhaps we could train all the parents? But no; this proposal does not hold out much hope. Parents are hard to reach, and the parents who need training the most are the very people whom we never see; so we must look for another way. Perhaps we could catch all the children, lock them up, put them under surveillance and keep a careful guard over them the whole time? This proposal does not seem much better.

There is, however, a way that is practicable and promises a real solution. We can make the teachers the instruments of our social progress. We can train our teachers to correct mistakes made in the family, to develop and extend children's social interest towards others. This is an entirely natural development in the role of the school. Because the family is not able to educate children for all the tasks of later life, humankind has already established schools as the extended arm of the family. Why not use the school to make humankind more sociable, more co-operative and more interested in human welfare?

You will see that our activities must be based upon the following ideas. I will put them very briefly. All the advantages we enjoy in our present culture have been made possible by the efforts of people who have *contributed*. If individuals have not been co-operative, have not been interested in others, have made no contribution to the whole, their life has been futile, they have disappeared from the face of the earth leaving no trace behind them. Only the work of those people who have contributed survives. Their spirit lives on and their spirit is eternal. If we make this the basis for teaching our children, they will grow up with a natural liking for co-operative work. When they are confronted with difficulties they will not weaken; they will be strong enough to face even the most difficult problems and solve them in a way that benefits everyone.

10

The Problem of Work

BALANCING THE THREE TASKS OF LIFE

The three ties binding human beings pose the three problems of life, but none of these problems can be solved independently. Each of them demands a successful approach to the other two. The first tie poses the problem of work. We live on the surface of this planet, with all this planet's resources, the fertility of its soil, its mineral wealth and its climate and atmosphere. It has always been the task of humankind to find the right answers to the problems these conditions present to us, and even today we cannot assume that we have found a satisfactory answer. In every era, humankind has succeeded in solving those problems to a certain extent. But there has always been scope for further improvements and accomplishments.

The best means of solving the first problem, that of work, comes from the solution to the second problem, that of society. The second tie binding us is the fact of belonging to the human race and the necessity of living in association with others. Our attitude and behaviour would be altogether different if we were the only one of our kind alive on earth. However, we always have to consider other people, to adapt ourselves to them and to interest ourselves in them. This problem is best solved by friendship, social feeling and co-operation. With the solution of this second problem we can take a huge stride towards the solution of the first.

It was only because people learned to co-operate that we were able to make the great discovery of the division of labour, a discovery that is the chief safeguard of the welfare of humankind. To preserve human life would not be possible if all individuals attempted to wrest a living from the earth by themselves without co-operation and with none of the results and benefits of past co-operation. Through the division of labour we can use the results of many different kinds of training and organize many different abilities so that all of them contribute to the common welfare and guarantee relief from insecurity as well as increased opportunity for all the members of society. It is true that we cannot yet claim to have achieved everything that could be done; but then we cannot yet claim that the division of labour is fully developed. Nevertheless, every attempt to solve the problem of work must take place within this framework of the division of human labour and the shared effort to contribute through our work to the common good.

Some people try to evade this problem of work, attempting to avoid work altogether or to busy themselves outside the usual field of human interests. We shall always find, however, that if they dodge this problem, they will in fact be demanding support from their fellows. In one way or another they will be living on the labour of others without making a contribution of their own. This is the life style of pampered children: whenever a problem faces them they demand that it should be solved for them by the efforts of others; and it is chiefly pampered children who hinder the co-operation of humankind and throw unfair burdens on those who are actively engaged in solving the problems of life.

Our third tie is that we can only be either male or female. Our part in the continuance of humankind depends on our approach to the other sex and the fulfilment of our sexual role. This relationship between the two sexes also presents a problem and, like the other problems in life, it cannot be solved in isolation. For a successful solution to the problem of love and marriage, an occupation contributing to the common good is necessary, as well as good and friendly contact with other human beings. As we have already seen, in our own day the most desirable solution to this problem, the solution that best fulfils the requirements of society and the division of labour, is monogamy. The degree of co-operation of individuals is revealed with particular clarity in the way in which they address this problem.

These three problems never occur separately; they all cast shadows across one another and the solution of one helps towards the solution of the others. Indeed we can say that they are all aspects of the same situation and the same problem – the necessity for human beings to preserve life, and to further life, in the environment in which they find themselves.

A person's career can sometimes be used as an excuse for evading the problems of society and love. Very often in our social life an exaggerated involvement in work can be chosen as a way to avoid the problem of love and marriage. Sometimes we find it used as an excuse for marital failure. One partner devotes himself furiously to his business and thinks, 'I have no time to spare for my marriage, and so I am not responsible for our unhappiness.' It is especially common for neurotic people to try to dodge these two problems of society and love. They make no approach to the other sex, and take no interest in other people, but they are occupied day and night with their business. They think of it and dream of it in bed. They work themselves into a state of tension, and in their tension, neurotic symptoms appear, such as stomach irritation or some such trouble. They then feel that their stomach trouble excuses them from facing the problems of society and love. In other cases individuals are always changing job. They can always think of a job that would suit them better, but the truth is that they cannot stick at one particular job but must always chop and change.

EARLY TRAINING

Home and school influences

A mother is the first influence in the development of her children's occupational interests. The efforts and training of the first four or five years of life have a decisive influence on the child's main sphere of activity in adult life. If ever I am called on for vocational guidance, I always ask about the early life of individuals and what they were interested in during their first years. Their memories of this period reveal conclusively what they have trained themselves for most consistently: they reveal their ideals and how they fit into their mental universe. I will return later on to the importance of first memories.

The next step in our training is taken by the schools, and I believe that our schools are now giving more attention to the ir pupils' future careers, to training their hands, ears and eyes, their faculties and functions. Such training is as important as the teaching of academic subjects. We should not forget, however, that the teaching of academic subjects is also important for the child's career development. In later life we often hear people say that they have forgotten the Latin or French they learned at school; nevertheless, it was still right to teach these subjects. In studying all these subjects, we have found, through the accumulated experience of the past, an excellent way of training all the functions of the mind. Some modern schools also pay great attention to craftsmanship and handiwork, and in this way we can broaden the experience of children and boost their self-confidence.

Correcting potential mistakes

There are some people who could choose any career and still never be satisfied. What they want is not a career but an easy guarantee of superiority. They do not wish to face up to the problems of life, since they feel it is unfair of life to present them with any problems at all. These are the pampered children who are happy to be supported by others.

Other children never wish to be placed in a leading position. Their chief interest is to find a leader to look up to, another child or adult to whom they can subordinate themselves. This is not a very favourable development and it would be better if such submissive tendencies could be discouraged. If we cannot stop them in childhood, such children will be unable to take a leading role in later life and will choose positions where they have the tasks of a minor official, where all their work is routine and where everything they have to do is controlled by regulations.

The mistaken tendency to avoid work, to be absent-minded or lazy, also begins early in life. When we see such children heading for difficulties, we must find out the reasons for their mistake in a scientific way and try to correct them by scientific means. If we lived on a planet that offered us everything we needed without having to work, it would perhaps be a virtue to be lazy and a vice to be industrious. But as far as we can understand from our relations with our own planet, earth, the logical answer and the one that accords with common sense, is that we should work, co-operate and contribute. Human beings have always felt this intuitively; we can now see its necessity from the scientific angle.

Geniuses and early striving

Early childhood training has always been evident in geniuses, and I believe that the question of genius can throw light on the whole subject. Only those individual geniuses who have contributed greatly to the common good are called geniuses. We cannot imagine geniuses who have left no benefit to humankind behind them. The arts are the product of the most co-operative of all individuals, and the great geniuses of mankind have raised the whole level of our culture. Homer in his poems makes mention of only three colours, and these three had to serve for all shades and nuances. Who has taught us to appreciate all the colour relationships we now surround ourselves with? We must admit that it is the work of artists and painters.

Composers have refined our hearing to an extraordinary degree. If we now sing in harmonious tones instead of in the harsh ones of our ancestors, it is the musicians who have taught us; it is they who have enriched our minds and taught us to train our ears and voices. Who deepened our feelings and taught us to express them more clearly and to understand them more fully? It was the poets. They enriched our language, made it more flexible and adapted it to all the purposes of life.

There can be no question but that geniuses have been the most co-operative of all human beings. In some aspects of their individual behaviour and attitudes we could perhaps lose sight of their co-operative ability, but we can see it clearly in the whole picture of their lives. It was not so easy for them to co-operate as it was for others because they chose a difficult path and had numerous obstacles to contend with. Often they started with severe physical disadvantages. In almost all outstanding people we find some physical imperfection, but one gets the impression that although they were sorely tried at the beginning of life, they struggled and overcame their difficulties. Most clearly of all, we see how early in life their interests began and how hard they trained themselves in their childhood. They sharpened their senses so that they could make contact with the problems of the world and understand them. From this early training we can conclude that their art and their genius were their own creation, not an undeserved gift of nature or inheritance. They strove and we are blessed in consequence.

Nurturing talents

This early striving is the best foundation for later success. Suppose we have a girl of three or four who has been left alone. She begins to sew a hat for her doll. When we see her at work we tell her what a nice hat it is and suggest how it could be made even better. The little girl is encouraged and stimulated. She redoubles her efforts and improves her skill. But suppose we had said to the girl, 'Put that needle down! You will hurt yourself. There's no need for you to make a hat at all. We'll go out and buy you a far nicer one.' She would give up her efforts. If we compared two such girls in later life we would find that the first had developed her artistic taste and was interested in working; the second would not know what to do with herself and would think that she could always buy better things than she could make.

IDENTIFYING CHILDREN'S INTERESTS

Childhood declarations

Children's development is much simpler if they know from childhood which career they would like to take up in later life. If we ask children what they would like to be, most of them will give an answer. Their answers are not usually clearly considered, however, and when they say that they want to be aeroplane pilots or engine drivers they do not know why they are choosing these occupations. It is our task to recognize the underlying motives, to see the direction their efforts are tending towards, to find out what is pushing them forward, what kind of goal they have and how they feel they can bring it about. The answer they give to our question about a future career shows us only one kind of occupation that seems to them to represent superiority; but from this occupation we can also identify other opportunities for helping them to reach their goal.

Children of twelve or fourteen should have a much clearer idea of the career they would like, and I am always sorry to hear that children of this age do not know what they wish to be in later life. Their apparent lack of ambition does not mean that they have no interest in anything. They are probably extremely ambitious, but not courageous enough to make their ambitions known. In such cases we must take pains to find out their chief interest and training. Some children, when they finish high school at the age of sixteen, are still unsettled about their future career. Often they are brilliant pupils but have no idea of how their life will continue. We can recognize that these children are very ambitious but not really co-operative. They have not found their place in the division of labour and they cannot find a practical method of achieving their ambitions in time.

It is thus an advantage to ask children at early age what career they would like to have, and I often put this question to classes so that the children have to consider the point and cannot forget the problem or try to conceal their answer. I also ask them why they have selected their chosen career and their answers are often very revealing. Children's whole life style can be observed in their choice of career. They are showing us the main direction of all their efforts and what they value most in life. We must let them value what they choose, since we ourselves have no means of saying which career is higher and which is lower in the scheme of things. If they really get down to work and spend their time contributing to the well-being of others, they are every bit as useful and important as anyone else. Their only task is to train themselves to try to support themselves and to pursue their interests within the framework of the division of labour.

process early in life, since otherwise their interests might already have crystallized.

Here we might repeat that a woman's contribution to the life of humankind through motherhood can never be overestimated. If she is concerned about the lives of her children and is paving the way for them to become useful, contributory members of society, if she is broadening their interests and training them in co-operation, her work is so valuable that it can never be adequately rewarded. In our own culture the work of a mother is undervalued and often regarded as a rather unattractive or worthless occupation. It is paid only indirectly and a woman who makes it her main career is generally placed in a position of economic dependence. The success of the family, however, depends equally upon the work of the mother and the work of the father. Whether the mother keeps house or works outside the home, her work as a mother is just as important as her partner's.

SOME INFLUENCES ON CAREER CHOICE

Children who encounter the problem of sickness or death without preparation always retain a keen interest in these matters. They wish to be doctors, nurses or chemists. Their efforts, I believe, should be encouraged, since I have always found that children with such interests who became doctors began their training very early and had a great liking for their profession. Sometimes a brush with death can be compensated for in another way. Children will have the ambition to survive death through artistic or literary creativity, or they may become devoutly religious.

One of the most common strivings is the attempt to outdo other members of the family, and especially to outdo the father or mother. This can be very valuable; we are glad to see the new generation outdistance the old and, to a certain extent, if children wish to surpass the achievements of their father in their own occupation, their father's experience can provide them with an excellent start. Often children born into a family where the father was a policeman have the ambition to be lawyers or a judges. If the father is employed in a hospital, the children want to be doctors

It is possible that for a great majority of men and women, their interests still lie in the direction they were training themselves in their first four or five years and they cannot forget this, but they later felt compelled by economic considerations or parental pressure to take up a career that does not interest them. This is another indication of the impact and importance of childhood training.

Early memories

In vocational guidance, first memories should be considered very carefully. If in children's first memories we see an interest in visual things, we can conclude that they will be more suited to an occupation in which they can use their eyes. Children might mention impressions of someone talking to them, of the sound of the wind or of a bell ringing. We would recognize that they are an acoustic type and we can guess that they might be suited for some profession connected with music. In other recollections we can see impressions of movement. These are individuals who need more activity; perhaps they would be interested in occupations demanding manual labour or travel.

Play-acting

By watching children we can often see them preparing themselves for a career in adult life. Many children show great mechanical and technical interest, and this also promises a fruitful career in later life if they can achieve their ambitions. Children's games can give us an insight into their interests. Sometimes, for example, children wish to be a teachers, and we can see how they gather younger children together and play at schools with them.

A girl who looks forward to being a mother will play with dolls and train herself to take a greater interest in babies. This interest in the role of a mother should be encouraged and we need not be afraid of giving little girls dolls to play with. Some people feel that if we give them dolls we are distracting them from reality, but in fact they are training themselves to identify with and fulfil tasks of a mother. It is important that they should begin or surgeons. If the father is a teacher, the children want to be university lecturers.

If the value of money is overstressed in family life, the children will be tempted to look at the problem of work only in the light of the money they can make. This is a great mistake, for such children do not follow an interest that enables them to contribute to humankind. True, everyone should earn their living; and it is also true that there are people who neglect this point and make themselves a burden to others. But if children are only interested in making money they can easily leave the path of co-operation and only look for their own advantage. If 'to make money' is their only goal and no social interest is involved, why should they not make money by robbing and swindling other people? Even if the position is less extreme, but there is still only a small degree of social interest combined with the goal, individuals may make plenty of money but their activities will not be of much benefit to their fellow human beings. In our complicated times, it is possible to become rich and successful by following this path. Even a mistaken path may sometimes seem to be successful in some respects. We cannot promise that individuals who go through life with the right attitude will obtain immediate success, but we can promise that they will keep their courage and will not lose their self-esteem.

LOOKING AT SOLUTIONS

Our first approach with problem children is to find out their main interest. Through this it is easier to help and encourage the whole child. In cases of young people who have not been able to settle on a career, or older people who have had professional problems, their real interests should be discovered and sympathetically used as the basis for vocational guidance, combined with an effort to find them employment. This is not always easy. Today high unemployment is a matter of great concern. This is not a good situation at a time when people are trying to improve co-operation. I believe, therefore, that everybody who has recognized the importance of co-operation should do their best to make sure that there are no unemployed people, and that there is work available to everybody who wants it.

We may improve the situation by furthering the development of training schools, technical schools and adult education. Many unemployed people are untrained and unskilled. Some of them, perhaps, have had little interest in social life. It is a great burden for humankind to have untrained members of society and people who are not interested in the common good. These people feel worthless and disadvantaged, and it is understandable that untrained and unskilled people make up a large proportion of criminals, neurotics and suicides. Because of their lack of training, they lag behind the rest of humanity. All parents and teachers, and all who are interested in the future development and improvement of humankind, should work to ensure a better training for all children, and to prepare them for a special place in the division of labour.

11

THE INDIVIDUAL
AND SOCIETY

THE HUMAN STRIVING FOR UNITY

The oldest of human strivings is to be at one with our fellow human beings. It is through interest in our fellow human beings that the human race has grown and progressed. The family is an organization in which interest in other people is essential, and from the dawn of time there has been this tendency for human beings to group themselves in families. Primitive tribes used common symbols to hold them together and give them a sense of shared identity, and the purpose of the symbol was to unite people in co-operation.

The role of religion

The simplest primitive religion is the worship of a totem. One group would worship a lizard, another a bull or serpent. Those who worshipped the same totem lived together and co-operated, and each member of the group considered himself a brother of the other members. These primitive customs were one of humankind's greatest means of gaining and retaining co-operation. At the festivals connected with these primitive religions, everyone who worshipped the lizard, for example, would join their companions, and they would discuss the harvest, and how to defend themselves against wild animals and the elements. This was the meaning of the festival.

Marriage was regarded as an affair in which the interests of the whole group were involved. Every man had to seek his partner outside his own group or totem, in accordance with social restrictions. Even today it is important to recognize that love and marriage are not private affairs, but common tasks in which the whole of humankind should take part in mind and spirit. There is a certain responsibility involved in marrying, since it is a step commended by the whole of society, and the whole of society is concerned that healthy children should be born and that they should be brought up in a spirit of co-operation. All humankind should therefore be willing to offer support to every marriage. The systems of primitive societies, their totems and their elaborate conventions to control marriage, may seem ridiculous to us now, but their importance in their own time can hardly be overstated; and their real aim was to increase human co-operation.

The most important duty imposed by religion has always been, 'Love thy neighbour.' Here again, in another form, we have the same attempt to increase our interest in our fellow human beings. It is interesting, too, that we can now confirm the value of this effort from a scientific standpoint. Pampered children ask us, 'Why should I love my neighbour? Does my neighbour love me?' and so reveal their lack of training in co-operation and their exclusive interest in themselves. It is those individuals who are not interested in their fellow human beings who have the greatest difficulties in life and cause the greatest injury to others. It is from among such individuals that all human failures spring. There are many religious and political initiatives that try in their own way to increase co-operation; and I, for my own part, would agree with every human effort that recognizes co-operation as the final goal. There is no need to fight, criticize and undervalue each other. None of us is blessed with the possession of the absolute truth and there are many paths that lead towards the ultimate goal of co-operation.

Political and social movements

In politics we know that even the best methods may be abused, but nobody could accomplish anything through politics if they did not also bring about co-operation. Every politician must have as their final goal the betterment of humankind; and this always means a higher degree of co-operation. We are often ill-equipped to judge which politician or which political party can truly bring progress. Individuals judge in accordance with their own life style.

But if a political party has people co-operating happily within its own circle, we have no cause to resent its activity. So, too, with social movements. If it is the aim of those engaged in such movements to bring up children as really good members of society and to improve their social feeling, those movements may follow their own traditions, promote their own culture, and attempt to influence and change the laws as they think best: we should not disapprove of their efforts. Class movement, also, is group movement and co-operation, and if its goal is the betterment of humankind, we should not be prejudiced against it.

So all political and social movements should be judged only on the basis of their ability to further our interest in our fellow human beings, and we will find there are many ways to help in increasing co-operation. Perhaps some ways are better than others, but if the goal of co-operation is there, it is useless to attack any one method on the grounds that it may not be the best.

LACK OF SOCIAL INTEREST AND THE FAILURE TO RELATE

Self-interest

What we must take issue with is the attitude of people who are motivated only by self-interest. This attitude is the greatest conceivable obstacle to individual and collective progress. It is only through our interest in our fellow human beings that any of our human capabilities develop. To speak, to read and to write all presuppose a bond with other people. Language itself is common to all humankind; it is a product of social interest. Understanding is a matter of sharing, not a private function. To understand means to comprehend in a way that we expect everybody else to share. It is to connect ourselves through a shared medium with other people, to submit to the common experience of all humanity.

There are some people who predominantly pursue their own interests and seek personal superiority. They give a private meaning to life; in their view, life should exist solely for their benefit. This is not a shared understanding, however; it is an

opinion that no one else in the whole world is likely to share.
We find, therefore, that such people are unable to relate to
their fellow human beings. Often, when we see children who
have been brought up to be self-centred, we find that they have
a hangdog or vacant look on their face, and we can see
something of the same look in the faces of criminals or of the
mentally ill. They do not use their eyes to relate to others. They
do not perceive the world in the same way as other people.
Sometimes such children and adults will not even look at their
fellow human beings; they turn their eyes away and look
elsewhere.

Mental disorders

The same failure to relate to others is shown in many neurotic
symptoms; it is particularly noticeable, for example, in compulsive
blushing, in stammering, in impotence or premature ejaculation.
These all reveal an inability to bond with other human beings,
and arise from a lack of interest in them.

The highest degree of isolation is represented by mental
illness. Even mental illness is not incurable if the sufferer's interest
in other people can be aroused, but it denotes a greater remoteness
from the rest of society than any other symptom except, perhaps,
suicide. It takes great skill to cure such cases. We must win the
patient back to co-operation, and we can only do this through
patience and the kindest and friendliest treatment. Once I was
called in to do what I could for a girl with schizophrenia. She had
suffered from this condition for eight years and for the last two
had been in a mental hospital. She barked like a dog, spat, tore
her clothes and tried to eat her handkerchief, which revealed just
how far she had turned away from interest in other human beings.
She wanted to play the role of a dog, and this can be understood:
she felt that her mother had treated her like a dog, and perhaps
she was saying, 'The more I see of human beings, the more I would
like to be a dog.' I spoke to her on eight successive days and she
did not say a word in reply. I continued to speak to her, and after
thirty days she began to talk in a confused and unintelligible way.
I was a friend to her and she felt encouraged.

If patients of this type are encouraged they do not know what to do with their courage. Their resistance to their fellow human beings is very strong. We can predict, to some degree, the behaviour they will exhibit when they courage comes back, but they still do not wish to be co-operative. They are like problem children. They will do their best to be a nuisance: they will break anything they can lay hands on, or they will hit the nurse. When I next spoke to this girl, she hit me. I had to consider what to do. The only reaction that would surprise her was to put up no resistance. This young girl did not have great physical strength. I let her hit me and looked at her in a friendly way. She had not expected this; it deprived her of every challenge.

She still did not know what to do with her reawakened courage. She broke my window and cut her hand on the glass. I did not reproach her, but simply bandaged her hand. The usual way of reacting to such violence, to confine her and lock her in her room, was the wrong way of treating her. We must act differently if we wish to win over someone like this girl. It is the greatest mistake to expect a mentally disturbed person to act like a normal person. Almost everyone becomes annoyed and irritated with them because mentally ill people do not respond like ordinary human beings. They do not eat, they tear their clothes, and so on. Let them do it. There is no other way to help them.

After this, the girl recovered. A year passed and she continued to be perfectly healthy. One day, on my way to visit the mental hospital in which she had been confined, I met her in the street.

'What are you doing?' she asked me.

'Come with me,' I answered. 'I am going to the hospital where you lived for two years.' We went to the hospital together and I asked for the doctor who had treated her there. I suggested that he should talk to her while I saw another patient. When I came back, the doctor was very put out.

'She is perfectly healthy,' he said, 'but there is one thing about her that displeases me. She does not like me.'

I still see this girl from time to time and she has remained in good health for ten years. She earns her own living, gets on well with other people, and no one who saw her would believe that she had ever suffered from mental illness.

Two conditions that reveal with particular clarity the estrangement of the sufferer from other human beings are paranoia and melancholia. In paranoia patients accuse all humanity; they think that everyone else is involved in a conspiracy against them. In melancholia, patients accuse themselves: they say, for example, 'I have ruined my whole family', or 'I have lost all my money and my children will starve'. Even if individuals accuse themselves however, this is only the outside face they show; they are really accusing others.

For example, a woman of considerable prominence and influence had an accident and could no longer continue with her social life. She had three daughters who had married and left home, and she felt very lonely; at about the same time she lost her husband. She had been pampered before and she tried to replace what she had lost. She began to travel abroad. However, she no longer felt as important as she had been, and while she was abroad she began to suffer from melancholia. Her new friends deserted her.

Melancholia is a disorder that is a great trial for anyone involved with the sufferer. She cabled for her daughters to come, but each of them had an excuse and none of them came to see her. When she returned home, her most frequent words were, 'My daughters have been so very kind.' Her daughters had left her alone, they had let a nurse take care of her, and now that she had come home they visited her only occasionally. Those words were an accusation, and everyone who knew the circumstances would recognize them as such. Melancholia is like a long-continued rage and reproach against others, with the aim of gaining care, sympathy and support, although the patients only seem to be dejected about their own guilt. A melancholic's first memory is generally something like this: 'I remember I wanted to lie on the couch, but my brother was lying there. I cried so much that he had to leave.'

Melancholics are often inclined to avenge themselves on others by committing suicide, and the doctor's first concern is to avoid giving them an excuse for suicide. I myself try to relieve their tension by suggesting to them, as the first rule in treatment, 'Never do anything you don't like'. This seems a small thing, but I believe that it gets to the root of the problem. If melancholics ae free to do anything they want, whom can they accuse? What have they got to take revenge for? 'If you want to go to the theatre', I tell her, 'or to go on a holiday, do it. If you find on the way that you don't want to, don't bother.'

It is the best situation anyone could be in. It satisfies their need for superiority. They are like God and can do what they please. On the other hand, it does not fit very easily into their life style. They want to dominate and accuse others and if the others agree with them there is no way of dominating them. This approach is usually highly effective and I have never had a suicide among my patients. It is understood, of course, that it is best to have someone to watch such patients, and some of my patients have not been watched as closely as I would have liked. So long as there is an observer, there is no danger.

Often, the patient replies to my proposition, 'But there is nothing I like doing'.

I am well prepared for this answer, because I have heard it so many times. 'Then refrain from doing anything you dislike', I say.

Sometimes, however, they will reply, 'I should like to stay in bed all day.'

I know that if I allow it, they will no longer want to do it. I also know that if I hinder them, they will start a war. I always agree with them. That is one strategy. Another attacks the life style even more directly. I tell them, 'You can be cured in fourteen days if you follow this prescription. Try to think every day how you can please someone.' Imagine what this means to them. They are usually occupied with the thought, 'How can I worry someone?'

The answers are very interesting. Some say, 'This will be very easy for me. I have done it all my life.'

They have never done it, of course. I ask them to think it over. They do not think it over. I tell them, 'You can make use of all the time you spend when you are unable to go to sleep by thinking how you can please someone, and your health will improve dramatically.' When I see them the next day, I ask them, 'Did you think over what I suggested?'

They answer, 'Last night I went to sleep as soon as I got into bed.' All this must be done, of course, in a modest, friendly manner, without a hint of superiority.

Others will answer, 'I could never do it. I am so worried.'

I tell them, 'Don't stop worrying; but at the same time you can think, now and then, of others.' I want to redirect their interest towards other people.

Many say, 'Why should I please others? Others don't try to please me.'

You must think of your health', I answer. 'The others will suffer later on.' Only rarely do patients reply, 'I have thought over what you suggested.' All my efforts are devoted towards increasing the social interest of the patients. I know that the real reason for their malady is their lack of co-operation and I want them to see it too. As soon as they can relate to their fellow human beings on an equal and co-operative footing, they are cured.

Criminal negligence

Another clear example of a lack of social interest is so-called 'criminal negligence.' Someone lets a lighted match fall and starts a forest fire. Or a worker leaves a cable stretched across a road when he goes home for the day; a car runs into it and the occupants are killed. In neither case did the individuals mean any harm. They do not seem to be guilty in a moral sense for the actual disaster. But they have not been trained to think of other people; they do not spontaneously take precautions to secure their safety. It is a higher degree of the same lack of co-operation that we see in untidy children and in people who stand on other people's toes, break dishes and plates, or knock ornaments off the mantelpiece.

SOCIAL INTEREST AND SOCIAL EQUALITY

Interest in our fellow human beings is taught in the home and at school, and we have already seen what obstacles may be put in the way of children's development. Social feeling is not, perhaps, an inherited instinct, but the potential for it is inherited. This potential is developed in accordance with the parents' skill and their interest in the children, and in accordance with the children's own judgement of their environment. If they feel that other people are hostile, if they feel that they are surrounded by enemies and have their back to the wall, we cannot expect them to make friends and to be a good friend to others. If they feel that others should be their slaves, they will wish, not to help others, but to rule them. If they are interested in their own sensations and in their physical irritations and discomforts, they will shut themselves off from society.

We have seen how it is best for children to feel that they are an equally valued member of their family and to take an interest in all the other members. We have seen that the parents should themselves be on friendly terms with each other and should have good and close friendships with others outside the family. In this way their children come to feel that trustworthy human beings exist outside the family circle as well as within it. We have also seen how, at school, children should feel a part of the class, a friend to the other children and able to rely on their friendship. Life in the family and life at school are preparations for life in the wider world. The aim of both family and school is to educate children to be a social human being, an equal member of the human race. Only in these conditions will they preserve their courage and meet the problems of life confidently, finding solutions to them that promote the well-being of others.

If they can be a good friend to everyone and contribute to society through useful work and a happy marriage, they will never feel inferior to other people or defeated by them. They will feel that they are at home in the world, in a friendly place, meeting people they like and equal to the task of coping with their difficulties. They will feel, 'This world is my world. I must act and organize, not wait and expect.' They will be completely sure that the present time is only one stage in the history of humankind, and that they belong to the whole human process – past, present and future; but they will also feel that this is the time in which they can fulfil their creative tasks and make their own contribution to human development. It is true that there are evils and difficulties, prejudices and disasters in this world; but it is our own world and its advantages and disadvantages are our own. It is our world, to work in and improve; and we can hope that if anyone faces up to their tasks in the right way they can play their part in improving it.

To face one's tasks means to assume responsibility for solving the three problems of human life in a co-operative way. All that we demand of human beings, and the highest praise that we can give them, is that they should be good work colleagues, good companions and true partners in love and marriage. In short, we may say that they should prove themselves to be human beings.

12

LOVE AND MARRIAGE

THE IMPORTANCE OF LOVE, CO-OPERATION AND SOCIAL INTEREST

In a certain district of Germany there is an old custom that tests whether an engaged couple are suited for married life together. Before the wedding ceremony, the bride and bridegroom are brought to a clearing where a tree has been cut down. Here they are given a two-handed saw and set to work to saw the trunk in two. This test reveals how far they are willing to co-operate with each other. It is a task for two people. If there is no trust between them, they will tug against each other and accomplish nothing. If one of them wishes to take the lead and do everything by himself, then, even if the other gives way, the task will take twice as long. They must both use their initiative, and their efforts must be co-ordinated together. These German villagers have recognized that co-operation is the chief prerequisite for marriage.

If I were asked to say what love and marriage mean, I would give the following definition, incomplete as it may be: *Love, and its fulfilment in marriage, is the most intimate devotion to a partner of the other sex, expressed in physical attraction, in companionship, and in the decision to have children. Love and marriage are essential to human co-operation – not just a co-operation for the welfare of two persons, but co-operation for the welfare of humanity as well.*

This standpoint, that love and marriage constitute a co-operation for the welfare of humankind, throws light on every aspect of the subject. Even physical attraction, the most important of all human impulses, has been a very necessary development for humankind. As I have explained so often, humankind with all its weaknesses, has been none too well equipped for life on earth. The only way to preserve human life was to propagate it; hence our fertility and the continual stimulus of physical attraction.

Today, we find difficulties and dissensions arising over all the problems of love. Married couples are confronted with these difficulties, parents are concerned with them, the whole of society is involved in them. If we are trying, therefore, to come to the right conclusion, our approach must be objective and unprejudiced. We must forget what we have learned and try, as far as we can, to investigate the subject without letting other considerations interfere with a full and free discussion.

I do not mean that we can judge the problem of love and marriage as if it were an entirely isolated problem. Human beings can never be wholly free in this way: they can never reach solutions to their problems purely on the basis of their private ideas. Indeed, all human beings are bound by definite ties; their development takes place within a certain framework and their decisions must conform with it. These three main ties, as we have seen, stem from the fact that we are living in one particular place in the universe and must develop within the limits and possibilities of our environment and circumstances; that we are living among others of our own kind to whom we must learn to adapt ourselves; and that there are two sexes, with the future of our race dependent on the good relations between them.

It is clear that if individuals are interested in their fellow human beings and in the welfare of humankind, everything they do will be guided by the interests of other people, and they will try to solve the problem of love and marriage as if the welfare of others were involved. They do not need to *know* that they are trying to solve it in this way. If you ask them, they will perhaps be unable to give an objective account of their aims. But they will spontaneously seek the welfare and betterment of humankind and this interest will be visible in all their activities.

There are other human beings who are not so concerned with the welfare of humankind. Instead of taking as their underlying view of life 'What can I contribute to my fellow human beings?', and 'How can I be a part of the whole?', they are more inclined to ask, 'What's in it for me? Are other people paying me enough attention? Am I properly appreciated?' If this attitude is behind an approach to life, the individuals will try to solve the problem of love and marriage in the same way. They will always ask: 'What can I get out of it?'

Love is not the purely natural function that some psychologists believe it to be. Sex is a drive or instinct, but the question of love and marriage is more than just how to satisfy this drive. Wherever we look, we find that our drives and instincts are developed, cultivated and refined. We have repressed some of our desires and inclinations. For the benefit of our fellow beings, we have learned how to avoid offending each other, for example. We have learned how to be clean and presentable. Even our hunger does not have a purely natural outlet; we have cultivated tastes and manners connected with eating. Our drives have all been adapted to our common culture; they all reflect the efforts we have learned to make for the welfare of humankind and for our life in society.

If we apply this understanding to the problem of love and marriage we will see, once again, that the interest of the whole, the interest in humanity, must always be involved. This interest is a primary one. There is no advantage in discussing any of the aspects of love and marriage, in proposing concessions, changes, new regulations or institutions, until we appreciate that the problem can only be solved by taking a broad view, by considering human welfare as a whole. Perhaps we will improve; perhaps we will find more satisfactory answers to the problem; but if we do find better answers they will be better because they take fuller account of the fact that humankind consists of two sexes living on this planet, and that co-operation is necessary for survival. In so far as our answers already take account of these conditions, the truth contained in them can stand for ever.

An equal partnership

When we use this approach, our first discovery about the love problem is that it is a task for two individuals. For many people this is bound to be a new task. Some of our early training has taught us to work alone, some to work in a team or a crowd. We tend to have had comparatively little experience of working in pairs. These new conditions, therefore, present a problem; but that problem is easier to solve if these two people are already interested in their fellow human beings, for then they can learn more easily to be interested in each other.

We could even say that for a full realization of this co-operation between two partners, each partner must be more interested in the other than in him- or herself. This is the only basis on which love and marriage can be successful. The misguidedness of many opinions on marriage, and many proposals for its reform, will at once be apparent. If each partner is to be more interested in the other partner than in him- or herself, there must be equality. If such intimacy and mutual devotion is to be achieved, neither partner must feel subdued or overshadowed. However, equality is only possible if both partners have this attitude. Each should be making every effort to ease and enrich the life of the other. In this way each partner is safe, each feels that they are worthwhile, each feels needed. Here we find the fundamental guarantee of marriage, the fundamental meaning of happiness in this relationship. It is the feeling that you are worthwhile, that you cannot be replaced, that your partner needs you, that you are behaving well, that you are a good companion and a true friend.

It is not possible for a partner in a co-operative task to accept a position of subservience. Two people cannot live together fruitfully if one wishes to rule and force the other to obey. In our present conditions many men and, indeed, many women are convinced that it is the man's part to rule and dictate, to play the leading role, to be the master. This is the reason why we have so many unhappy marriages. Nobody can endure a position of inferiority without anger and resentment. Partners must be equal, and when people are equal, they will always find a way to settle their difficulties. They will agree, for example, on the question of having children. They know that a decision to remain childless reflects an unwillingness to help secure the future of humankind. They will agree on questions of education; and they will be stimulated to solve their problems as they occur, because they know that the children of unhappy marriages are disadvantaged and cannot develop well.

PREPARATION FOR MARRIAGE

In our present society people are rarely well-prepared for co-operation. Our training has focused too much on individual success, and on considering what we can get out of life rather than what we can put into it. It is easy to understand that when we get two people living together in the intimacy that marriage demands, any failure in co-operation, in the ability to be concerned about somebody else, will have the gravest results. Most people are experiencing this close relationship for the first time. They are unaccustomed to considering another human being's interests and aims, desires, hopes and ambitions. They are not prepared for the problems of a *shared* task. This explains the many mistakes we see around us, but it is now time to examine the facts and learn how to avoid mistakes in the future.

Life style, parents and attitudes to marriage

Every crisis of adult life is met in accordance with our previous training: our response always conforms with our life style. Our preparation for marriage does not take place overnight. We can see in children's characteristic behaviour, in their attitudes, thoughts and actions, how they are training themselves for adult situations. In its main features their approach to love is already established by their fifth or sixth year.

Quite early in children's development we can see that they are already forming their outlook on love and marriage. We should not imagine that they are feeling sexual promptings in our adult sense of the term. They are making up their mind about one aspect of social life in general of which they feel a part. Love and marriage are features of their environment: they enter into their conception of their own future. They must have some comprehension of them, and take a stance on these problems.

When children give such early evidence of their interest in the other sex and choose partners for themselves, we should never interpret it as a mistake, or a nuisance, or a precocious sexual urge. Still less should we deride it or make a joke of it. We should take it as a step forward in their preparation for love and marriage. Instead of belittling it, we should rather agree with the children that love represents a marvellous challenge, a challenge for which they should be prepared, a challenge they should undertake on behalf of the whole of humankind. Thus we can implant an ideal in children's minds, and later in life they will be well-prepared to respond to each other as companions and friends in an intimate relationship. It is revealing to observe that children are spontaneously and wholeheartedly in favour of monogamy despite the fact that the marriages of their parents are not always harmonious and happy.

We are always better prepared if our parents' marriage has been harmonious. Children gain their earliest impressions of what marriage is like from the life of their parents, and it is not surprising that most failures in life are children from broken homes and an unhappy family life. If the parents are not able to co-operate themselves, it will be impossible for them to teach co-operation to their children. It often happens that we can best consider the fitness of individuals for marriage by learning whether they were brought up in the right family atmosphere, and by observing their attitude towards their parents, sisters and brothers.

The most important factor is where they gained their preparation for love and marriage. We must be careful on this point, however. We have already learned that individuals are not determined by their environment but by their interpretation of that environment. Their interpretation can be useful. It is possible that they had very unhappy experiences of family life in their parents' home, but this may simply stimulate them to do better in their own family life and they may be striving to prepare themselves well for marriage. We must never judge or exclude human beings because they have an unfortunate family life behind him.

The importance of friendship and work
One of the ways in which social interest can be developed is through friendship. We learn in friendship to look with the eyes of

others, to listen with their ears and to feel with their heart. If children are frustrated, if they are always watched and protected, if they grow up isolated, without friends and companions, they do not develop this ability to identify with others. They always consider themselves the most important people in the world and are always anxious to ensure their own welfare.

Training in friendship is a preparation for marriage. Games might be useful if they entailed training in co-operation, but in children's games we find only too often competition and the desire to excel. It is very useful to establish situations in which two children work together, study together and learn together. I believe that we should not undervalue dancing. Dancing is a pastime in which two people take part in a shared activity, and I think it is good for children to be trained in dancing. I do not mean the dancing we have today, which is more of a performance than of a shared activity. If, however, we had simple and easy dances for children, it would greatly help their development.

Another problem that also helps to prepare people for marriage is the problem of work. Today this problem is usually encountered before the problem of love and marriage. One partner, or both, must have a job so that they can earn their living and support a family. It is clear that preparation for marriage also includes preparation for work.

Sex education

I would never encourage parents to explain the physical aspects of sex too early in life or to explain more than their children wish to learn. It is clear that the way children view the problems of marriage is very important. If this subject is handled badly, they will see these problems as a danger or as something altogether beyond them. In my own experience, children who were introduced to the facts of adult relationships in early life, at four, five or six years of age, and children who had precocious experiences, are always more scared of love in later life. Physical attraction also suggests to them the idea of danger. If children are more grown-up when they have their first explanations and experiences, they are not nearly so frightened: and there is far less opportunity for them to make mistakes in their relationships.

The key is never to lie to children, never to evade their questions, to understand what is behind their questions, to explain only as much as they wish to learn and only as much as we are sure they can understand. Officious and intrusive information can do a great deal of damage. In this problem of life, as in all others, it is better for children to be independent and learn what they want to know by asking. If there is trust between them and their parents they can come to no harm.

There is a common superstition that children can be misled by the explanations of their peers. Children whose training in co-operation and independence has been good will never be harmed by playground whisperings, and I have never seen otherwise healthy children suffer harm in this way. Children do not swallow everything their school friends tell them. For the most part they are very critical and, if they are not sure whether what they have been told is true, they will ask their parents or their brothers and sisters. I must also confess that I have often found children more delicate and tactful in these affairs than their elders.

Influences on partner choice

Even the beginnings of the physical attraction of adult sexuality is learned in childhood. The impressions children gain with regard to sympathy and attraction, the impressions given by the members of the other sex in their immediate surroundings – these are the beginnings of physical attraction. When a boy gains these impressions from his mother, his sisters or the girls around him, his selection of physically attractive people in later life will be influenced by their similarity to those who were part of his early environment. Sometimes he is also influenced by works of art: everybody is drawn in this way by an ideal of personal beauty. Thus in later life individuals no longer have a free choice in the broadest sense, but a choice that is influenced by their upbringing.

This search for beauty is not a meaningless search. Our aesthetic emotions are always based on a desire for health and for the betterment of humankind. All our functions, all our abilities, draw us in this direction. We cannot escape it. We regard as beautiful those things that look towards eternity, that contribute to the benefit and the future of humankind, that symbolize the way in which we wish our children to develop. This is the beauty that never ceases to attract us.

Sometimes if a boy experiences difficulties with his mother, and a girl with her father (as often happens if the co-operation in a marriage is not satisfactory), they look in later life for a contrasting type of person. If, for example, the boy's mother has nagged and bullied him, if he is weak and afraid of being dominated, he may find sexually attractive only those women who do not appear domineering. It is easy for him to make mistakes: he can look for a partner who also seems to be strong, either because he prefers strength or because he finds in her more of a challenge to prove his own strength. If the rift between himself and his mother is very wide, his preparation for love and marriage may be hindered and even physical attraction to the other sex may be obstructed. There are many degrees of this obstruction; where it is complete he will exclude the other sex entirely.

COMMITMENT AND RESPONSIBILITY IN MARRIAGE

The worst preparation is that of individuals who have learned always to seek to further their own interests. If they have been brought up in this way, they will spend all their time wondering what pleasure or excitement they can get out of life. They will always be demanding freedom and concessions, never considering how they can ease and enrich the life of a partner. This is a disastrous approach. I would compare such people to those who try to put a horse's collar on from the tail end. It is a mistaken way of going about things.

In preparing our attitude to love, therefore, we should not be constantly looking for excuses and ways of avoiding responsibility. The companionship of love cannot flourish in the presence of hesitation and doubt. Co-operation demands a life time's commitment; a marriage is not a marriage unless a firm and unalterable commitment has been made. In this commitment we include the decision to have children, the decision to educate them and train them in co-operation and to make them, as far as we can, genuinely useful members of society, truly equal and responsible members of the human race. A good marriage is the best means we have for bringing up a future generation, and marriage should always have this aim. Marriage is really a job of work; it has its own rules and laws. We cannot choose to focus on one aspect and ignore the others without infringing the eternal law of co-operation.

It is impossible to achieve true intimacy and devotion in love if we limit our responsibility to five years or regard the marriage as a trial run. If men or women keep open the option of such an escape, they do not put their all into the task. We never arrange such a 'get-out clause' in any of the other serious and important tasks of life. We cannot limit our love. All those well-meaning and good-natured people who are trying to find an alternative for marriage are on the wrong path. The alternatives they propose would hamper the efforts of couples who were entering marriage; they would make it easier for them to opt out and to shirk the effort they should make in the task they have set themselves.

I know that there are many difficulties in our society and that they hinder people from solving the problem of love and marriage in the right way, even though they would like to solve it. It is not love and marriage, however, that I feel should be scrapped; I want to do away with the difficulties of our society. We know what characteristics are necessary for a loving partnership – to be faithful and honest and trustworthy, not to be reserved, not to be self-seeking . . .

Common evasions

It is obvious that if people believe that unfaithfulness is all in a day's work, they are not properly prepared for marriage. It is not even possible to achieve true companionship if both partners have agreed to preserve their 'freedom'. This is not partnership. In a partnership we are not free to move in any direction we choose. We have committed ourselves to co-operation. Let me give an example of how such a private agreement, poorly adapted to marital success and the welfare of humankind, can harm both the partners. A divorced man and a divorced woman married. They were cultivated and intelligent people and each sincerely hoped that their new venture in marriage would be better than their previous ones. They did not know, however, why their first marriages had failed; they were looking for an improved relationship without realizing that they lacked social interest. They professed themselves to be free-thinkers and wanted a modern marriage in which they would never run the risk of being bored by each other. They proposed, therefore, that both of them should be perfectly free in every respect; they would do whatever they wanted, but they would trust each other enough to tell each other everything that happened.

On this point the husband seemed more adventurous than the wife. Whenever he came home he had many lively experiences to tell her and she seemed to enjoy them enormously and to be very proud of her husband's successes. She was always meaning to begin a flirtation or an affair herself, but before she had taken the first step she began to suffer from agoraphobia. She could no longer go out alone; her neurosis kept her to her room. If she took a step outside the door she was so scared that she was compelled to return. This agoraphobia was a protection against the decision she had made, but there was more to it than this. At last, since she was unable to go out alone, her husband was compelled to stay by her side. You see how the logic of marriage broke through their decision. The husband could no longer be a free-thinker because he had to stay with his wife. She herself could not make any use of her freedom because she was afraid to go out alone. If this woman were to be cured, she would be forced to reach a better understanding of marriage, and the husband would have to regard it as a co-operative partnership too.

Other mistakes are made at the very beginning of a marriage. Children who have been indulged at home often feel neglected in marriage. They have not been trained to adapt to the demands of social life. Pampered children may develop into great tyrants in marriage; the other partner feels victimized and trapped, and begins to resist. It is interesting to observe what happens when two pampered children marry each other. Both demand interest and attention and neither can be satisfied. The next step is to look for an escape; one partner begins a flirtation with someone else in the hope of gaining more attention.

Some people are incapable of falling in love with only one person; they must fall in love with two at the same time. They thus feel free: they can escape from one to the other, and never shoulder the full responsibilities of love. Both, in effect, means neither.

There are other people who invent a romantic, ideal or unattainable love; they can thus luxuriate in their feelings without the necessity of approaching a partner in reality. A romantic ideal can effectively exclude all candidates, since no real-life lover can possibly live up to it.

Many men and women, through mistakes in their development, have trained themselves to dislike and reject their sexual role. They have suppressed their natural functions and are physically incapable, without treatment, of achieving a successful marriage. As mentioned, this is what I have termed the 'masculine protest', and it is provoked by the overvaluation of men in our present culture. If children are left in doubt about their sexual role, they are apt to feel insecure. So long as the masculine role is taken to be the dominant one, it is natural that children should feel, whether they are boys or girls, that the masculine role is enviable. They will doubt their own ability to fulfil this role, will overstress the importance of manliness, and will try to avoid being put to the test.

In our culture we frequently come across people who are ill at ease with their sexual role. This may be the root cause of all cases of frigidity in women and psychosomatic impotence in men. In these cases there is a resistance to love and marriage revealed through a physical resistance. It is impossible to avoid these diffi-culties unless we truly believe that men and women are equal; and as long as half the human race has reason to be dissatisfied with its status, this dissatisfaction will be a huge obstacle to the success of marriage. The remedy here is training for equality and, at the same time, we should never permit children to remain in doubt about their own future role.

I believe that the intimate devotion of love and marriage is most readily attained if there have been no premarital sexual relations. I have found that secretly most men do not really like it if their sweetheart is no longer a virgin when she marries. Sometimes they regard it as a sign of easy virtue and are shocked by it. Moreover, in our culture, if there are sexual relations before marriage the emotional strain is greater for the woman. It is also a great mistake if a marriage is contracted out of fear and not out of courage. We can understand that courage is one side of co-operation, and if men and women choose their partners out of fear it is a sign that they do not want real co-operation. This also holds good when they choose partners who drink heavily or are vastly inferior in social status or education. They are afraid of love and marriage and wish to establish a situation in which their partner will look up to them.

COURTSHIP

The degree of courage and the degree of individuals' ability to co-operate is revealed in their approach to the other sex. All individuals have their characteristic approach, their characteristic demeanour and temperament in courtship, and this is always consistent with their life style. The way they behave when in love reveals whether they say 'Yes' to the future of humanity, are confident and co-operative, or whether they are interested only in themselves, suffer from stage fright, and torture themselves with the question, 'What kind of impression am I making? What do they think of me?' A man may be slow and cautious in his approach to a woman, or rash and precipitate; in every case, his courtship behaviour is shaped by his goals and his life style and is yet another expression of it. We cannot judge a man's fitness for marriage entirely by his courtship behaviour, for here he already has a direct goal before him while in other respects he may be indecisive. Nevertheless it gives some sound clues to his personality.

In our own culture (and only in these conditions) it is generally expected that the man should be the first to express interest, that he should make the first approach. So long as this convention exists, therefore, it is necessary to train boys in the masculine attitude – to take the initiative, not to hesitate or look for a way out. They can only be trained, however, if they feel themselves to be a part of society as a whole, and accept its advantages and disadvantages as their own. Of course, girls and women are also engaged in courtship; they also take the initiative, but in our prevailing cultural climate in the West they feel obliged to be more reserved, and their approach is expressed in their appearance, in the way they dress, the way they move, the way they look, speak and listen. A man's approach, therefore may be called simpler and shallower, a woman's deeper and more complex.

MAKING MARRIAGE WORK

The physical side of marriage

Sexual attraction towards the other partner is necessary, but it should always be directed along the lines of a desire for human welfare. If the partners are really interested in each other, they will never suffer from waning sexual attraction. This problem always implies a lack of interest; it tells us that individuals no longer feel on equal, friendly and co-operative terms with their partner, and no longer wish to enrich the life of their partner. People may think, sometimes, that the interest continues but the physical attraction has ceased. This is never true. Sometimes the mouth lies, or the mind does not understand; but the functions of the body always speak the truth. If the functions are deficient, it follows that there is no true agreement between these two people. They have lost interest in each other. One of them, at least, no longer wishes to face the task of love and marriage but is looking for a way out.

In one other way the sex drive in human beings is different from the sex drive among other creatures. It is continuous. This is another way in which the welfare and preservation of humanity is guaranteed; it is a way by which humanity can increase, multiply and thus secure its welfare and survival. In other creatures, nature has used other means to ensure this survival: in many, for example, we find that the females produce a vast number of eggs that never come to maturity. Many of them are lost or destroyed but their great numbers ensure that some will survive.

With people, also, one method of ensuring survival is to have children. We find, therefore, that in this problem of love and marriage those people who are most spontaneously interested in the welfare of humankind are the most likely to have children, and those who are not interested, consciously or unconsciously, in their fellow human beings, refuse the burden of procreation. If they are always demanding and expecting, never giving, they will not like children. They are interested only in themselves and they regard children as a burden and a nuisance; something that will occupy time and attention that they would prefer to spend on themselves. We can say, therefore, that for a full solution of the problem of love and marriage a decision to have children is necessary. A good marriage is the best means we know for bringing up the future generation of humankind, and this should always be a part of marriage.

Monogamy, hard work and realism

The solution to the problem of love and marriage in our practical and social life is monogamy. Anyone who starts a relationship that demands such intimate devotion and such concern for another person cannot shake the fundamental basis of this relationship and search for an escape. We know that there is the possibility that the marriage will break down. Unfortunately we cannot always avoid it, but it is easier to avoid if we regard marriage and love as a social function that confronts us, a task we are expected to perform. We will then try every means to solve the problem.

Break-ups generally happen because the partners are not working together as hard as they might; they are not working to make their marriage a success, but are merely waiting for success to be handed to them on a plate. If they face the problem in this way, of course they will fail. It is a mistake to regard love and marriage as an ideal state, or as the happy ending of a story. It is when two people are married that the possibilities of their relationship begin; it is during marriage that they are faced with the real tasks of life and the real opportunity to create for the sake of society.

The other point of view, the point of view of marriage as an end, as a final goal, is far too prominent in our culture. We can see it, for example, in thousands of novels, which end with a newly married couple, who are really only at the beginning of their life together. Yet the situation is often treated as if marriage itself had solved everything satisfactorily: as if the couple had won through to the end and would now live happily ever after. Another important point to realize is that love by itself does not settle everything. There are all kinds of love, and it is better to rely upon work, interest and co-operation to solve the problems of marriage.

There is nothing at all miraculous in the marital relationship. As we have seen, the attitude of all individuals towards marriage is an expression of their life style; thus we cannot understand it unless we understand the whole individual. It is consistent with all their efforts and aims. We can discover, for example, why so many people are always looking for a way out. I can tell exactly which people have this escapist attitude: all the people who are still pampered children. This type of person can be a danger to society – these grown-up spoilt children whose life style was fixed in the first four or five years of life:

'Can I get all I want?' they ask in every situation. If they cannot have everything they want, they think life is purposeless. 'What is the use of living', they ask, 'if I cannot have what I want?' They become pessimistic: they conceive a 'death wish'. They make themselves sick and neurotic, and out of their mistaken life style they construct a whole social philosophy. They feel that their mistaken ideas are of unique and tremendous importance; they feel that it is pure spite on the part of the universe if they have to repress their drives and emotions. That is the way they were brought up. Once, long ago, they lived in a golden age when they were given everything they wanted. Some of them, perhaps, still feel that if they cry long enough, if they protest enough, if they refuse to co-operate, they will once more get what they want. They do not see life and society as a whole, but only focus on their own personal interests.

The result is that they do not want to contribute, they always want to have everything handed to them on a plate. Marriage too is, for them, something to have on 'sale or return'. They want companionate marriages, trial marriages, easier divorces: at the very beginning of marriage they demand freedom and a right to be unfaithful if the feeling takes them. Now if one human being is really concerned for another, they must show all the characteristics of that concern: they must be reliable and faithful, responsible and a true friend. Unless a person's marriage and love life meet these requirements, they have failed in this, the third great problem of life.

It is also necessary to be concerned about the welfare of children, and if a marriage is based upon different outlooks from the one I have described, there will be great difficulties in bringing up children. If the parents quarrel and undervalue their marriage, if they do not view it positively, as an ongoing concern whose problems can be solved, it is not a very favourable situation for helping the children to be sociable.

Solving marital problems

There may be reasons why people should not live together; there are probably cases in which it would be better for them to live apart. Who should decide? Are we going to put it in the hands of people who themselves do not understand that marriage is a task, who are only interested in their own lives? They would look at divorce in the same way as they look at marriage: 'What can be got out of it?'

These are obviously not the people to decide. You often find that people divorce and remarry again and again and always make the same mistake. Then who ought to decide? Perhaps we might imagine that if something is wrong with a marriage, a psychiatrist should decide whether or not it should be broken up. There is a problem there. I do not know whether it holds true in America, but in Europe I have found that most psychiatrists think that personal welfare is the most important thing. Generally, therefore, if they are consulted in such a case, they advise the patient to take a lover and think that this might be the way to solve the problem.

I am sure that in time they will change their minds and stop giving such advice. They can only propose such a solution if they have failed to understand the problem of love and marriage as a whole; the way it relates to the other problems of our life on earth; and it is this holistic perspective that I have been offering for your consideration.

A similar mistake is made when people look upon marriage as a solution for a personal problem. Here again I cannot speak of America, but I know that in Europe, if a boy or girl becomes neurotic, psychiatrists often advise them to take a lover and to begin sexual relations. They give similar advice to adults, too. This is really reducing love and marriage to a mere patent medicine, and those who take the 'medicine' are bound to lose by it. The proper solution of the problem of love and marriage belongs to the highest fulfilment of the whole personality. There is no problem more closely bound up with happiness and a useful and worthwhile role in life. We cannot treat it as a trifle. We cannot look on love and marriage as a remedy for a criminal career, for alcoholism or neurosis. Neurotic people need to have the right treatment before they are fit for love and marriage, and if they embark upon them before they are capable of approaching them correctly, they are bound to encounter new dangers and misfortunes. Marriage is too high an ideal, and the solution of the task demands too much effort and creative activity for us to load it with additional burdens of this kind.

Some people enter into marriage with other inappropriate aims. Some people marry for the sake of economic security; they marry because they are sorry for someone; or they marry because they want a servant. There is no place for such irrelevancies in marriage. I have even known cases where people have married in order to increase their difficulties. Perhaps a young man is in difficulties with his studies or his future career. He feels that he is likely to fail, and he wants an excuse for his failure. Consequently, he takes on the additional task of marriage to give himself an excuse.

MARRIAGE AND THE EQUALITY OF MEN AND WOMEN

I am sure we should not try to underestimate or belittle the problem of love. Instead, we need to set it on a higher level. In all the remedies I have heard proposed, it is always the women who really suffer the disadvantages. There is no doubt that in our culture men have an easier time of it than women. This is a result of the mistaken way society approaches marriage. It cannot be overcome by personal revolt. Especially in marriage itself, a personal revolt would affect both the relationship and the welfare of the partner. It can only be overcome by recognizing the general attitude of our culture and working to change it. A pupil of mine, Professor Rasey of Detroit, did a survey and found that forty-two per cent of the girls she questioned would like to have been boys, which means that they were dissatisfied with their own sex. How can we solve the problems of love and marriage while half of humankind is disappointed and discouraged, and resents its social position and the greater freedom of the other half? Can it be easy to solve such problems if women are always expecting to be undervalued, and believe themselves to be mere sex objects for men, or believe that it is natural for men to be fickle and unfaithful?

From all we have said we can draw a simple, obvious and helpful conclusion. Human beings are by nature neither polygamous nor monogamous. But we all live together on this planet, and although we are all equals we are nevertheless divided into two sexes. We have seen that all of us must solve the three problems life presents us with. These facts will show us that the fullest and highest development of the individual in love and marriage can best be secured by monogamy.

GLOSSARY
OF KEY TERMS

Individual Psychology The study of the individual as an indivisible whole, as a unitary, goal-directed self, which in the normal, healthy state is a full member of society and a participant in human relationships.

Inferiority complex Feelings of inferiority or inadequacy that produce stress, psychological evasions and a compensatory drive towards an illusory sense of superiority.

Life style A key concept in Individual Psychology: the complex of the personal philosophy, beliefs and characteristic approach to life of individuals, and the unifying feature of their personality. The life style represents the creative response to early experiences of individuals, which in turn influence all their perceptions of themselves and the world, and thus their emotions, motives and actions.

Masculine protest A reaction, by either sex, to the prejudices of our society about masculinity and femininity. A man's behaviour may constitute a protest against the demands made on him by the myths of male superiority; a woman's may be a protest against the denigration of femininity and the limitations placed on women.

Misguided behaviour An attempt to compensate for a feeling of inadequacy or insecurity in an indirect manner, based on a mistaken 'private logic'.

Organ inferiority A physical defect or weakness that often gives rise to compensatory behaviour.

Other sex Adler's term for 'opposite sex', emphasizing that male and female are not opposite but complementary.

Pampering Over-indulgence or over-protectiveness of children, stunting the development of their self-reliance, courage, responsibility and capacity for co-operation with others.

Psyche The mind, the whole personality both conscious and unconscious, which directs personal drives, gives significance to perceptions and sensations, and originates needs and goals.

Social feeling (or social interest) Community spirit, the sense of human fellowship and identity with the whole of humanity that entails positive social relationships. For Adler, these relationships should incorporate equality, reciprocity and co-operation if they are to be constructive and healthy. Social feeling begins with the ability to empathize with fellow human beings, and leads to the striving for an ideal community based on co-operation and personal equality. This concept is integral to Adler's view of the individual as a social being.

Tasks of life The three broad areas of human experience that each individual must confront: the tasks of pursuing a socially useful profession or occupation; of building fruitful human relationships; and of fulfilling one's role in love, marriage and family life.

BIBLIOGRAPHY

BOOKS BY ALFRED ADLER

The Case of Miss R: The Interpretation of a Life Story. New York: Greenberg, 1929

The Education of Children. Chicago: Regnery Gateway Ed, 1970

The Neurotic Constitution. New York: Arno Press, 1974

The Pattern of Life. New York: Rinehart & Co, 1930

The Practice and Theory of Individual Psychology. New York: Harcourt, Brace & Co, 1927

Problems of Neurosis: A book of case histories. New York: Harper Torchbooks, 1964

Social Interest. Oxford: Oneworld Publications, 1998

Understanding Human Nature. Oxford: Oneworld Publications, 1998

Understanding Life. Oxford: Oneworld Publications, 1997

BOOKS ABOUT ALFRED ADLER AND HIS WORK

H. L. & Rowena R. Ansbacher (eds). *The Individual Psychology of Alfred Adler: A systematic presentation in selection from his writings.* New York: Harper Torchbooks, 1964

P. Bottome. *Alfred Adler: A Portrait from Life.* New York: Vanguard, 1957

D. C. Dinkmeyer, D. C. Dinkmeyer, Jr., & L. Sperry. *Adlerian Counseling and Psychotherapy.* Columbus: Merrill Publishing Company, 1987

R. Dreikurs. *Fundamentals of Adlerian Psychology.* Chicago: Adler School, 1953

B. Handlbauer. *The Freud–Adler Controversy.* Oxford: Oneworld Publications, 1998

G. Manaster & R. Corsini. *Individual Psychology: Theory and Practice.* Chicago: Adler School, 1982

H. Orgler. Alfred Adler: *The Man and His Work.* New York: Capricorn Books, 1965

INDEX